"IT 英语"系列教程

中级IT英语
读写教程 ② （第二版）

总主编　司炳月
主　编　胡晓玉　于　芳
副主编　崔永光　詹　灵
编　者　王晓华　刘　欣　曹　麟
　　　　张雅欣　张婉婷　石文迪

清华大学出版社
北　京

内 容 简 介

为顺应经济全球化和信息技术的发展趋势，培养兼具 IT 专业技能和外语能力的人才，以适应 IT 行业发展需要，特编写了本教材。全书共有 8 个单元，内容涉及 IT 职业规划、教育网络信息化、编程语言、增强现实技术、人工智能、互联网经济、网络安全和 IT 领军人物八个方面。每个单元分为 Section A 和 Section B 两大部分，每部分包含一篇主课文和与主课文相关的生词和短语，并设计了大量形式多样、内容丰富的练习，同时还配有科技文写作和学术写作技能方面的指导，以全面提高学生的阅读、写作和翻译能力。本书每个单元均配有单元小测，读者可先扫描封底的"文泉云盘防盗码"解锁资源，再扫描书中对应处的二维码，通过"文泉考试"进行单元测验。

本书是《中级 IT 英语读写教程 2》的第二版。本书适合作为 IT 及其相关专业本科高年级学生和科技英语专业学生的英语教材，也可作为从事 IT 相关工作人士自我提升的参考资料。

版权所有，侵权必究。举报：010-62782989，beiqinquan@tup.tsinghua.edu.cn。

图书在版编目（CIP）数据

中级 IT 英语读写教程 . 2 / 司炳月总主编；胡晓玉等主编. -- 2 版.
北京：清华大学出版社，2024.11（2025.7重印）. -- （"IT 英语"系列教程）. -- ISBN 978-7-302-66784-1
Ⅰ. F49
中国国家版本馆 CIP 数据核字第 2024EV7139 号

责任编辑：徐博文
封面设计：李伯骥
责任校对：王荣静
责任印制：宋　林

出版发行：清华大学出版社
    网　　址：https://www.tup.com.cn, https://www.wqxuetang.com
    地　　址：北京清华大学学研大厦A座　　　邮　编：100084
    社 总 机：010-83470000　　　　　　　　邮　购：010-62786544
    投稿与读者服务：010-62776969, c-service@tup.tsinghua.edu.cn
    质量反馈：010-62772015, zhiliang@tup.tsinghua.edu.cn
印 装 者：涿州汇美亿浓印刷有限公司
经　　销：全国新华书店
开　　本：185mm×260mm　　　印　张：17.75　　　字　数：403 千字
版　　次：2017 年 11 月第 1 版　　2024 年 12 月第 2 版　　印　次：2025 年 7 月第 2 次印刷
定　　价：72.00 元

产品编号：104173-01

第二版前言

一、编写背景

为响应《大学英语教学指南（2020版）》（以下简称《指南》）中"鼓励各高校建设符合本校定位与特点的大学英语校本数字化课程资源；鼓励本区域内同类高校跨校开发大学英语数字化课程资源"的号召，本系列教材于2018年首次出版，自出版以来，以其科学的编写理念和丰富多元的学习体验取得了良好的教学效果，受到广大师生的好评。

为进一步配合各高校全面贯彻执行《国家中长期教育改革和发展规划纲要（2010—2020年）》（以下简称《纲要》）中适应国家和区域经济社会发展需要，优化学科专业、类型、层次结构，促进多学科交叉和融合，扩大应用型、复合型、技能型人才培养的要求，"IT英语"系列教程编写团队深入教学一线，进行广泛调研，在充分了解第一版教材使用情况的基础上，推出了第二版"IT英语"系列教程。第二版教程继承了第一版教程的优势与特色，贯彻"分类指导、因材施教"的原则，体现"以教师为主导，以学生为主体"的教学理念，并充分考虑新时代高等教育课程改革、教学模式创新和学生个性化学习的需求，对教材设计理念、教材体系、教材内容等方面进行全面升级，旨在助力高等教育教学改革实践中课程、教材、资源一体化进程，全面提高国际型、应用型人才的培养质量。

此外，《高等学校课程思政建设指导纲要》明确指出课程思政建设的重点是要紧紧围绕坚定学生理想信念，以爱党、爱国、爱社会主义、爱人民、爱集体为主线，围绕政治认同、家国情怀、文化素养、宪法法治意识、道德修养等重点，优化课程思政内容供给。因此，第二版教程在内容选择上融入了社会主义核心价值观和中华优秀传统文化方面的主题知识，并基于语言与知识并重、内容并置、主题统领和分享拓展等原则，将课程思政元素有机融入教材中。同时，在当今这个全球化互联的时代，网络信息的无国界自由流通已成为常态，培养批判性思维技能以及深化对信息技术伦理问题的认识，对学生而言显得尤为关键。通过IT英语教育，学生不仅能够跨越语言障碍，还能够深入探讨数据安全、网络安全、数字伦理等前沿议题，以及技术进步对社会的广泛影响，有助于培养学生的社会责任感与公民参与意识。

二、编写原则

"IT 英语"系列教程(第二版)贯彻《纲要》和《关于全面提高高等教育质量的若干意见》的精神,遵循外语学习规律,在充分考虑新时代大学生的认知水平、专业特点和未来职业发展需求等因素的基础上,通过严谨的编写、科学的设计和多媒介教学资源的支持,旨在帮助学生有效地提升 IT 英语综合应用能力、跨文化交际能力以及综合人文素养,全面助力实现复合型人才的培养目标。第二版教程在设计与编写过程中遵循的具体原则如下:

1. 服务国家战略发展对复合型国际人才培养的需求

随着我国国际化进程不断加快,兼具专业知识与跨语言交际能力、能够直接参与国际交流与竞争的国际化通用型人才已经成为提升综合国力和国际竞争力的战略资源,也是高等教育人才培养的重点和难点。因此,第二版教程的编写和设计不仅关注 IT 领域的前沿知识,而且重视跨文化沟通能力、知识信息运用和处理能力、对抗多元文化冲击能力、中华民族人格和国格的培养与相互融合,力求满足新形势下对复合型国际人才培养的需求。

2. 满足学生对专业知识与外语知识相结合的需求

高校开设大学英语课程,一方面服务于国家、社会发展的需求,助力国家改革开放和经济社会发展;另一方面,也满足了学生专业学习、国际交流、继续深造、工作就业等方面的需要。第二版教程深度融合 IT 前沿知识与最新信息,使学生通过知识结构的调整带动英语综合运用能力的整体提升,满足其对专业知识与外语知识相结合的需求。

3. 满足大学英语教学大纲和教学目标的要求

第二版教程旨在帮助学生在 IT 专业领域中,能够运用英语进行顺畅的跨文化交流,合理地运用语用学、跨文化交际学等方面的知识,较为准确地理解有一定语言难度、内容较为熟悉或与本人所学专业相关的口头或书面材料,对不同来源的信息进行科学的综合、对比、分析,并得出自己的结论或形成自己的认识,培养其逻辑思维能力和批判思维能力。

4. 体现新时代外语教育中科学价值与思想价值的融合

《指南》提出大学英语课程应该培养学生对中国文化的理解和阐释能力,服务中国文化对外传播,强调将社会主义核心价值观渗透在课程内容之中。大学英语教学应主动融入学校课程思政教学体系,使之在高等学校落实立德树人根本任务中发挥重要作用。因此,第二版教程在设计与编写时,注重外语类课程在价值观引导方面的重要作用,培养学生的文化自信与民族自豪感,为向世界讲好中国故事奠定必要的基础。

三、教程特色

1. 注重真实性与实效性，兼顾专业性和人文性的有机结合

"IT 英语"读写教程（第二版）在选材上与 IT 相关专业学生的职业需求紧密结合，同时秉承第一版教程与时俱进的理念，从大量国内外专业书籍、期刊、媒体和公司网站中精选出涉及 IT 职场主要情景和任务的最新文章。这些文章既体现 IT 产业的动态与发展，又隐含对 IT 行业的人文关怀。通过学习与阅读相关文章，学生能够掌握 IT 专业相关英语词汇和表达方式，为未来的职业发展打下坚实基础，增强对人类自身精神家园的关注。

2. 以专业知识为媒介，凸显 IT 英语的实用性

"IT 英语"读写教程（第二版）进一步突显 IT 英语实用性的特点。每单元对学习目标做了进一步细化，完善单元学习的多角度评价。每单元不仅包括阅读版块、翻译版块和写作版块，还针对 IT 相关专业的英语阅读、翻译、学术写作等技能进行系统的学习和训练，适用于教师开展合作式课堂口语交际、调查问卷及汇报展演等教学活动，实现英语语言知识与专业实践操作有机结合，着力提升学生在 IT 工作场景的英语综合运用能力。

3. 提升文化自信意识，充分融入课程思政内容

"IT 英语"读写教程（第二版）编写团队充分发挥中西文化背景结合的优势，在教材编写过程中融入各国科技文化发展内容，引导学生了解和探讨中西文化差异。每个单元都穿插了与中国传统文化紧密相连的内容，特别是聚焦于中国科技发展的辉煌成就，潜移默化地传授中国传统文化知识，培养文化包容的态度，提升学生对中西文化差异的理解，增强学生对母语文化的自豪感。

4. 满足个性化教学需求，促进教师专业化发展

《纲要》明确指出："严格教师资质，提升教师素质，努力造就一支师德高尚、业务精湛、结构合理、充满活力的高素质专业化教师队伍。"而教师的专业发展能力受多种主客观因素的影响，需要外在环境和管理机制的保障。使用第二版教程在一定程度上能够促进教师更新教学理念和提高教学技能。同时，第二版教程为教师提供了丰富的教学资源，教师可以根据具体教学情况和学生需求，因材施教。教师用书、教学课件等配套资源能够为教师提供全面、系统的教学支持。

四、教程结构

"IT 英语"读写教程（第二版）由《初级 IT 英语读写教程》（第二版）和《中级

英语读写教程 2（第二版）
Intermediate IT English Reading and Writing 2 (2nd Edition)

IT 英语读写教程》（第二版）两套教程组成，每套教程分为 1、2 两册，每册包含 8 个单元，内容涵盖信息技术领域的前沿热门话题，以专门用途英语课程代替通用英语课程，打破通用英语与专业英语的界限，使英语教学过程服务于 IT 职业教育和应用，在夯实学生英语综合运用能力的同时，培养其从事 IT 领域相关工作时应具备的英语沟通能力。此外，第二版教程增加了中国科技发展的相关内容，从科技视角阐释中国文化，凸显课程思政的内涵。

《初级 IT 英语读写教程 1》（第二版）中的每个单元涉及一个主题，并围绕主题安排具体教学内容和任务设计，每单元由 Section A 和 Section B 两部分组成。Section A 分为 Pre-Reading Activities、Text A、Reading Comprehension、Language Focus、Structure Analysis and Writing 和 Translation 六部分。其中，Pre-Reading Activities 围绕单元主题设计一些简单有趣、实用性强的教学内容，例如，IT 常见职业及其职责辨识、计算思维在生活中的应用举例、因特网知识小测验、物联网情景填空等。这些内容不仅能够导入单元主题，而且能够激发学生的学习兴趣，为师生、生生间交流知识与生活经验创造良好的教学平台，也为后续学习做好准备；Text A 围绕一篇阅读材料展开一系列活动，并配有注释、单词表、短语表、专有名词表和相关练习。Section B 分为 Reading Skill、Text B、Reading Comprehension、Language Focus 和 Translation 五部分。其中，Reading Skill 详细介绍了常见的阅读技巧，帮助学生在理论和实践技巧层面上提高阅读水平与效率。

《初级 IT 英语读写教程 2》（第二版）延续《初级 IT 英语读写教程 1》（第二版）注重英语综合运用能力提升以及 IT 英语重实用性的特点。每单元由 Section A 和 Section B 组成。Section A 包含一篇精读课文，并配有生词表、短语和惯用表达、缩略词表、术语表和课后练习。其中，生词、短语和惯用表达均从课文中精心选取。课后练习紧紧围绕课文中的重点和难点展开，包括课文理解、词汇练习、选词填空、短语和惯用表达练习、结构分析和写作、翻译等题型。Section B 按照英语专业学生的培养目标和要求进行编写，包含一篇与 Section A 同主题的阅读文章，旨在补充和强化专业阅读内容。Section A 与 Section B 所选的两篇文章一易一难，针对不同英语水平、不同 IT 知识与技能掌握程度的学生，教师可灵活调整教学内容。

《中级 IT 英语读写教程 1》（第二版）在难度上有所提升。Section A 和 Section B 两部分的文章及练习设计针对性强，具有丰富性和系统性，严格遵循语言学习的规律，针对不同层次、不同年级的学生，难易程度和侧重点均有所不同，以满足分级教学的需求。Section A 部分有形式多样的课前导入练习，课后有生词表、重要短语及表达、注释及课后练习。课后练习包括问答题、填空题、词形转换、选词填空、写作和翻译练习。Section B 包含一篇与 Section A 同主题的精读文章，旨在补充和强化专业阅读内容。课前有阅读技巧总结，课后有生词表、关键短语、注释及课后练习。课后练习包含问答、词汇短语练习、句型练习、词语搭配及项目实操建议。

《中级 IT 英语读写教程 2》（第二版）进一步突出 IT 英语的专业特色，各单元主题划分更加清晰。第 1 单元和第 2 单元关注当下 IT 行业热点问题；第 3 单元至第 5 单元聚焦 IT 行业日常工作；第 6 单元至第 8 单元聚集于计算机网络技术发展与社会以及人与人之间关系的深度思考与展望。Section A 和 Section B 包含主题相同、难度不同的两篇文章，既体现"因材施教"的教学理念，又为学有余力的学生提供有针对性的自学材料。此外，《中级 IT 英语读写教程 2》（第二版）的框架设计与编写延续《中级 IT 英语读写教程 1》（第二版）的风格，课后练习的设计除了帮助学生巩固和深化课文内容，还能够使其通过分析文本，理解作者的写作意图，形成自己的观点，这不仅可以提高学生的语言能力，亦可以培养他们的逻辑推理和批判性思维能力。

五、教学建议

"IT 英语"读写教程（第二版）提供系列教程、教师用书、教学课件等教学资源，为实施分级教学、分类指导与创新教学模式提供较大的选择空间。教师可根据院校教学条件、课程学时数及具体教学目标以及学生的实际情况，自主选择教学材料。

对于英语课程学时数比较少的学校，在日常教学中教师可在 Section A 和 Section B 中选择一篇文章作为主要教学内容，引导学生了解和学习各种阅读技巧，并运用相关技巧充分理解阅读文章。此外，写作应作为日常教学必不可少的一部分，尤其是在信息泛滥的互联网时代，学生通过学习英语写作，可以对信息进行批判性吸收，对观点和证据进行鉴别，并形成有逻辑支撑的论证。

对于英语课程学时数比较充足的学校，所有版块内容都可以在课堂上完成。建议两周内完成读写教程一个单元的教学内容。根据具体的教学安排和教学进度，教师可将部分单元练习题作为课后作业，并在下次课堂教学中进行检查和评估，通过这些活动教师不仅可以检验教学效果，而且可以培养学生自主学习和协作学习的能力。

本系列教程在编写过程中，经过多次研讨、听取多方意见，反复修改完成。总主编大连外国语大学司炳月教授从宏观策划到具体细节都提出了许多宝贵意见。编写团队成员均为大学一线英语专业教师，具有多年 IT 英语教学经验。另外，第二版教程在编写过程中得到清华大学出版社和大连外国语大学软件学院的大力支持，谨在此一并感谢。

由于编者水平有限，教材难免存在问题与不足，在此也欢迎各位专家、读者在审阅和使用本系列教程的过程中提供宝贵的意见和建议，以使教材不断完善。

编者
2024 年 9 月

第一版前言

一、编写背景

1.《国家中长期教育改革和发展规划纲要（2010—2020年）》

信息时代的悄然而至，使得我国教育在面临难得的改革与发展机遇的同时，也面临着全新的挑战。传统的教育教学理念、教育模式、教学内容、教学方式、教学手段、教育结构乃至整个教育体制都将随之发生变革。2010年，教育部颁发了《国家中长期教育改革和发展规划纲要（2010—2020年）》（以下简称《纲要》），《纲要》中提出要"优化学科专业、类型、层次结构，促进多学科交叉和融合。扩大应用型、复合型、技能型人才培养规模"。在对创新人才培养模式的论述中提出，要"加强教材建设，确定不同教育阶段学生必须掌握的核心内容，形成教学内容更新机制"。

2.《全民科学素质行动计划纲要实施方案（2016—2020年）》

2016年3月，国务院办公厅印发了《全民科学素质行动计划纲要实施方案（2016—2020年）》（以下简称《方案》）。《方案》中对高等教育中的教材要求有清楚的阐述："加强各类人群科技教育培训的教材建设。结合不同人群特点和需求，不断更新丰富科技教育培训的教材内容，注重培养具有创意、创新、创业能力的高层次创造性人才。将相关学科内容纳入各级各类科技教育培训教材和教学计划。"

3.《大学英语教学指南》

《大学英语教学指南》（以下简称《指南》）是新时期普通高等学校制定大学英语教学大纲、进行大学英语课程建设、开展大学英语课程评价的依据。《指南》在对教材建设和教学资源的论述中明确阐述了："鼓励各高校建设符合本校定位与特点的大学英语校本数字化课程资源；鼓励本区域内同类高校跨校开发大学英语数字化课程资源。"

二、编写原则

本套教材是与IT及其相关专业密切相关的知识课程，符合新形势下国家对复合型人才培养提出的要求，符合语言学习规律和新时代大学生的认知水平，也满足大学生专业学习和未来职业发展的实际需要，有利于促进复合型人才培养目标的实现。本套教材在设计与编写过程中遵循以下原则：

1. 满足社会对于复合型人才培养的需求

当代大学生正面临多元化社会带来的冲突和挑战，复合型人才的培养成为国家、社会发展的需求。因此，为社会提供既具有专业知识又具备跨语言交际能力、能够直接参与国际交流与竞争的国际化通用型人才是高校人才培养的重点和难点，也是全球化对人才提出的更高、更新的要求。

2. 满足学生对于专业与外语知识相结合的需求

高校开设大学英语课程，一方面满足了国家、社会发展的需求，为国家改革开放和经济社会发展服务；另一方面，也满足了学生专业学习、国际交流、继续深造、工作就业等方面的需要。本套教材旨在满足 IT 及其相关专业学生的需求，帮助他们在掌握专业知识的同时提高英语水平。此外，教材亦体现了专门用途英语理论对大学英语教学课程设置的具体要求。

3. 满足大学英语教学大纲和教学目标的要求

大学英语的教学目标是培养学生的英语应用能力，增强学生的跨文化交际意识和交际能力；同时发展其自主学习能力，提高综合文化素养，使他们在学习、生活、社会交往和未来工作中能够有效地使用英语，满足国家、社会、学校和个人发展的需要。本套教材编写的目的就是使学生能够在 IT 专业领域中使用英语进行有效的交流；能够有效地运用有关篇章、语用等知识；能够较好地理解有一定语言难度、内容较为熟悉或与本人所学专业相关的口头或书面材料；能够对不同来源的信息进行综合、对比、分析，并得出自己的结论或形成自己的认识。

三、编写依据

1. "专业知识"+"外语能力"的"复合型"人才培养目标

大学英语课程作为高等学校人文教育的一部分，兼具工具性和人文性。在进一步提高学生英语听、说、读、写、译基本能力的基础上，学生可以通过学习与专业或未来工作有关的学术英语或职业英语获得在学术或职业领域进行交流的相关能力。本套教材是根据大学英语教学大纲和教学目标的要求，采用系统、科学的教材编写原则和方法编写而成。从教材的前期策划和准备、单元设计、教学资源开发、编写团队、内容设置和编排到教学效果的评价和评估都有整体的体系构建，以满足教学大纲和课程目标的要求。本套教材不但注重培养学生听、说、读、写、译这些语言基本技能，而且强化学生思辨、创新能力的培养。

2. "学生为主体"+"教师为主导"的"双主"教学理念

《指南》中提出大学英语教学应贯彻分类指导、因材施教的原则,以适应个性化教学的实际需要。新一轮的大学英语教学改革中也明确提出了"以教师为主导,以学生为主体"的"双主"教学理念。在教学过程中,教师的主导作用主要体现在课堂教学设计、教学组织、教学策略使用、教学管理和协调、课堂教学评价和评估等方面,而教师对课堂的主导方向要以满足学生的个性需求、促进学生的个性发展和自主学习为目的,只有两者相互结合,方能相得益彰,顺利实现大学英语教学改革目标。

3. "语言输入"+"语言输出"的"双向"驱动教学体系

本套教材在课堂教学活动和课后练习中设计了很多"语言输入"和"语言输出"的互动环节,教材采用任务式、合作式、项目式、探究式等教学方法,体现以教师为主导、以学生为主体的教学理念,使教学活动满足从"语言输入"到"语言输出"的需求。课后练习的设计关注学生自主学习能力的培养,引导和帮助他们掌握学习策略,学会学习;促使学生从"被动学习"向"主动学习"转变,真正让学生成为学习过程中的主体,实现课内和课外学习"不断线"。

4. "平面教材"+"立体化教材"的"双辅"交互优势

本套教材将大力推进最新信息技术与课程教学的融合,凸显现代学习方式的自主性、移动性、随时性等特点,发挥现代教育技术的推介作用。积极创建多元的教学与学习环境,利用互联网等信息基础设施和网络交流平台,使"平面教材"呈现出信息化教育的特征,形成"立体化教材"的特征。

此外,本套教材鼓励教师建设和使用微课、慕课,拓展教学内容,实施基于"教材平面内容"和"网上立体课件"的混合式教学模式,使学生朝着主动学习、自主学习和个性化学习方向发展,实现教学资源网络化、教学环境虚拟化、教学个性化、学习评估过程化等。

5. 以教材为引导、推动教师的自主专业发展,实现"教""学"相长

《纲要》明确指出,要"严格教师资质,提升教师素质,努力造就一支师德高尚、业务精湛、结构合理、充满活力的高素质专业化教师队伍"。教师的专业发展能力受多种主客观因素的影响,需要外在环境和管理机制的保障。教师专业发展的规律性特点可归纳为长期性、动态性、实践性和环境依托性。本套教材的编写和使用正是根据实践性和环境依托性的特点,编写和使用新教材的过程也是教师更新教学理念、提高教学技能的专业发展必经过程。

四、教材结构

本套教材共包含"读写"和"听说"两大系列。其中,"读写"系列分为初级、中级、高级三个级别,共六个分册。"听说"系列分为初级和中级两个级别,共四个分册。

在"读写"系列中,每册书有 8 个单元。每个单元分为 Section A 和 Section B 两部分。Section A 根据大学英语教学大纲的要求编制,包含一篇精读课文,课文后有生词表、短语和表达、缩略词、术语和课后练习。Section B 是按照专业英语学生的培养目标和要求编写,包含一篇与 Section A 同主题的阅读文章,旨在补充和强化专业阅读内容。两篇文章一易一难,每个单元都可以满足分级教学的需要和不同程度学生水平的需求,两个部分的练习形式多样,具有丰富性和系统性的特点。练习设计遵循语言学习的规律,针对不同层次、不同年级的学生,选材的难易程度、知识侧重点等方面均有所不同。

在"听说"系列中,每册书有 16 个单元,每个单元分为 Section A、Section B 及 Section C 三部分。其中,Section A 为听力技能训练,听力内容围绕 IT 相关主题展开。该部分由 Text A 和 Text B 两部分组成,前者针对 IT 及相关专业(非英语专业)学生,题目设计相对简单;后者针对英语专业(如科技英语)学生,题目设计难度有所增加。Section B 为口语技能训练,旨在培养学生的口头交际能力。Section C 为听力考试强化训练,该部分侧重应试,根据当下国内外几大英语考试(如大学英语四六级、托福、雅思等),全方位、多角度满足学生对英语学习的需求。希望通过题型多样、题量丰富的强化训练,让学生一方面熟悉并适应听力考试的多样题型,另一方面检测自己的英语听力水平,提高自主学习能力。

五、教材特色

1. 素材原汁原味

本套教材的所有阅读和听力文本均选自英美国家真实的 IT 专业文本,包括 IT 相关专业的学术网站、期刊及英语原版教材。编者在选择文本时尽量选择新颖、有趣的分支话题,文章的语言也尽量避免过于严肃和刻板,使学生在理解和分析课文的过程中既能利用专业知识进行思考和判断,又不觉枯燥。

2. 内容注重实用性

本套教材的"读写"系列避免了国内同类教材培养目标单一、片面的缺陷,注重提高学生的多种技能。每个单元不仅包括阅读板块、翻译板块和写作板块,还针对 IT 及其相关专业的英语阅读、翻译、学术写作等技能进行系统的学习和训练。而在"听说"系列中,编者在选择听说文本的话题时,一方面迎合当今 IT 产业就业的发展趋势,另一方面也考虑与高校 IT 专业课程紧密相关,并参考国内各大重点高校 IT 专业设置,挑选出IT领域相关的热门话题，这些话题广泛涉及IT相关专业学生所关心的IT就业方面的问题、IT专业知识的学习方法、全国重点高校IT相关专业课程中开设的典型编程语言、当今的网络环境、时下IT领域多项前沿技术等内容，以便在提升学生英语语言能力的同时了解和学习与IT相关的专业知识，突出语言运用，通过文本传递IT知识，重现真实IT场景。

3. 练习内容和形式丰富多样

本套教材在阅读和听力理解、语言知识学习及技能训练方面都设计了大量的练习，而且练习形式富于变化，如简答、判断、填空、选择、配对、翻译、图表、口语交际等，学生不仅可以学习词汇、短语等语言点，还可以提高阅读和听力理解能力、分析语言的能力及表达能力。

六、适用对象

本套教材特别适合计算机科学与技术、信息管理与信息系统、软件工程和网络工程等与IT相关专业的学生学习和使用，可以分阶段或分学期选用；也特别适合从事软件系统需求分析、设计、开发、测试、运行及维护工作的工程师和管理人员查阅和参考。编者在选材上保证与IT信息技术密切相关的同时，努力确保文章内容贴近生活，所选材料涵盖了当前教育、工作和社会领域的诸多热点，文字形象生动、可读性强。因此，本套教材也比较适合那些有一定英语基础，同时也喜爱计算机应用技术和互联网文化的人士阅读，以扩展知识，开拓视野。

七、编写团队

本套教材由大连外国语大学软件学院教师担任主编团队。参与编写的编者有来自全国各高校的大学英语教师、专业英语教师、计算机专业的教师、IT职场的企业专家以及旅居海外的专家和学者。

本套教材在编写过程中得到校企合作教材编写组的大力支持，在此表示衷心感谢。校企合作编写组成员包括李鸿飞、王文智、姜超、韩参、蒋振彬、梁浩、刘志强（排名不分先后）。

本套教材在编写过程中也得到了大连外国语大学软件学院的领导与英语教研室所有老师的鼎力支持，在此表示感谢。

由于编者水平有限，错误与缺点在所难免，恳请读者批评指正。

司炳月
2017年6月

Contents 目录

Unit 1 Stay Current in IT 1
Section A 3
    Text A Never Stop Learning 4
Section B 17
    Text B How to Stay Current with Technology Trends? 18

Unit 2 Strive for Professionalism in IT 31
Section A 33
    Text A What Is a Professional Programmer? 34
Section B 47
    Text B A Broken Window's Crisis 49

Unit 3 How We Begin Matters 63
Section A 65
    Text A The Importance of a Kickoff Meeting 65
Section B 78
    Text B The Truth About Making a Schedule 80

Unit 4 Project Management 93
Section A 95
    Text A Develop Leadership Skills to Succeed as a Project
            Manager 96
Section B 111
    Text B The Art of Project Management 112

英语读写教程 2（第二版）
Intermediate IT English Reading and Writing 2 (2nd Edition)

Unit 5 Reach out to Customers ... 127

Section A ... 129
  Text A Make Customer Feedback Actionable ... 130
Section B ... 144
  Text B What Customer-Centric IT Really Looks Like? ... 145

Unit 6 Gender Discrepancy in IT ... 159

Section A ... 161
  Text A Women in Technology: A Brightening Outlook? ... 161
Section B ... 175
  Text B Grace Hopper: A Pioneering Programmer in History ... 177

Unit 7 Get Advancement in IT ... 189

Section A ... 191
  Text A Getting Started with a "BANG" ... 192
Section B ... 205
  Text B What If You Don't Want to Manage in Tech? ... 208

Unit 8 Why Corporate Culture Counts ... 221

Section A ... 223
  Text A Five Dangerous Myths About Corporate Culture ... 223
Section B ... 238
  Text B How to Read Corporate Culture? ... 240

Glossary ... 253

Unit 1

Stay Current in IT

Learning objectives

In this unit you will:
- learn about the importance of keeping learning in the IT field;
- learn how to keep up with new technology;
- learn how to write a biographical narrative essay;
- learn how to use previewing as a reading strategy.

> You are never too old to learn more than you already know and to become able to do more than you already can.
>
> —*Isaac Asimov*
>
> When we are no longer able to change a situation—we are challenged to change ourselves.
>
> —*Viktor E. Frankl*

Preview

Technology is moving at lightning speed. Many new skills, software and platforms are being created and put to use at work. It seems that there is always a lot to catch up with and if you slow down your steps, you are way falling behind. As for college students who major in information technology and want to transform tech skills into a tool at work, they might feel that what they have accumulated in college is not enough, not directly relevant, and not customized for their first job requirement. Naveen Jain, former CEO of InfoSpace, once said, "We are now living in a fast paced technological era where every skill that we teach our children becomes obsolete in the 10 to 15 years due to exponentially growing technological advances." So is there really a skill gap between education and employment? What can students do to bridge the gap so that they can smoothly transfer from college to work? What else should students possess so that they can make a success in the tech world?

Section A

 Pre-reading activities

1. **Answer the following questions briefly based on the given pictures.**

    (1) What do the pictures above describe?

    (2) What technology trend can you see from them?

    (3) Do these products make life convenient?

2. **Work in pairs and discuss the following questions.**

    (1) What can you conclude from the pictures above?

    (2) What do you think of the development trend of technology?

    (3) What should people prepare for the future of technology?

Text A

Never Stop Learning

1. This past May Day in the UK was a rare day to catch up on gardening and other household tasks for the always-busy Ed Baker, technical **evangelist** at Microsoft UK. But sitting in his home office in between **sporadic** rainfalls, he was already looking ahead to the meetings, events and keynotes set for the coming weeks. If it were not a public holiday, he would, from the same base of operations, be fielding calls with clients **assisting** with higher-level technical development and deployment for Microsoft products—and he would **undoubtedly** have his webcam on. As his current professional title implies, Baker is serious about using and **promoting** the latest cutting-edge technology. Likewise, he's serious about preparing and **smoothing** the way for students of all ages and backgrounds to take part in, **facilitate** and **prosper** in today's tech-**savvy** world. Baker is a **seasoned** IT educator with a strikingly impressive list of training roles on his resume. CompTIA certifications and other industry **accreditations** have been **instrumental** both in confirming his own skills and setting him up to **propagate** IT knowledge and career readiness to students of all walks throughout the UK—and each class has offered Baker its own sense of **gratification**.

2. "Any student can learn something. It doesn't matter what age or background he has. If he can come out of it and feel positive and happy, then I've done my job," Baker said.

3. Baker got his start in IT in a place some might see as unexpected. Baker was a police officer beginning in the 1980s and, for 14 years, he did everything from walking the beat to motorcycle **patrol** to criminal investigation. But during his free time, he was **tinkering** with personal computers. He had jumped in around the **precinct** to **troubleshoot** computer problems as necessary, so when his supervisors were looking for someone to **implement** an online crime mapping system, they tapped Baker to handle it. In short order, he had jumped from **hobbyist** to professional. He learned, too, the value of certifications. Getting his first certification taught him the **ins-and-outs** of the hardware he would be working on and confirmed to anyone he was working with or for that he knew his stuff.

4. As his career **progressed**, Baker struck out on his own as a self-employed IT project manager. There, he began to view certification and training from a new **standpoint**. He had just locked down a big contract, and realized he needed an **apprentice** working with him who had the kind of tech skills and professionalism that would help his business shine. But he found such skills **sorely** lacking in his interviewees. Seeing the need, he resolved to change things himself, first by putting his apprentice through an online training course and later by moving into being a trainer himself.

5. "I decided to change jobs and try to get a job as a full-time trainer training apprentices to give something back," Baker said.

6. From that point on, Baker lived and breathed IT training. In a **litany** of roles full-time and part-time, he has spread the word of IT and the skills it takes to be successful. And as he's done so, he picked up CompTIA A+, CompTIA Network+, CompTIA Security+, CompTIA Server+ and CompTIA IT Fundamentals himself, along with no fewer than 50 other industry certifications. "I did all those certifications as well and then got **hooked**, became a certified trainer and just took exams for fun," Baker said.

7. Baker has **molded** young people into career-ready adults and helped them take their first step into the workforce. He has taught A+ and Network+ boot camps to help IT pros meet their immediate career needs. He has helped adults who never thought themselves capable of working in tech learn the right skills and confirm them with the right certifications. He has approached all these different audiences, and many more with a **tangible** enthusiasm for the field and for making the world better through IT training and certification. Hearing his story and seeing the busy schedule he keeps, even on holidays, it's clear that one could benefit not only by having him as an instructor, but by watching his approach to IT success.

8. In his two-and-a-half years at Microsoft UK, Baker has focused mainly on the company's products. But his advice about having a career in IT, now and in the future, **resonates** industry-wide. "To succeed in IT you just have to be willing to never stop learning," Baker said. "You have to be willing to change."

9. And as CompTIA continues to keep its finger on the pulse of what's going on throughout the IT field, and build its certification exams around the hands-on needs of the rapidly-changing IT industry, CompTIA certifications offer a way to keep skills fresh and **applicable**, and to **heed** Baker's **sage** advice for success in the field.

10. Baker has got a whole bunch in the industry at the moment who are his age or slightly younger, who have done something in the same way their whole career. That is changing. They're moving into things like cloud technology, DevOps, a whole bunch of different skills that are required, and that will leave them on the **sidelines** if they do not change. And that's exactly the same at every level of the industry.

11. The culture of learning must be **instilled** in a person's whole life in order to reach greater heights of success. Once people start learning, they will be more open and **adaptable** to change; they will develop natural abilities, have **inquisitive** minds and ask questions that will bring positive changes to current business practices. When people make learning a habit, they'll be surprised by how often they will develop new ideas, how often they can find new ways to solve problems, and how **evolved** they'll become as an entrepreneur, as a business owner, and as a professional, **irrespective** of their industry. So work hard, learn hard and never stop learning, and never lose the willingness to change what you do.

(996 words)

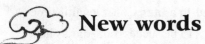

New words

evangelist	/ɪˈvændʒɪlɪst/	n.	[C] preacher of the Gospel, esp. one who travels around holding evangelical religious meetings 福音传道者；尤指布道家
sporadic	/spəˈrædɪk/	a.	happening or seen only occasionally or in a few places; occurring irregularly 偶发的；偶见的；零星的
assist	/əˈsɪst/	vt.	(fml.) to help 帮助；援助；协助
undoubtedly	/ʌnˈdaʊtɪdli/	ad.	[attrib.] not doubted or questioned; indisputably 无疑地；毋庸置疑地
promote	/prəˈməʊt/	vt.	1. to help the progress of (sth.); to encourage or support 促进；增进（某事物）；鼓励；支持 2. to raise sb. to a higher position or rank 提升或晋升某人 3. to publicize (sth.) in order to sell it 宣传（某物）以促进销售
smooth	/smuːð/	vt.	~ sth. (away, back, down, out, etc.) to make sth. smooth or flat 使某物光滑、平坦、平静或顺利
facilitate	/fəˈsɪlɪteɪt/	vt.	(fml.) (of an object, a process, etc. but not of a person) to make (sth.) easy or less difficult; to make an action or a process possible or easier（指物体、过程等，但不用于指人）使（某事物）容易或减少困难；促进；促使；使便利
prosper	/ˈprɒspə/	vi.	to be successful; to thrive 成功；兴旺
savvy	/ˈsævi/	n.	[U] (slang) common sense; understanding 常识；理解
		a.	(infml. AmE) having practical knowledge and understanding of sth.; having common sense 有常识的；聪慧的
seasoned	/ˈsiːzənd/	a.	[only before noun] used to describe someone who has a lot of experience of a particular thing 经验丰富的；老练的
accreditation	/əˌkredɪˈteɪʃ(ə)n/	n.	official approval to do sth., especially because of having reached an acceptable standard 任命；鉴定；给予的信任；权威的代表；授权
instrumental	/ˌɪnstrəˈmentəl/	a.	[pred.] 1. the means of bringing sth. about 作为促成某事物之手段；有帮助；起作用 2. of or for musical instruments 乐器的；为器乐用的
propagate	/ˈprɒpəˌɡeɪt/	vt.	1. (fml.) to spread (views, knowledge, beliefs, etc.) more widely 传播（观点、知识、信仰等）2. to increase the number of (plants, animals, etc.) by a natural process from the parent stock 繁殖（动植物等）；使增殖

gratification	/ˌgrætɪfɪˈkeɪʃ(ə)n/	n.	[U, C] (fml.) the state of feeling pleasure when sth. goes well for you or when your desires are satisfied 满足；喜悦；满意
patrol	/pəˈtrəʊl/	v.	to go round (a town, an area, etc.) to check that all is secure and orderly or to look for wrongdoers, an enemy or people who need help 在（某城、地带等）巡逻；巡查
		n.	action of patrolling 巡逻；巡查
tinker	/ˈtɪŋkə/	n.	[C] person who travels from place to place repairing kettles, pans, etc.（走街串巷的）小炉匠
		vi.	~ (at/with sth.) to work in a casual or inexpert way, esp. trying to repair or improve sth. 随便地或以外行方式做（尤指试着修理或改进某物）
precinct	/ˈpriːsɪŋkt/	n.	[C] 1. area enclosed by definite boundaries, esp. the walls of a cathedral, church or college（有界限围成的）区域；（尤指）教堂或大学墙以内的境域 2. (Brit.) area in a town for specific or restricted use, esp. one where vehicles may not enter 城镇中有某用途的或受限制的地区；（尤指禁止机动车通行的）行人专用区
troubleshoot	/ˈtrʌblʃuːt/	vt.	to solve problems 检修
implement	/ˈɪmplɪmənt/	n.	[C] tool or instrument 工具；器具
		vt.	to put (sth.) into effect; to carry out 使（某事物）生效；履行；实施；贯彻
hobbyist	/ˈhɒbɪɪst/	n.	[C] (fml.) a person who is very interested in a particular hobby 沉溺于某种嗜好成癖者
ins-and-outs		n.	[pl.] all the exact details of a complicated situation, problem, system, etc. 详细情形
progress	/prəʊˈgres/	vi.	to improve, develop, or achieve things so that you are then at a more advanced stage 前进；行进；进步；进展
standpoint	/ˈstændˌpɔɪnt/	n.	[C] position from which things are seen and opinions are formed; point of view 立场；立脚点；看问题的角度
apprentice	/əˈprentɪs/	n.	[C] 1. a person who has agreed to work for a skilled employer for a fixed period in return for being taught his trade or craft 学徒；徒弟 2. beginner or novice 生手；新手
sorely	/ˈsɔːlɪ/	ad.	very much or very seriously 非常；强烈地
litany	/ˈlɪtənɪ/	n.	1. [C] series of prayers to God for use in church services, spoken by a priest with set responses by the congregation 连祷；启应式祈祷 2. [C] (fig.) ~ (of sth.) long boring recital 枯燥冗长的述说

英语读写教程 2（第二版）
Intermediate IT English Reading and Writing 2 (2nd Edition)

hook	/hʊk/	*n.*	[C] curved or bent piece of wire, plastic, etc. for catching hold of sth. or for hanging sth. on 钩子；吊钩；挂钩
		vi.	**to be/get hooked (on sth.)** (slang) to be/become addicted (to sth.); to be/become completely committed (to sth.) 迷上（某事物）；完全陷于（某事物）之中
mold	/məʊld/	*n.*	[C] hollow container with a particular shape, into which a soft or liquid substance is poured to set or cool into that shape 模子；铸模；铸型
		vt.	1. to shape (a soft substance) into a particular form or object 使（软材料）成形 2. to shape or influence sb. or sth. 指导或控制某人或某事物的发展；塑造或影响某人或某事
tangible	/ˈtændʒəbəl/	*a.*	(fml.) 1. that can be perceived by touch 可触知的 2. clear and definite; real 明确的；确切的；真实的
resonate	/ˈrezəˌneɪt/	*vi.*	(of a voice, an instrument, etc.) to make a deep, clear sound that continues for a long time 共鸣；共振；起回声
applicable	/ˈæplɪkəbəl/	*a.*	[pred.] **~ (to sb./sth.)** that can be applied; appropriate or suitable 可适用的；合适的；适当的
heed	/hiːd/	*vt.*	(fml.) to pay attention to (advice, etc.); to take notice of (sth.) 注意或听从（劝告等）；留心（某事物）
sage	/seɪdʒ/	*n.*	[C] (fml.) very wise man 圣人；贤哲；智者
		a.	[usu. attrib.] (fml.) wise or wise-looking 贤明的；貌似聪明的
sideline	/ˈsaɪdˌlaɪn/	*n.*	[C] (*on the ~*) not taking part in an activity even though you want to or should do 旁观；不直接参与
instill	/ɪnˈstɪl/	*vt.*	**~ sth. (in/into sb.)** to cause sb. gradually to acquire a particular desirable quality 逐渐使某人获得（某种可取的品质）；逐步灌输
adaptable	/əˈdæptəbəl/	*a.*	[usu. after noun] able to change in order to be successful in new and different situations 适合的；适应性强的
inquisitive	/ɪnˈkwɪzɪtɪv/	*a.*	1. very interested in learning about many different things 好学的；好奇的；兴趣广泛的 2. (too) fond of inquiring into other people's affairs（太）好打听别人的事情的
evolve	/ɪˈvɒlv/	*v.*	**~ (sth.) (from sth.) (into sth.)** to develop gradually, esp. from a simple to a more complicated form; to develop sth. in this way（使）逐渐形成；逐步发展；逐渐演变
irrespective	/ˌɪrɪˈspektɪv/	*a.*	(**~ of sth./sb.**) not taking account of or considering (sth./sb.) 不顾或不考虑（某事物 / 某人）

Unit 1 Stay Current in IT

 New expressions

catch up	to be or get involved in sth. 赶上
look ahead	to think about and plan for what might happen in the future 计划未来；预测未来
tinker with	to make small changes to sth. in order to repair it or make it work better 鼓捣；胡乱地修补
lock down	to make sth. become fixed and unable to move or change 锁定
keep one's finger on the pulse	to be well-informed about the current events 了如指掌
be instilled in sb.	to cause sb. gradually to acquire a particular desirable quality 逐渐使某人获得某种可取的品质；逐步灌输
be adaptable to sth.	to be able to change in order to be successful in new and different situations 适应
irrespective of	not taking account of or considering (sth./sb.) 不顾或不考虑

 Notes

1. Microsoft (微软): founded by Paul Allen and Bill Gates on April 4, 1975. It is an American multinational technology company headquartered in Redmond, Washington, that develops, manufactures, licenses, supports and sells computer software, consumer electronics and personal computers and services.

2. CompTIA (Computing Technology Industry Association, 美国计算机行业协会): a provider of professional certifications for the information technology industry which are vendor-neutral.

3. Cloud technology (云技术): a type of Internet-based computing that provides shared computer processing resources and data to computers and other devices on demand.

4. DevOps (Development 和 Operations 的组合): a culture, movement or practice that emphasizes the collaboration and communication of both software developers and other information technology professionals while automating the process of software delivery and infrastructure changes.

Reading comprehension

Understanding the text

1. Answer the following questions.

(1) Who is Ed Baker?

(2) What is he looking ahead to?

(3) What is he serious about doing?

(4) Does he think anyone is able to learn something?

(5) What did he work as before he entered the IT field?

(6) Why did he want to transform from a self-employed IT project manager to an IT trainer?

(7) What advice did he give to those who wanted to succeed in the IT world?

(8) Why is keeping learning important in the IT world?

Critical thinking

2. Work in pairs and discuss the following questions.

(1) What's your opinion of Ed Baker? What personalities do you think he possessed?

(2) Can you imagine the difficulties he encountered when he changed his job from a police officer to an IT engineer?

(3) Majoring in IT, what preparation do you need to do before entering the workforce?

(4) After working in the IT field, what should you keep learning?

Word building

The suffix *-ly* combines with adjectives to form adverbs. Adverbs formed in this way express the idea that something is done in the way described by the adjective. Such adverbs can often be used with adverbs of degree such as *very* to show the extent to which the qualities described are true. A final *y* is replaced by *i* before adding *-ly*.

Examples

Words learned	Add -*ly*	New words formed
sore	→	sorely
literal	→	literally
superficial	→	superficially
obvious	→	obviously
consequent	→	consequently

The prefix *un-* combines with adjectives to form new adjectives. Adjectives formed in this way express the idea that the state referred to by the original adjectives is reversed.

Examples

Words learned	Add *un-*	New words formed
expected	→	unexpected
doubted	→	undoubted
lucky	→	unlucky
believable	→	unbelievable
able	→	unable

3. Add -*ly* or *un-* to the following words to form new words.

Words learned	New words formed
-ly	
evident	
respective	
even	
absolute	
noble	
un-	
certain	
important	
pleasant	
accustomed	
acceptable	

4. **Fill in the blanks with the newly-formed words in Activity 3. Change the form where necessary. Each word can be used only once.**

   (1) The prospects for the country are fairly _____ balanced between peaceful reform and revolution.

   (2) Imprisonment without trial is totally _____ in a democratic country.

   (3) The big problem is that people are _____ to thinking and acting in a responsible and independent way.

   (4) He understands his age; he has brains; he is _____ born and gently bred.

   (5) The old cat was _____ incurable and the old couple had to get it put away.

   (6) Carol was _____ what she wanted to read, and her mother suggested law on the grounds that it would be much more useful than the arts.

   (7) Scholars describe these two styles of reasoning as "formalist" and "functionalist" _____.

   (8) She was _____ incapable of tolerating this insignificant incident.

   (9) The matter was so _____ that she dismissed it from her mind.

   (10) Again she nodded and her eyes took on the glaze of somebody remembering _____ things.

Banked cloze

5. **Fill in the blanks by selecting suitable words from the word bank. You may not use any of the words more than once.**

A. payoff	B. absolutely	C. out-of-date	D. dependent	E. tangible
F. irrespective	G. diminish	H. strategies	I. inquisitive	J. achievement
K. adapt	L. relevant	M. implement	N. standpoint	O. demonstrate

In today's world of technology, things change so rapidly, and knowledge, even the most specialized kind, can get (1) _____ very quickly. Given the accelerating pace of change, one has to ask: Does investing time and money in education still have the same (2) _____ it once did? Does the particular expertise you acquire remain (3) _____ and put you at an advantage in the real world? There is no need to (4) _____ anyone's education, because we have to admit the fact that education itself is (5) _____ essential. Becoming an expert in a field is, and will continue to be important only if you keep learning.

To become successful in the IT field, an area full of fast change and possibilities, a person can never stop learning.

As an individual IT pro, your career success is first of all built on skills. How much you are worth and how much you make are (6) _____ on the value of your skills in the industry. One of the proven (7) _____ for IT career success is to keep developing new skills. Besides, it's industry standard that almost all established vendors offer certifications on their products, systems, and tools. Getting certified is a popular (8) _____ among IT professionals. Certification is not your ticket to a dream job, not the destination of your learning road, but something that can be used to (9) _____ your learning ability.

No matter what kind of specific skill and certification you acquire, the most valuable kind of learning you can do is to learn how to (10) _____ and innovate; not to memorize, but to contribute; not to consume, but to create. So keep going, since we have a lot to learn.

Structured analysis and writing

I. Structure analysis

Write a biographical narrative essay

In this unit, you'll learn how to write a narrative essay in chronological order, which is frequently used in biographies.

A biography is a detailed description of a person's life. It involves more than just basic facts like education, work, relationships, and death; it portrays a person's experience of these life events. A biography analyzes and interprets the events in a person's life. It tries to find connections, explain the meaning of unexpected actions or mysteries, and make arguments about the significance of the person's accomplishments or life activities. A biography is usually about famous or infamous people, but a biography of an ordinary person can tell us a lot about a particular time and place. It is often about historical figures, but it can also be about people still living. Generally, a biography is written in chronological order. There may be some time periods grouped around a major theme. Still, others focus on specific topics or accomplishments. For example, from Paragraph 3 to Paragraph 6 in Text A, the early working experience of Ed Baker is presented in chronological order, describing how he transformed from a police officer to a professional IT trainer.

To write a narrative essay in chronological order, you should:

1) select a person you are interested in;

2) find out the basic facts of the person's life, and start with the encyclopedia and almanac;

3) think about what else you would like to know about the person, and what parts of the life you want to write most about. Some questions you might want to think about include:

- What makes this person special or interesting?
- What kind of effect did he or she have on the world or other people?
- What examples from their life illustrate those qualities?
- What events shaped or changed this person's life?
- Did he or she overcome obstacles? Take risks? Get lucky?

4) Do additional research at your library or on the Internet to find information that helps you answer these questions and tell an interesting story.

Now let's look at the following sentences taken from Text A, and pay attention to the underlined parts to see how different periods of life are connected to tell the life story of Ed Baker.

> <u>Baker got his start in IT in a place some might see as unexpected.</u> *Baker was a police officer beginning in the 1980s and, for 14 years, he did everything from walking the beat to motorcycle patrol to criminal investigation.* (Para. 3)

↓

> <u>As his career progressed</u>, *Baker struck out on his own as a self-employed IT project manager. There, he began to view certification and training from a new standpoint.* (Para. 4)

↓

> <u>From that point on</u>, *Baker lived and breathed IT training. In a litany of roles full-time and part-time, he has spread the word of IT and the skills it takes to be successful.* (Para. 6)

As can be seen from the above sentences, time signals are properly used to introduce the early working experience of Ed Baker.

II. Structured writing

Read the sample essay and see how it develops in chronological order.

> **Topic**
>
> Charles Dickens: A great writer of the Victorian period
>
> **Details might be organized in the chronological order:**

- When he was born;
- What his childhood was like;
- How he became a writer;
- When he died.

Sample essay

Charles Dickens is regarded as the greatest novelist of the Victorian period.

He was born in Portsmouth on February 7th, 1812. He had a well-off family in his early years, but his parents often banqueted guests and used money without restraint. As a result, his father was imprisoned for bad debt when Charles Dickens was 10 years old.

Charles was later sent to work in Warren's blacking factory and endured appalling conditions as well as loneliness and despair. He worked 10 hours every day. After three years, luckily, his father inherited the legacy of the family, so their financial conditions were improved. He was returned to school, but the experience was never forgotten and became fictionalized in two of his better-known novels *David Copperfield* and *Great Expectations*. At the age of 15, he graduated from Wellington College, and worked into a lawyer line. Later he turned to the newspaper, becoming a reporter at the age of 20.

Besides a huge list of novels, he published an autobiography, edited weekly periodicals and wrote travel books. His energy was inexhaustible and he spent much time abroad—for example, lecturing against slavery in the United States and touring Italy.

However, too much hard work and disappointment at reform seriously impaired his health. He died of a stroke in 1870 and was buried at Westminster Abbey. His tombstone wrote: He was a sympathizer to the poor, the suffering, and the oppressed; and by his death, one of England's greatest writers was lost to the world.

6. Write an essay of no less than 200 words on one of the following topics. One topic has an outline that you can follow.

Topic

A legendary figure in the IT world

Details might be organized in the chronological order:

- When he was born;
- What educational background he had;

- How he started his career;
- What he has achieved.

More topics:

- A great basketballer
- A hero who changed the world

Translation

7. Translate the following paragraph into Chinese.

As the son of a dentist and psychologist, Mark Zuckerberg has received a good education and has always been a whiz kid on the PC since he was a child. By the time he began classes at Harvard, Zuckerberg had already achieved a reputation as a programming prodigy. Together with his college roommates and fellow students, he launched Facebook from Harvard's dormitory rooms. Facebook grew phenomenally, and within the next year, it was immediately scaled out to other colleges in the United States. Eventually, it grew into a public service that anyone could access, whether to network with friends and family, to play games, or to meet past colleagues. Zuckerberg has remained true to his initial vision—to create a website that the entire world can use to communicate openly and easily with one another. Although its true value is debatable, it's safe to say that Facebook, and its creator Mark Zuckerberg, are two of the 21st century's most influential, controversial, and potentially powerful figures.

8. Translate the following paragraph into English.

低碳生活（low-carbon life）倡导人们在生活中减少二氧化碳的排放，是一种低能量、低消耗和低开支的生活方式。它要求人们以更健康、更安全和更自然的方式进行人与自然的活动。如今，这股风潮逐渐在中国一些大城市兴起，不知不觉地改变着人们的生活。为了实行低碳生活，人们需要改变一些生活细节，如节约用电、不使用塑料袋和一次性产品、优先乘坐公共交通工具等。低碳生活节能环保，大大有利于减缓全球气候变暖和环境恶化的速度。

Section B

 Reading skills: *Previewing*

Previewing means that you get an idea of what the reading material is about without actually reading the whole text. Previewing the text can help you activate prior knowledge, set reading goals, study important words, and predict the content, which will lead to improved comprehension of the reading material. By using previewing as a reading strategy, you will not only increase your understanding, but you will also have higher-level discussions and do more in-depth post-reading activities.

There are four steps to follow when previewing an article:

1) Read the title of the article and the subtitles if there are any. The title and subtitles often reveal the topic or subject of the reading material.

2) Read the first paragraph of the article. The first paragraph is often an introduction to the main idea of the article.

3) Read the last paragraph. The last paragraph usually summarizes the main content of the article, so you can get an idea as to what the author thinks is most important.

4) Read the first sentence of each remaining paragraph. Very likely the first sentence of a paragraph is the topic sentence; in other words, it very likely tells the main idea of that paragraph.

After you finish previewing, you may start reading the article from the beginning to the end. After your first reading, look back at the predictions you made about the article and see how accurate they are.

For example, when you see the title of Text A "Never Stop Learning", you might ask yourself some questions and make some predictions. The questions may be: What is the passage about? Who should keep learning? Why should people keep learning?

By reading the first paragraph and the last paragraph, you should be able to answer these questions. The first paragraph describes Baker's work and his achievements. The last paragraph is about the importance of continuous learning.

Next, read the first sentences of Paragraphs 2–10 of Text B, which are very likely to be the main ideas of these paragraphs. After reading the first sentences, you can learn about Baker's learning process, his entrepreneurial process and training, and how he helps young people enter the workforce, and Baker's work and approach at Microsoft.

By following the above steps and making predictions, you will have a better understanding of the reading material and the author's purpose in writing it.

Now make predictions about the following questions by using the reading skills of previewing.

(1) What may be the topic of the text?

    A. How to keep up with technology trends.

    B. How to join a professional organization.

    C. How to become an IT Talent.

(2) How many suggestions does the author give to keep up with the trends?

    A. 4   B. 5   C. 6

(3) What's the purpose of writing this article?

    A. To tell the importance of the IT industry.

    B. To show how to keep up with technology trends.

    C. To give advice to people on how to innovate.

Text B

How to Stay Current with Technology Trends?

1. Human nature **dictates** that we should always be moving forward, and for the better. This is the core **trait** that drives our constant pursuit of innovation. The IT industry always offers something new around the corner, always something much better than the previous

iteration, something that revolutionizes our way of thinking on how we solve problems.

2. As an IT professional, being up to date with the latest technologies is one of the most challenging yet necessary aspects you would have to face. You need to love technology to stay motivated and always study. You need to keep up with the latest trends and demands, to have a **satisfying** career, and to be successful at what you do.

3. Whether you are coding, **manufacturing** products or managing a project, staying current with technology can help you be more effective at work. It's evident that the knowledge of technology trends can help you stay relevant, stay organized, improve productivity, reach out to **potential** customers, and **accelerate** your growth as a person and help you grow your career in today's world.

4. Though it may seem **daunting**, there are many steps you can take to keep up with new technology.

Join a professional organization

5. Joining a professional organization can be a great way to stay on top of emerging technology that directly affects your industry. Many professional organizations produce magazines filled with current news and tech advances. The growing trend of technology-focused businesses is well patrolled by the industry's leading technology experts. With their **insights**, they can provide valuable advice on tips on keeping up with the latest trends and ideas. In addition to providing valuable insight, these experts can also **collaborate** with other members of the tech community in order to stay ahead of new technologies. So whether you're looking to stay informed about the latest in technology or just want to collaborate with **like-minded** people, a conversation with a top-tier technology expert is a beneficial way to achieve both.

Follow tech thought leaders by utilizing social media

6. A second box to tick on your tech to-do list to keep up with trends is to hit social media. Follow thought leaders and tech **outlets**. Turn on your **notifications** and check new articles and high-profile posts as soon as they're published.

7. Don't **restrict** yourself to tech **titans** like Elon Musk or Jeff Bezos. While these are undoubtedly top players, they're by far not the only—nor the most innovative—ones. And, as we have seen in Musk's Twitter **saga**, their technological **acumen** may not always be on point.

8. Instead, also follow tech editors at **trustworthy** media outlets, CEOs at smaller companies, and fast-growing startups. Product leads at large tech companies, such as YouTube and Google, can also be fantastic sources of information. When new features are being **launched**, for instance, they're often the first to share the news with the world.

9. Social media offers an additional advantage. It lets you assess how much each new trend resonates right away based on engagement—likes, shares, and mentions. By keeping an eye on social media, you're sure to know which trend is currently blowing up.

Prioritize learning and look for new avenues to upskill

10. Knowledge is the new **currency** in the IT industry. Continuous learners can **leverage** their knowledge of new trends, tools, coding languages, etc. to **boost** their professional growth. Both IT professionals and leaders must cultivate continuous learning habits for their teams to stay on top of the latest information.

11. In the IT industry, it is becoming less **compulsory** to have specific degrees or even formal education to pursue a career. Companies are moving toward skill-based hiring rather than **pedigree** hiring. However, it's important to always be on the lookout for new avenues to upskill. The **pandemic** has led to more e-learning opportunities, including a **plethora** of content and courses relevant to IT, such as Coursera, the Odin project, Udemy, and even YouTube videos.

12. You might start with courses that are not too time-consuming to keep a balance between professional and academic life. E-learning offers the flexibility to learn and upskill at your own pace, so once you are comfortable with time management, you can consider tackling the **lengthier** ones or even multiple courses.

Be willing to experiment

13. Practice and experimentation are key parts of staying up to date with technology. If you are a programmer, you can write code for side projects. A passion project keeps your technical skills sharp while experimenting with a new coding language or platform. Many sites offer **tutorials** and space to work on projects, allowing you to learn as you write code.

Avoid fads

14. Tech companies invent new tools all the time, but not every new tech is appropriate for you or your workplace. When investigating new technologies, consider how they meet your current or future needs. Even the most **revolutionary** product isn't necessary if it doesn't serve a purpose in your workplace. Spend your time and energy on products and processes that will benefit you as an employee and your company in the long run.

15. With the help of these tips, you can strive to remain updated and keep a better pace in this period of ever-advancing technology. Experts have estimated that the technology tools we use within our workplace evolve to the next generation every 24 months. So, there's no better time than the present to get yourself clued up.

(893 words)

New words

dictate	/dɪkˈteɪt/	vt.	1. to control or influence how sth. happens 支配；摆布；决定 2. ~ (sth.) (to sb.) to say words for sb. else to write down 口述
trait	/treɪt/	n.	a particular quality in your personality（人的个性的）特征；特性；特点
satisfying	/ˈsætɪsfaɪɪŋ/	a.	giving pleasure because it provides sth. you need or want 令人满意的；令人满足的
manufacture	/ˌmænjuˈfæktʃə/	vt.	to make goods in large quantities, using machinery（用机器）大量生产；成批制造
potential	/pəˈtenʃəl/	a.	that can develop into sth. or be developed in the future 潜在的；可能的
accelerate	/ækˈseləˌreɪt/	vt.	to happen or to make sth. happen faster or earlier than expected（使）加速；加快
daunt	/dɔːnt/	vt.	to make sb. feel nervous and less confident about doing sth. 使胆怯；使气馁；使失去信心
daunting	/ˈdɔːntɪŋ/	a.	frightening in a way that makes you feel less confident 令人生畏的；使人畏惧的；令人胆怯的；让人气馁的
insight	/ˈɪnˌsaɪt/	n.	[U] (approving) the ability to see and understand the truth about people or situations 洞察力；领悟
collaborate	/kəˈlæbəreɪt/	vi	~ (with sb. on sth.) ~ (with sb. in sth./in doing sth.) to work together with sb. in order to produce or achieve sth. 合作；协作
like-minded	/ˌlaɪk ˈmaɪndɪd/	a.	having similar ideas and interests 想法相同的；志趣相投的
outlet	/ˈaʊtlet/	n.	a way of expressing or making good use of strong feelings, ideas or energy（感情、思想、精力发泄的）出路；表现机会
notification	/ˌnəʊtɪfɪˈkeɪʃən/	n.	[C, U] (fml.) the act of giving or receiving official information about sth. 通知；通告；告示
restrict	/rɪˈstrɪkt/	vt.	to limit the size, amount or range of sth. 限制；限定（数量、范围等）
titan	/ˈtaɪtən/	n.	a person who is very large, strong, intelligent or important 巨人；高人；伟人
saga	/ˈsɑːɡə/	n.	a long story about events over a period of many years 长篇故事；长篇小说
acumen	/ˈækjuˌmen/	n.	[U] the ability to understand and decide things quickly and well 精明；敏锐

英语读写教程 2（第二版）
Intermediate IT English Reading and Writing 2 (2nd Edition)

trustworthy	/ˈtrʌstˌwɜːði/	a.	that you can rely on to be good, honest, sincere, etc. 值得信任的；可信赖的；可靠的
launch	/lɔːntʃ/	vt.	1. to make a product available to the public for the first time（首次）上市；发行 2. to start an activity, especially an organized one 开始从事；发起；发动（尤指有组织的活动）
prioritize	/praɪˈɒrɪˌtaɪz/	v.	1. to put tasks, problems, etc. in order of importance, so that you can deal with the most important first 按重要性排列；划分优先顺序 2. (fml.) to treat sth. as being more important than other things 优先处理
avenue	/ˈævɪˌnjuː/	n.	1. a choice or way of making progress towards sth. 选择；途径；手段 2. a street in a town or city（城镇的）大街
upskill	/ˈʌpˌskɪl/	v.	to improve the aptitude for work of (a person) by additional training（通过额外的培训）使技能提升
currency	/ˈkʌrənsi/	n.	the system of money that a country uses 通货；货币
leverage	/ˈliːvərɪdʒ/	vt.	to use to obtain a desired effect or result 充分利用（资源、观点等）
		n.	[U] (fml.) the ability to influence what people do 影响力
boost	/buːst/	vt.	to make sth. increase, or become better or more successful 使增长；使兴旺
compulsory	/kəmˈpʌlsəri/	a.	that must be done because of a law or a rule（因法律或规则而）必须做的；强制的；强迫的
pedigree	/ˈpedɪˌɡriː/	n.	a person's family history or the background of sth., especially when this is impressive 家谱；门第；世系；起源
pandemic	/pænˈdemɪk/	n.	a disease that spreads over a whole country or the whole world（全国或全球性）流行病；大流行病
plethora	/ˈpleθərə/	n.	an amount that is greater than is needed or can be used 过多；过量；过剩
lengthy	/ˈleŋθi/	a.	very long, and often too long, in time or size 很长的；漫长的；冗长的
tutorial	/tjuːˈtɔːriəl/	n.	a short book or computer program that gives information on a particular subject or explains how sth. is done 教程；辅导材料；使用说明书
fad	/fæd/	n.	an activity or topic of interest that is very popular for a short time, but which people become bored with very quickly 一时的狂热
revolutionary	/ˌrevəˈluːʃənəri/	a.	involving a great or complete change 彻底变革的；巨变的

New expressions

stay current with	to keep up with 跟上时代；保持同步
up to date	reflecting the latest information or changes 最新的；最近的；现代的
reach out to	to come in contact with 把手伸向；接触
restrict to	to stop sb./sth. from moving or acting freely 限制
keep an eye on	to follow with the eyes or the mind 照看；留意；密切注视
on the lookout for	to look carefully for sth./sb.; to examine a particular place when looking for sb./sth. 寻找；注意；警戒
keep a balance between	to give equal importance to two contrasting things or parts of sth. 保持平衡
at one's own pace	out of one's own rhythms and cycles 按自己的节奏
in the long run	after a very lengthy period of time 长远；终究
get clued up	to have a great deal of detailed knowledge and information about sth. 对……十分在行；十分了解某事

Notes

1. Elon Musk (埃隆·马斯克): born on June 28, 1971. An entrepreneur, engineer, inventor, philanthropist, founder and CEO of Tesla, CEO and Chief Technology Officer of SpaceX, Chairman of the Board of Directors of Solar City, CEO of Twitter, Fellow of the US National Academy of Engineering, Fellow of the Royal Society, Co-founder of OpenAI; he received his bachelor's degree in Economics and Physics from the University of Pennsylvania.

2. Jeff Bezos (杰夫·贝佐斯): born on January 12, 1964. He graduated from Princeton University. The entrepreneur who founded Amazon, the world's largest online bookstore; Executive Chairman of the Board of Amazon.com.

Reading comprehension

Understanding the text

1. Choose the best answer to each of the following questions.

(1) As an IT professional, what is one of the most challenging yet necessary aspects you would have to face?

   A. Being up to date with the latest technologies.

   B. Moving forward.

   C. Manufacturing products.

   D. Managing a project.

(2) How can the knowledge of technology trends help you?

   A. Stay relevant, stay organized, and improve productivity.

   B. Reach out to potential customers, and accelerate your growth as a person.

   C. Help you grow your career in today's world.

   D. All of the above.

(3) If you want to stay informed about the latest in technology or just want to collaborate with like-minded people, what is a beneficial way?

   A. A patrol by the industry's leading technology experts.

   B. A conversation with a top-tier technology expert.

   C. A collaboration with other members of the tech community.

   D. All of the above.

(4) Turn on your notifications and check new articles and high-profile posts as soon as _____.

   A. they're criticized   B. they're gone

   C. they're published   D. they're signed

(5) How to know which trend is currently blowing up?

   A. By keeping an eye on social media.

   B. By keeping an eye only on tech titans like Elon Musk or Jeff Bezos.

   C. By keeping an eye on technology experts.

   D. By keeping an eye on members of the tech community.

(6) What is the new currency in the IT industry?

   A. Knowledge.   B. Collaboration.

   C. Conversation.   D. Technology.

(7) What will benefit you as an employee and your company in the long run?

   A. Investigating new technologies.

   B. Spending your time and energy on products and processes.

   C. Inventing new tools.

   D. Producing the most revolutionary product.

(8) The purpose of the text is _____.

   A. to prove to us that it is impossible to stay current with technology trends

   B. to demonstrate that technology trends have five primary purposes

   C. to help us realize the importance of staying current with technology trends

   D. to suggest how to stay current with technology trends

Critical thinking

2. Work in pairs and discuss the following questions.

(1) Do you think it is important to stay current with technology trends?

(2) In your opinion, what factors are the main considerations in staying current with technology trends?

(3) How can we stay current with technology trends except for the points mentioned in the text?

 **Language focus**

Words in use

3. Fill in the blanks with the words given below. Change the form where necessary. Each word can be used only once.

| collaborate | compulsory | revolutionary | accelerate | lengthy |
| leverage | plethora | daunt | pandemic | dictate |

(1) When we take our vacations is very much _____ by Greg's work schedule.

(2) From climate change to the ongoing _____ and beyond, the issues facing today's world are increasingly complex and dynamic.

(3) Exposure to the sun can _____ the aging process.

(4) After _____ talks, the two sides finally reached a compromise.

(5) We don't have much political _____ in this matter.

(6) Only an effective _____ between filmmakers and art historians can create films that will enhance viewers' perceptions of art.

(7) Computing environment: data services could be consumed from a(n) _____ of platforms.

(8) In the new curriculum, some courses are _____, while others are optional for middle school students.

(9) When I stayed in a corner and was so scared, a friend of mine came to me, and said: in this world, nothing can _____ us, in addition to our own.

(10) The region at the time was fertile ground for _____ movements.

Expressions in use

4. **Fill in the blanks with the expressions given below. Change the form where necessary. Each expression can be used only once.**

on the lookout for	keep an eye on	stay current with	at one's own pace
keep a balance between	reach out to	restrict to	in the long run

(1) Do not tell yourself that it is not possible—no matter how old you are, just go _____.

(2) But scientists are always _____ any evidence that might suggest an alternative to the Big Bang.

(3) In my opinion, we should _____ amusement and study or work.

(4) He had extraordinary emotional intelligence, an ability to _____ people.

(5) The virus alert system _____ the websites customers' visit to stop them from accidentally going to places riddled with viruses.

(6) He can choose from different jobs and probably changes his work more frequently as he is not _____ a choice within a small radius.

(7) Companies are more likely to succeed _____ if they compete on quality or performance instead of price.

(8) You are supposed to take time to _____ your customer's changing needs.

Sentence structure

5. Rewrite the sentences by using the accompanying adverbials. Make changes where necessary.

Model:	The pandemic has led to more e-learning opportunities. They include a plethora of content and courses relevant to IT, such as Coursera, the Odin project, Udemy, and even YouTube videos.
⟶	The pandemic has led to more e-learning opportunities, including a plethora of content and courses relevant to IT, such as Coursera, the Odin project, Udemy, and even YouTube videos.

(1) We show our true feelings with our eyes, faces, bodies, and attitudes. At the same time, it causes a chain of reactions.

(2) She refused to attend the party. She didn't want to meet John there.

(3) The bus driver arrived one hour late. This caused me to miss the beginning of the game.

(4) The marine sat there in the dimly lit ward. At the same time, he held the old man's hand and offered words of hope and strength.

(5) I realized he was too sick to tell whether or not I was his son. I guessed he really needed me.

Collocation

Ed Baker emphasizes the value of continuous learning and career adaptability in the ***ever-advancing IT industry*** (Text B). With a passion for IT training and certification, he has empowered ***students of all ages and backgrounds*** (Text A), instilling in them the importance of staying up-to-date and embracing change for success. Continuous learning and ***staying current*** (Text B) with technology trends are essential for IT professionals. Join professional organizations, follow tech thought leaders on social media, prioritize upskilling, and experiment with side projects while avoiding fads to maintain a ***competitive edge*** (Text B) in the highly competitive tech industry.

6. **Replace the underlined words in the following sentences with the words provided in the box to form collocations you have learned from this unit.**

fantastic	accelerating	high-profile	compulsory
acumen	trustworthy	previous	stay

(1) There were no historical records of Homer, and no <u>reliable</u> biography of the man exists beyond a few self-referential hints embedded in the texts themselves.

(2) Education is valued greatly in Chinese culture; maths is recognized as an important <u>mandatory</u> subject throughout schooling; and the emphasis is on hard work coupled with a focus on accuracy.

(3) The Constitution requires the president to seek the <u>prior</u> approval of Congress for military action.

(4) People who live longer <u>keep</u> motivated and are always looking forward to their next accomplishment.

(5) Economist Helena Leurent says this period of rapid change in manufacturing is a(n) <u>brilliant</u> opportunity to make the world a better place.

(6) My dear students, I want you to know that each of your attention is truly helpful in <u>improving</u> the steps of development and growth of our university.

(7) It's no surprise that <u>famous</u> athletes can influence children's eating behaviors, but the scientists were able to quantify how prevalent these endorsements are in the children's environment.

(8) When you have business <u>wisdom</u>, you realize the importance of every job at every stage of your career.

Translation

7. Translate the following passage into English.

新技术是机遇也是风险和挑战。科学发现和技术创新的每一次重大突破都促进了人类社会的发展和进步，也会带来价值链、产业链、供应链的重构，打破现有的经济、社会、国家乃至地区间的平衡，挑战旧的规则和秩序。国家内部的经济社会管理、全球经济治理都需做出相应的调整。

Unit project

Write a report on self-learning for IT majors.

> Based on this unit theme, you will be expected to engage in writing a report on self-learning for IT majors. To make sure the report is as reliable and profound as possible, follow these specific steps.

(1) Work in groups and design a survey on self-learning for IT majors. The following questions can be included in your survey. Add more questions if you can.

- What should IT majors learn in college?
- What courses are necessary for them to learn?
- Besides professional basic knowledge, what else should they possess?
- Through what way can they improve themselves?
- What should they learn by themselves after graduation?
- Which is more important for IT majors' future success, solid professional knowledge or the ability to adapt to the tech world?
- …

(2) Each of your group members interviews 5–10 students on campus. Take down their answers to your questions.

(3) Write a report. Decide what findings should be included in the report and draw a conclusion.

(4) Report to the whole class about your conclusion.

Unit 2

Strive for Professionalism in IT

Learning objectives

In this unit you will:
- learn what a professional programmer is and how to become one;
- learn what broken window crisis is and how to deal with it;
- learn how to write an expository essay;
- learn how to read for main ideas and recognize important details.

> Being a professional is doing the things you love to do, on the days you don't feel like doing them.
>
> —*Julius Irving*
>
> In business "professionalism" is not a tactic but a moral value.
>
> —*Amit Kalantri*

Preview

IT stands for "Information Technology". It refers to anything related to computing technology, such as networking, hardware, software, the Internet, or the people that work with these technologies. Many companies now have IT departments for managing the computers, networks, and other technical areas of their businesses. IT jobs include computer programming, network administration, computer engineering, Web development, technical support, and many other related occupations. We are now living in the "information age", and information technology has become a part of our everyday lives. But what kind of people are capable of becoming professionals in the IT field? What qualities should an IT professional have? Do you want to be a member of them? What do you think is the best way to improve professional competency?

Section A

 Pre-reading activities

1. **Listen to the talk about the job responsibilities of computer programmers. Fill in the blanks based on what you hear.**

   (1) Computer programmers use programming languages to write, test, and _____ code. These essential tech professionals create programs and software that millions of people use every day.

   Computer programmers work _____ as part of larger software teams. Together with software developers and engineers, programmers create the _____ computers use to execute tasks. A programmer's job also includes finding bugs, eliminating errors, and _____ issues. These professionals need a detail-oriented and _____ outlook, along with skills in several programming languages.

   (2) What are the job responsibilities of a professional programmer? Summarize them with key words.

   a. _____
   b. _____
   c. _____

2. **Discuss the following questions with your partner.**

   (1) What is a programmer?

   (2) What do you think a professional programmer can do?

   (3) What does the word "professional" mean in the IT field?

Text A

What Is a Professional Programmer?

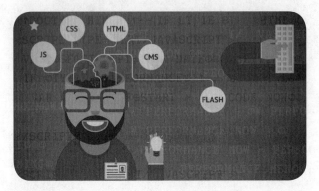

1. How do people become professional programmers? Many people go the "traditional" path through a computer science or software engineering education and from there into professionally **adroit** programming work.

2. Others become professional programmers by accident. A person writes a **trivial** program to help at work, and their workmates say, "Oh Gee, you can write programs! You're our programmer now!"

3. Other people start out as **amateurs** and follow a less conventional path, not always getting a degree, but clearly **craving** for the dream from the outset and working **earnestly** towards that goal.

4. I've been a hobbyist programmer since I was 6. I wasn't writing anything **stunning** back then but I had started writing and soon found it was **engrossing** most of my time. Since I never really stopped, that gives me 24 years of "programming experience" and counting.

5. At first I was keen on writing computer games. Later people asked me to write programs for them, and sometimes I even got paid. From this, I learned that programs are not **self-sustained** worlds of their own. People expect things out of a program that have more to do with Japanese or **Geophysics** or Engineering or whatever they've got in mind than with how a computer works. I had to learn something about all those domains in order to write programs for them.

6. At university it didn't take long before I became a tutor, and that's where I found teaching, especially teaching programming was **gratifying**.

7. While I was at university I got my first "real" job, writing Visual C++ code for a financial database company. In terms of design and theory, it was **lightweight** stuff. But in terms of working with others on a large project, I was being thrown into the deep end! They had **gigabytes** of source code, growing **cancerously** through the efforts of a dozen developers

of wildly differing skill levels.

8. In spite of my programming skills being well above average there, I learned to settle for being a junior programmer, a little fish in a large pond.

9. Skipping along a few more jobs and a lot more years, today I am a senior developer in a small research group—a big fish in a little pond. I've had to teach my co-workers a lot about professional programming, because most of them haven't been in the industry to get that taste of what large code bases and **diverse** skill levels mean to programs if you aren't using those "professional" skills to keep everyone pointed in the same direction.

10. There's quite a gap between "being able to program" and "being a professional programmer". It took me 15 years to go from beginner to **hotshot** programmer, then another 10 years to go from hotshot to professional—and I'm still learning.

11. Whatever the path we follow, most professional programmers have in common the fact that they learned to code first and how to be a professional later.

12. So what does it mean to be a professional programmer? Some definitions simply say to be a professional is "to make money from a skill", but true professionals also have a set of qualities often described as "**professionalism**". In my opinion, these qualities are trustworthiness, communication, constant updating of skills, and an interest in accountability. Each of these affects the professional programmer in certain ways.

13. The concept of trustworthiness applies in several different ways for programmers. Can you be trusted with a job? Can you be trusted to ask for help when you need it? If you're given clients' data or have signed a **non-disclosure** agreement, then you are **entrusted** to respect privacy. You are trusted to check license agreements on third party tools or libraries and to get licenses or permission as required. And like any professional, you are trusted to simply do a good job.

14. While some media sources portray programming as a loner's craft, the truth is that it really involves a lot of communication and working with others. If you work for a company, you'll be part of a development team and be expected to communicate and work well with others.

15. Respecting the people you work with and really listening to them is a critical part of communication. Spend your time communicating clearly, **concisely** and **convincingly**, thinking from the perspective of the **recipient**, over e-mail to co-workers, managers, clients/partners and hopefully one day executives. Teamwork can't happen without good communication.

16. Technology is always **evolving**, and with it, so should a developer's knowledge base. If you want to stay relevant in your field, it's important to keep up with new and **updated**

programming languages, software, and hardware.

17. You must be willing to examine new tech, analyze its merits and **pitfalls**, **assimilate** it rapidly, fully absorb, understand, and integrate this new thing into your skill set. You can view learning as a skill that you should focus on mastering. Once you do, you'll have an easier time rolling with the **punches** of technology, and staying ahead of the competition in your field.

18. Writing code for others is a responsibility. You need to make sure your software is reliable. You need to make sure you and the client truly understand the requirements and specifications. You need to have **documentation** of your work, all current and past bugs, your progress, any problems, signed-off milestones, and more. You are also required to know about some basic legal issues, like software licensing, the terms of your employment contract, and intellectual property law.

19. As you can see, there is a huge gap between "coding" and "professional programming". Most programming courses focus on the coding side of things, and the professional skills tend to be **glossed** over or not covered at all. I have found myself regularly teaching these skills to new co-workers, which highlighted the need for "professionalism skills training". Teaching my co-workers reminded me how much I enjoy teaching.

20. These days I consider myself to be a professional programmer, though I am still discovering the depth and breadth of what exactly that means. Perhaps that **perpetual** exploration of programming and of professionalism is what makes this for me a career and not just a job.

(1,017 words)

New words

adroit	/əˈdrɔɪt/	*a.*	skillful; clever 熟练的；机敏的；灵巧的
trivial	/ˈtrɪviəl/	*a.*	small and of little importance 微不足道的；价值不高的
amateur	/ˈæmətə/	*n.*	[C] a person who practices a sport or artistic skill without receiving money for it 业余爱好者（不为金钱而从事体育或艺术活动的人）
crave	/kreɪv/	*vi.*	~ *(for) sth.* to have a strong desire for sth. 渴望；渴求某事物
earnestly	/ˈɜːnɪstli/	*ad.*	in a serious manner 认真地；诚挚地；热切地
stunning	/ˈstʌnɪŋ/	*a.*	extremely attractive or beautiful 极好的；出色的
engross	/ɪnˈɡrəʊs/	*v.*	(usu. passive) to occupy all the time or attention of (sb.) 占去某人的全部时间或注意力；使全神贯注

Unit 2 Strive for Professionalism in IT

self-sustained	/ˈselfsəˈsteɪnd/	a.	independent, complete and not needing other things or help from 自持的；自立的
geophysics	/ˌdʒiːəʊˈfɪzɪks/	n.	[U] scientific study of the physics of the Earth, e.g. its magnetism, meteorology 地球物理学
gratifying	/ˈɡrætɪfaɪɪŋ/	a.	pleasing and satisfying 悦人的；令人满足的
lightweight	/ˈlaɪtˌweɪt/	a.	not very important or skillful in a particular area of activity 无足轻重的；不足取的
gigabyte	/ˈɡɪɡəˌbaɪt/	n.	[C] written abbreviation GB or Gb, a unit for measuring computer information, equal to 1,024 megabytes, and used less exactly to mean a billion bytes 十亿字节
cancerously	/ˈkænsərəslɪ/	ad.	related to or affected with cancer 像癌症般地；步步扩散地
diverse	/daɪˈvɜːs/	a.	of different kinds; varied 多种多样的；不同的
hotshot	/ˈhɒtˌʃɒt/	n.	[C] someone who is dazzlingly skilled in any field 高手；能人
professionalism	/prəˈfeʃənəˌlɪzəm/	n.	[U] 1. (approve.) skill or qualities of a profession or its members 专业技能；特长；职业特性 2. practice of employing professionals in sport 在体育竞赛中雇用职业选手的做法
disclosure	/dɪsˈkləʊʒə/	n.	1. [U] making sth. known 公开；透露 2. [C] thing, esp. a secret that is made known 被公开的事情；（尤指）被透露的秘闻
non-disclosure		n.	failure or refusal to make sth. known 不揭露；守秘密；不提供资料
entrust	/ɪnˈtrʌst/	vt.	to trust sb. or to take charge of sth./sb. 委托某人负责或照看某事物/照看某人
concisely	/kənˈsaɪslɪ/	ad.	in a concise manner; accurately 简明地
convincingly	/kənˈvɪnsɪŋlɪ/	ad.	making you believe that something is true or right 令人信服地；有说服力地
recipient	/rɪˈsɪpɪənt/	n.	[C] a person who receives sth. 接受者
update	/ˌʌpˈdeɪt/	vt.	to bring (sth.) up to date; to modernize 更新（某事物）；使现代化；更新
updated	/ˌʌpˈdeɪtɪd/	a.	to moderize 最新的；现代化的；适时的；校正的
pitfall	/ˈpɪtˌfɔːl/	n.	[C] unsuspected danger or difficulty 意想不到的危险或困难
assimilate	/əˈsɪmɪˌleɪt/	vt.	1. (cause sth. to) become absorbed into the body after digestion （使某物）经消化而吸收 2. (allow sb./sth. to)

			become part of another social group or state（让某人/某事物）同化 3. to absorb (ideas, knowledge, etc.) in the mind 吸收（思想、知识等）
punch	/pʌntʃ/	vt.	to strike (sb./sth.) hard with the fist 用拳猛击（某人/某物）
		n.	1. [C] blow given with the fist（用拳的）一击；一拳 2. [U] (fig.) effective force or vigor 力量；活力
documentation	/ˌdɒkjʊmenˈteɪʃən/	n.	[U] official documents, reports, etc. that are used to prove that something is true or correct 文件
gloss	/glɒs/	vi.	(~ over sth.) to treat sth. briefly, or in a superficial or an incomplete way, so as to avoid embarrassing details 简略地、浮皮潦草地或敷衍地处理某事（以求避开难堪的细节）
perpetual	/pəˈpetjʊəl/	a.	1. (usu. attrib.) continuing indefinitely; permanent 永久的；永恒的 2. without interruption; continuous 不间断的；持续的

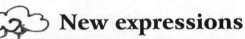

New expressions

by accident	as a result of chance 偶然；意外地
crave for sth.	to have a strong desire for sth. 渴望；渴求某事物
in terms of	as regards sth. 在某事物方面；以某说法来表达
a dozen of	a lot of 成打的；许多的
settle for	to accept sth. even though it is not the best, or not what you really want 勉强接受
in common	in the same way as someone or sth. else 常见的；共有的
keep up with	to manage to do as much or as well as other people 跟上；保持一致
roll with the punches	to deal with problems or difficulties by doing whatever you need to do, rather than by trying only one method 想方设法地应对
stay ahead of	to be in the lead over (sb./sth.) 保持领先
gloss over sth.	to treat sth. briefly, or in a superficial or incomplete way, so as to avoid embarrassing details 简略地或敷衍地处理某事（以求掩盖错误）

Unit 2 Strive for Professionalism in IT

 Notes

1. gigabyte (千兆字节): a unit for measuring computer information, equal to 1,024 megabytes, and used less exactly to mean a billion bytes.
2. software license (软件许可证): a legal instrument (usually by way of contract law, with or without printed material) governing the use or redistribution of software.
3. intellectual property (知识产权): creations of the intellect for which a monopoly is assigned to designated owners by law.

 Reading comprehension

Understanding the text

1. Answer the following questions.

(1) According to the text, what are the three paths people go through to become programmers?

(2) How did the writer become a programmer?

(3) Why did he have to teach co-workers a lot about professional programming?

(4) What do most professional programmers have in common?

(5) What qualities should true professionals have?

(6) What does the concept of trustworthiness mean for programmers?

(7) Why should professional programmers update their skills?

(8) According to the text, what is the huge gap between coding and professional programming?

Critical thinking

2. Work in pairs and discuss the following questions.

(1) What's your opinion of a professional programmer? What qualities do you think they should have?

(2) In your viewpoint, what is the most difficult challenge for a professional programmer?

(3) Do you agree with the sentence "there is a huge gap between coding and professional programming"?

Word building

The suffix *-ness* can be added to adjectives to form nouns with the meaning of "the quality or condition of being..." A final *y* is replaced by *i* before adding *-ness*.

Examples

Words learned	Add *-ness*	New words formed
great	→	greatness
cold	→	coldness
weak	→	weakness
ill	→	illness
happy	→	happiness

The prefixes *in-*, *im-*, *il-*, and *ir-* are added to adjectives to make them negative in meaning.

Examples

Words learned	Add *in-*, *im-*, *il-*, *ir-*	New words formed
complete	→	incomplete
responsible	→	irresponsible
logical	→	illogical
possible	→	impossible

3. Add *-ness, in-, im-, il-* or *ir-* to the following words to form new words.

Words learned	New words formed
-ness	
sad	
nervous	
dark	
lazy	
careless	
in- il-, im-, ir-	
direct	
proper	
sensitive	
literate	
regular	

Unit 2 Strive for Professionalism in IT

4. Fill in the blanks with the newly-formed words in Activity 3. Change the form where necessary. Each word can be used only once.

(1) I was _____ in the old society, but now I can read.

(2) I know that we will get through this _____, just as each of us must when we go through loss.

(3) Some children prefer a more _____ way to cope with their emotions. Role-play is the best way to help them.

(4) Our surveyors stated that _____ on the part of the manufacturer caused the shortage of the goods.

(5) The police have been criticized for being _____ to complaints from the public.

(6) Those are days of _____, when many of them spent most of their lives enduring all kinds of hardships.

(7) Joking with everyone at this official celebration is _____ behavior for such a serious occasion.

(8) Emphasizing the importance of persistence and hard work will help a child avoid the _____ trap.

(9) I have difficulty learning French _____ verbs; I just can't seem to get them into my head.

(10) Excessive smiling in a job interview is seen for what it is— _____ and a lack of confidence.

Banked cloze

5. Fill in the blanks by selecting suitable words from the word bank. You may not use any of the words more than once.

A. challenge	B. cultivate	C. slight	D. critical	E. prosperous
F. inspire	G. consistent	H. accordingly	I. adept	J. lead
K. esteem	L. preserve	M. behalf	N. famous	O. map

As many (1) _____ business people already know, preparation is often the key to success in any endeavor. You may be socially (2) _____ at work and have a pleasant enough personality, but you'll be more likely to convince others that your solution is the right one if you have the facts on your side. Doing your homework means taking the initiative to be prepared for any (3) _____: making a presentation, advancing a new idea to your boss, etc. And doing your homework also means doing the basic research necessary to back up whatever claims you are making. One especially (4) _____ factor to consider is the culture of the organization you work for: The ideals that are held in high (5) _____ by management and used as models for good employee behavior. For your initiatives to be successful, you have to tailor your approach (6) _____. Here are some suggestions: First of all, research your organization's culture by talking with your colleagues about what norms, values, and beliefs are most important to your organization. Secondly, (7) _____ out your organization's decision-making channels and take time to get to know each person in the channels you wish to influence. Thirdly, (8) _____ networks of co-workers who can support you in your efforts and influence others on your (9) _____. At last, as you prepare to influence others in your organization, be sure that your anticipated approach is (10) _____ with the organization's culture.

Structured analysis and writing

Structure analysis

Write an expository essay

The expository essay requires the student to investigate an idea, evaluate evidence, expound on the idea, and set forth an argument concerning that idea in a clear and concise manner. It may use the techniques of compare and contrast, cause and effect, examples, statistics or definitions in order to meet its goal.

The structure of the expository essay usually follows the format of three parts: introduction, body and conclusion. The introduction is a statement of the essay's thesis and the sub-topics that will be developed within the essay body. Each paragraph of the body part must have a dominant point that directly relates to the essay thesis. All supporting sentences within each body paragraph must have a direct and factual relationship to the dominant point. The expository essay is usually concluded by restating the thesis and summarizing the points that lead to the conclusion.

Now let's look at the following sentences taken from Text A, and pay attention to how the author uses his own experience as an example to show one way of becoming a professional programmer.

> How do people become professional programmers? Many people go the "traditional" path through a computer science or software engineering education and from there into professionally adroit programming work. (Para. 1)

↓

> *Other people start out as amateurs and follow a less conventional path, not always getting a degree, but clearly craving for the dream from the outset and working earnestly towards that goal. (Para. 3)*

↓

> *At first, I was keen on writing computer games. Later people asked me to write programs for them, and sometimes I even got paid. (Para. 5)*

↓

> *At university, it didn't take long before I became a tutor, and that's where I found teaching, especially teaching programming was gratifying. (Para. 6)*

↓

> *In spite of my programming skills being well above average there, I learned to settle for being a junior programmer, a little fish in a large pond. (Para. 8)*

↓

> *There's quite a gap between "being able to program" and being a "professional programmer". It took me 15 years to go from beginner to hotshot programmer, then another 10 years to go from hotshot to professional—and I'm still learning. (Para. 10)*

As can be seen from the paragraphs above, procedures and facts are properly used to explain how people can become professional programmers.

Structured writing

Read the sample essay and see how an expository essay is structured.

Topic

What does friendship mean?

Introduction

A general definition of the term "best friend"

Body

Cite three specific examples to illustrate the term

Conclusion

Friendship is a treasure in our life.

Sample essay

Friendship—What Does It Mean?

In my definition, a best friend is a twin soul, a person with whom I feel totally at ease. Just as fish cannot live without water, we cannot live without friends. Friends are companions who share both our joys and sadness. Friends are mirrors through which we can see our own.

Everyone needs friendship. No one can sail the ocean of life single-handedly. We need help from, and also give help to, others. In the modern age, people attach more importance to relations and connections. A man of charisma has many friends. His power lies in his ability to give.

The term, friend, covers a wide range of meanings. It can be a nodding acquaintance, a comrade, a confidant, a partner, a playmate, a brother, an intimate, etc. A best friend is a life constant in one's heart.

Ms. W is one of my best friends. We met since childhood and our friendship has lasted for 47 years. We've come in and out of each other's lives at different times, and witnessed many changes throughout our lives yet our friendship is a bond that remains unbreakable.

Ms. R is a friend I have made in college, and we often joke that we share a brain. She was then studying at another university in the city and we spoke on the phone on an average of once a week from 2–3 hours per call. She has provided me with so much sparklingly academic and mental support that we're bonded in both creativity and emotional growth.

Mr. Z is the love of my life and the male "best friend" as my boyfriend. We met in the mid-1980s and I fell in love with him because of his kindness and gentle nature. Although I would happily spend the rest of my life with him, I have no need for that to happen—I love him conditionally and I desire his happiness, whatever that entails.

Friendship, a treasure in our lives, is like a bottle of wine. The longer it is kept, the sweeter it will be. It is also like a cup of tea. When we are thirsty, it is our best choice, but when we have enough time to enjoy ourselves, it is also the most fragrant drink.

6. Write an essay of no less than 200 words on one of the following topics. One topic has an outline that you can follow.

Topic
How to keep lifelong learning
Introduction
What lifelong learning means
Body
Tips and examples to keep lifelong learning
Conclusion
What can be reached in lifelong learning

More topics:

- The benefits of volunteering
- How to keep a good mood

Translation

7. Translate the following paragraph into Chinese.

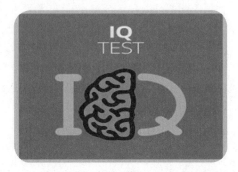

  There is more agreement on the kinds of behavior referred to by the term—intelligence than there is on how to interpret or classify them. But it is generally agreed that a person of high intelligence is one who can grasp ideas readily, make distinctions logically and make use of verbal and mathematical symbols in solving problems. An intelligence test is a rough measure of a child's capacity for learning, particularly for learning the kinds of things required in school. It does not measure character, social adjustment, physical endurance, manual skills or artistic abilities. It is not supposed to—it was not designed for such purposes. To criticize it for such failure is roughly comparable to criticizing a thermometer for not measuring wind velocity. Now since the assessment of intelligence is a comparative matter, we must be sure that the scale with which we are comparing our subjects provides a valid or fair comparison.

8. Translate the following paragraph into English.

吸烟之危害可谓大矣，其严重性是不能低估的。吸烟污染空气，损害健康，使肺癌发病率大大增加。为了使各国人民关注烟草的盛行及预防吸烟导致的疾病和死亡，世界卫生组织已将每年的5月31日定为"世界无烟日"。瘾君子们说："一天不吃饭可以，一个时辰不抽烟就难捱了，不能戒。"只有当他们意识到吸烟有百害而无一利，于人于己都是一种祸害，并真正坚持戒烟时，才有可能最终摆脱烟草的诱惑。

Section B

 Reading skills: *Reading for main ideas and recognizing important details*

Reading for Main Ideas

An important skill in reading is learning to comprehend the main idea of a text. This is accomplished by first determining the thesis statement of the text. The thesis statement, or topic sentence, tells the reader what the text is about; it is the most important sentence in the text. Sometimes the main idea is implied rather than directly stated in a sentence and the reader must learn how to infer as to what the main idea of the text is in order to comprehend the material as a whole.

Look at the following example from Text A:

<u>Writing code for others is a responsibility</u>. You need to make sure your software is reliable. You need to make sure you and the client truly understand the requirements and specifications. You need to have documentation of your work, all current and past bugs, your progress, any problems, signed-off milestones, and more. You are also required to know about some basic legal issues, like software licensing, the terms of your employment contract, and intellectual property law. (Para. 18)

The first sentence is the topic sentence of this paragraph. The rest of the paragraph illustrates specifically why writing code for others is a responsibility.

Recognizing Important Details

To understand the main idea thoroughly, you must recognize the important facts or details which help develop or support it. These facts and details give you a deeper understanding of the main idea. Here are some ways to help you recognize the important facts or details:

1) Read for the main idea. If you have identified the main idea, you can recognize more easily the important facts that support it.

2) Keep in mind that not all facts or details are equally important. Look only for the facts related to the main idea.

3) Check on your understanding of the material you have read, review the facts or details

which you have decided are the most important. Then consider if they support what you have identified as the main idea. If adding up the facts or details does not lead logically to the main idea, you have failed either to identify the main idea or to recognize the important supporting details.

Now let us look at the following example from Text A:

The concept of trustworthiness applies in several different ways for programmers. <u>Can you be trusted with a job? Can you be trusted to ask for help when you need it? If you're given clients' data or have signed a non-disclosure agreement, then you are being entrusted to respect privacy. You are trusted to check license agreements on third party tools or libraries and to get licenses or permission as required. And like any professional, you are trusted to simply do a good job.</u> (Para. 13)

As can be seen from the paragraph above, the underlined sentences are the important details closely related to the main idea of the paragraph, trying to explain how trustworthiness is applied to the work of programmers.

Skim the following paragraphs of Text B quickly and work out the main ideas and important details of them.

(1) There are many factors that can engender software rot. The most important one seems to be the psychology, or culture, at work on a project. Even if you are a team of one, your project's psychology can be a very delicate thing. Despite the best laid plans and the best people, a project can still experience ruin and decay during its lifetime. (Para. 2)

The main idea of the paragraph is _____

Important details are _____

(2) One broken window, left unrepaired for a considerable length of time, instills in the inhabitants of the building a sense of abandonment—a sense that powers neglect the building. So another window gets broken. People start littering. Graffiti appears. Serious structural damage begins. In a comparatively short space of time, the building becomes damaged beyond the owner's desire to fix it, and the sense of abandonment becomes a reality. (Para. 6)

The main idea of the paragraph is _____

Important details are _____

Text B

A Broken Window's Crisis

1. While software development is **immune** from almost all physical laws, **entropy** hits us hard. Entropy is a term from physics that refers to the amount of disorder in a system. Unfortunately, the laws of **thermodynamics** guarantee that the entropy in the universe tends toward a **maximum**. When disorder increases in software, programmers call it "software **rot**".

2. There are many factors that can **engender** software rot. The most important one seems to be the psychology, or culture, at work on a project. Even if you are a team of one, your project's psychology can be a very **delicate** thing. Despite the best laid plans and the best people, a project can still experience ruin and **decay** during its lifetime. Yet there are other projects that, despite enormous difficulties and constant **setbacks**, successfully fight nature's tendency toward disorder and manage to come out pretty well.

3. What makes the difference?

4. In inner cities, some buildings are beautiful and clean, while others are rotting **hulks**. Why? Researchers in the field of mine and urban decay discovered a fascinating **trigger** mechanism, one that very quickly turns a clean, **intact**, inhabited building into a **smashed** and abandoned **derelict**.

5. A broken window.

6. One broken window, left unrepaired for a **considerable** length of time, instills in the **inhabitants** of the building a sense of **abandonment**—a sense that powers **neglect** the building. So another window gets broken. People start **littering**. **Graffiti** appears. Serious structural damage begins. In a **comparatively** short space of time, the building becomes damaged beyond the owner's desire to fix it, and the sense of abandonment becomes a reality.

7. The "broken window theory" has inspired police departments in New York and other major cities to crack down on the small stuff in order to keep out the big stuff. It works;

keeping on top of broken windows, graffiti, and other small infractions has reduced the serious crime level.

8. Don't leave "broken windows" (bad designs, wrong decisions, or poor code) unrepaired. Fix each one as soon as it is discovered. If there is **insufficient** time to fix it properly, then **board** it up. Perhaps you can comment out the offending code, or display a "Not Implemented" message, or **replace dummy** data instead. Take some action to prevent further damage and to show that you are on top of the situation.

9. We've seen clean, functional systems **deteriorate** pretty quickly once windows start breaking. There are other factors that can contribute to software rot, and we'll touch on some of them elsewhere, but neglect accelerates the rot faster than any other factor.

10. You may be thinking that no one has the time to go around cleaning up all the broken glass of a project. If you continue to think like that, then you'd better plan on getting a **dumpster**, or moving to another neighborhood. Don't let entropy win.

11. By contrast, there is the story of an **obscenely** rich **acquaintance** of Andy's. His house was **immaculate**, beautiful, loaded with priceless antiques, **objects d'art**, and so on. One day, a **tapestry** that was hanging a little too close to his living room fireplace caught on fire. The fire department rushed in to save the day—and his house. But before they **dragged** their big, dirty **hoses** into the house, they stopped—with the fire raging—to roll out a mat between the front door and the source of the fire.

12. They didn't want to mess up the carpet.

13. A pretty extreme case, to be sure, but that's the way it must be with software. One broken window—a badly designed piece of code, a poor management decision that the team must live with for the duration of the project—is all it takes to start the decline. If you find yourself working on a project with quite a few broken windows, it's all too easy to slip into the mindset of "all the rest of this code is crap, I will just follow suit". It doesn't matter if the project has been fine up to this point.

14. As a program evolves, it will become necessary to rethink earlier decisions and rework portions of the code. This process is perfectly natural. Code needs to evolve, it can never come to a **standstill**. Rewriting, reworking, and re-architecting code is collectively known as **refactoring**. When you come across a **stumbling** block because the code doesn't quite fit anymore, or you notice two things that should really be **intermingled**, or anything else at all strikes you as being "wrong", don't **procrastinate** to change it.

15. Refactoring your code—moving **functionality** around and updating earlier decisions—is really an exercise in pain management. Many developers are reluctant to start **ripping** up code just because it isn't quite right. When you go to the boss or client and ask for

another week to refactor the code, time pressure is often used as an excuse for not allowing it. But this excuse just doesn't hold up: fail to refactor now, and there'll be a far greater time investment to fix the problem down the road—when there are more **dependencies** to reckon with.

16. You might want to explain this principle to the boss by using a medical **analogy**: think of the code that needs refactoring as a "growth". Removing it requires **invasive** surgery. You can go in now, and take it out while it is still small. Or, you could wait while it grows and spreads—but removing it then will be both more expensive and more dangerous. Wait even longer, and you may lose the patient entirely.

17. So keep track of the things that need to be refactored. As a professional software engineer, if you can't refactor something immediately, make sure that it gets placed on the schedule. Make sure that users of the affected code know that it is scheduled to be refactored and how this might affect them.

(973 words)

New words

immune	/ɪˈmjuːn/	a.	~ (to/against sth.) that cannot be harmed by a disease or illness, either because of inoculation or through natural resistance 有免疫力（因接种疫苗或自发的）
entropy	/ˈentrəpɪ/	n.	[U] [technical] a lack of order in a system, including the idea that the lack of order increases over a period of time 熵
thermodynamics	/ˌθɜːməʊdaɪˈnæmɪks/	n.	[U] branch of physics dealing with the relations between heat and other forms of energy 热力学
maximum	/ˈmæksɪməm/	n.	[C] greatest amount, size, intensity, etc. possible or recorded 最大的量、体积、强度等
rot	/rɒt/	n.	[U] rotting; rottenness 腐烂；腐坏
engender	/ɪnˈdʒendə/	vt.	(fml.) to be the cause of (a situation or condition) 产生（某形势或状况）；造成；引起
delicate	/ˈdelɪkɪt/	a.	1. easily injured or damaged; fragile 容易受伤或受损的；易碎的；脆弱的 2. soft or tender when touched; made of sth. fine or thin 柔软的；柔和的；娇嫩的 3. (of the senses or of instruments) able to detect or show very small changes or differences; sensitive（指感官、仪器）精密的；灵敏的

decay	/dɪˈkeɪ/	n.	[U] state reached by the process of decaying 腐败衰退的状态
setback	/ˈsetbæk/	n.	[C] an unfortunate happening that hinders 挫折；退步
hulk	/hʌlk/	n.	[C] 1. body of an old ship which is no longer in use（废弃的旧船的）船体 2. very large and usu. clumsy person or thing 很大的而且通常为很笨的人或物
trigger	/ˈtrɪɡə/	n.	[C] lever that releases a spring, esp. so as to fire a gun（释放弹簧的）扳柄；（尤指枪的）扳机
intact	/ɪnˈtækt/	a.	undamaged; complete 无损伤的；完整的
smash	/smæʃ/	vt.	~ sth. (up); ~ sth. open (cause sth. to) be broken violently into pieces（使某物）粉碎；破碎
derelict	/ˈderɪlɪkt/	n.	[C] 1. sth. abandoned 废弃物 2. a person without a home, job, or property 被遗弃的人
		a.	deserted and allowed to fall into ruins; dilapidated 弃置的；破旧的
considerable	/kənˈsɪdərəbəl/	a.	great in amount or size 相当多的；相当大的
inhabitant	/ɪnˈhæbɪtənt/	n.	[C] one of the people who live in a particular place 居民
abandon	/əˈbændən/	vt.	to go away from (a person or thing or place) not intending to return; to forsake; to desert 离开（某人、某物或某地）而不返回；遗弃；抛弃；离弃
abandonment	/əˈbændənmənt/	n.	[U] the act of abandoning 放弃；放任；遗弃
neglect	/nɪˈɡlekt/	vt.	to give no or not enough care or attention to (sb./sth.) 疏忽；忽略某人/某事物
litter	/ˈlɪtə/	v.	to make (a place) untidy with scattered rubbish 乱扔垃圾使（某处）凌乱
		n.	[C] light rubbish (e.g. bits of paper, wrappings, bottles) left lying about, esp. in a public place 乱扔的杂物（如纸屑、包装纸、瓶子）；（尤指在公共场所乱扔的）垃圾
graffiti	/ɡræˈfiːtiː/	n.	[U] drawings or writing on a public wall, usu. humorous, obscene or political（在公共墙壁上涂写的）图画或文字（通常含幽默、猥亵或政治内容）
comparatively	/kəmˈpærətɪvlɪ/	ad.	as compared to something else or to a previous state 比较地；相当地
insufficient	/ˌɪnsəˈfɪʃənt/	a.	~ (for sth./to do sth.) not sufficient 不充足的；不充分的；不足的；不够的
board	/bɔːd/	vt.	~ sth. (up/over) to cover sth. with boards 用木板覆盖（某物）

replace	/rɪˈpleɪs/	vt.	to take the place of (sb./sth.) 代替；取代某人/某事物
dummy	/ˈdʌmɪ/	n.	[C] 1. model of the human figure, used for displaying or fitting clothes, etc.（用于展示或试穿装等的）人体模型 2. a thing that appears to be real but is only an imitation 仿制品
dummy data		n.	benign information that does not contain any useful data, but serves to reserve space where real data is nominally present 虚假数据；伪数据
deteriorate	/dɪˈtɪərɪəˌreɪt/	vi.	~ (into sth.) to become worse in quality or condition 变坏；变质；恶化
dumpster	/ˈdʌmpstə/	n.	[C] container designed to receive and transport and dump waste 垃圾箱
obscene	/əbˈsiːn/	a.	(of words, thoughts, books, pictures, etc.) indecent, esp. sexually; disgusting and offensive; likely to corrupt（指词语、思想、书画等）下流的；可憎的；伤风败俗的
obscenely	/əbˈsiːnlɪ/	ad.	in a sexually offensive, disgusting, or indecent manner 淫秽地；下流地
acquaintance	/əˈkweɪntəns/	n.	1. [U] ~ with sth./sb. (often slight) knowledge of sth./sb. 对某事物/某人了解 2. [C] a person with whom you are acquainted 熟人
immaculate	/ɪˈmækjʊlɪt/	a.	perfectly clean and tidy; spotless 整洁的；无污迹的；无瑕的
objet d'art	/ˈɒbʒeɪˌdɑː/	n.	[C] (pl. objets d'art) (French) small decorative or artistic object 小饰物；小艺术品
tapestry	/ˈtæpɪstrɪ/	n.	[C] (piece of) cloth into which threads of colored wool are woven or embroidered by hand to make pictures or designs, used for covering walls and furniture 绣帷；织花帷；壁毯；挂毯
drag	/dræg/	vt.	to pull (sb./sth.) along with effort and difficulty 拖；拉；扯；拽（某人/某物）
hose	/həʊz/	n.	[C] flexible tube made of rubber, plastic or canvas and used for directing water onto fires, gardens, etc. 软管（橡皮、塑料或帆布制成，用于输水救火、浇花等）
standstill	/ˈstændˌstɪl/	n.	[sing.] halt; stop 停顿；中止
refactor	/rɪˈfæktə/	n./v.	to restruct, to reconstitute 重构
stumble	/ˈstʌmbəl/	vi.	~ (over sth.) to strike one's foot against sth. and almost fall 绊脚

stumbling block		n.	a circumstance that causes difficulty or hesitation 绊脚石
intermingle	/ˌɪntəˈmɪŋgəl/	vt.	(cause people, ideas, substances, etc.) to mix together（使人、思想、物质等）混合
procrastinate	/prəʊˈkræstɪˌneɪt/	vi.	(fml.) to delay or postpone action 拖延；耽搁
functionality	/ˌfʌŋkʃənˈælɪtɪ/	n.	[U] one or all of the operations that a computer, software program, or piece of equipment is able to perform 功能；功能性
rip	/rɪp/	v.	~ (up) to divide or make a hole in (sth.) by pulling sharply; to tear sth. into pieces 撕裂或拉破（某物）
dependency	/dɪˈpendənsɪ/	n.	1. [U] dependence 依赖 2. [C] a country governed or controlled by another 附属国；附属地
analogy	/əˈnælədʒɪ/	n.	[C] ~ (between sth. and sth.) partial similarity between two things that are compared 类似；相似；类比
invasive	/ɪnˈveɪsɪv/	a.	tending to spread harmfully 有扩散危害的；扩散性的；蔓延性的

 ## New expressions

refer to	to mention or speak of sb./sth.; to allude to sb./sth. 提到、说到或涉及某人/某事物
come out	to become known 为人所知
a sense of	a feeling or understanding 感觉；感知
crack down	to try harder to prevent an illegal activity 严厉打击或镇压
board sth. up	to cover with wooden boards 用木板封住
save the day	to prevent failure or defeat when this seems certain to happen 反败为胜；转危为安
mess up	to spoil sth. or do sth. badly 弄糟；胡乱地做
follow suit	to do what someone else is doing 跟着做；照着做；如法炮制
come to a standstill	to stop 处于停顿状态
come across	to meet or find sb. by chance 偶遇
fix... down	to solve problem 解决问题
keep track of	to have information about what is happening or where sb./sth. is 与某人/某事保持联系

 **Notes**

1. entropy（熵；平均信息量；负熵）: a measure of the unavailable energy in a closed thermodynamic system that is also usually considered to be a measure of the system's disorder, that is a property of the system's state, and that varies directly with any reversible change in heat in the system and inversely with the temperature of the system.

2. thermodynamics（热力学）: a branch of science concerned with heat and temperature and their relation to energy and work.

3. objects d'art（艺术品）: literally "art object", or work of art, in French, but in practice, the term has long been reserved in English to describe works of art that are paintings, large or medium-sized sculptures, prints or drawings.

 Reading comprehension

Understanding the text

1. Choose the best answer to each of the following questions.

(1) What is the most important factor that can contribute to software rot?

   A. The best laid plan.

   B. The psychology, or culture, at work on a project.

   C. The best people.

   D. Enormous difficulties and constant setbacks.

(2) Which of the following can illustrate the fascinating trigger mechanism in the field of mine and urban decay in Para. 4?

   A. In inner cities, some buildings are beautiful and clean, while others are rotting hulks.

   B. After one window gets broken, people start littering.

   C. A clean, intact, inhabited building very quickly turns into a smashed and abandoned derelict.

   D. There are some projects that successfully fight nature's tendency toward disorder and manage to come out pretty well.

(3) What does a broken window cause?

   A. A sense of abandonment.   B. A new window.

   C. A repaired window.   D. A high building.

(4) Which is NOT mentioned to deal with the broken window?

   A. Fix each one as soon as it is discovered.

   B. Board it up.

   C. Comment out the offending code.

   D. Take the window away.

(5) What would happen if you find yourself working on a project with quite a few broken windows?

   A. Correct the mistake immediately.

   B. Slip into the mindset of "all the rest of this code is crap, I will just follow suit".

   C. Work hard to change it.

   D. Start ripping up code.

(6) According to the passage, what is NOT known as refactoring?

   A. Rethinking earlier decisions.   B. Rewriting.

   C. Rearchitecting code.   D. Reworking.

(7) When you go to the boss or client and ask for another week to refactor the code, what is often used as an excuse for not allowing it?

   A. Difficulty.   B. Time pressure.

   C. Lack of money.   D. Lack of confidence.

(8) What is NOT included to deal with the things that need to be refactored?

   A. Keep track of the things.

   B. Make sure that it gets placed on the schedule.

   C. Make sure that users of the affected code know that it is scheduled to be refactored.

   D. Keep it still and ignore it.

Critical thinking

2. **Work in pairs and discuss the following questions.**

(1) What is the figurative meaning of the broken window crisis in this unit? How is the story of the broken window related to a software programmer's career?

(2) Have you suffered a similar broken window experience? What do you think is the best strategy to reckon with the problem?

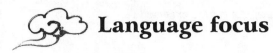

Language focus

Words in use

3. Fill in the blanks with the words given below. Change the form where necessary. Each word can be used only once.

| immaculate | obscene | abandon | deteriorate | neglect |
| smash | setback | delicate | maximum | immune |

(1) He warns the situation of the flood victims will _____ further unless the international community acts quickly.

(2) We have suffered a serious _____. Nevertheless, we must not be discouraged.

(3) Only a very _____ thermometer can measure such tiny changes in temperature.

(4) While strengthening international non-proliferation efforts, we shall not _____ the importance of advancing arms control and disarmament process.

(5) When he was a child, his life contained noble ambitions and _____ thought.

(6) He sought to extract the _____ political advantage from the cut in interest rates.

(7) The father of a baby, who was bothered by the stuffiness, tried to _____ windows to get air into the carriages.

(8) Since publication, his writings were branded as _____ and a blasphemy against God.

(9) In the effort to understand AIDS, attention is moving from the virus to the _____ system.

(10) The storm got worse and worse. Finally, I was obliged to _____ the car and continue on foot.

Expressions in use

4. Fill in the blanks with the expressions given below. Change the form where necessary. Each expression can be used only once.

| come across | a sense of | save the day | keep track of |
| mess up | crack down | come out | refer to |

(1) The government _____ hard on those campaigning for greater democracy.

(2) It's also been emphasized that no major policy changes can be expected to _____ of the meeting.

(3) No matter where the emergency is, the fire chief is ready to speed to the scene and _____!

(4) Whenever you _____ something that is meaningful and noteworthy, incorporate that into your book.

(5) It is important to budget your income so you can _____ how your money is being spent.

(6) One of the main reasons people _____ their lives is that they have no godly friends to give them feedback.

(7) This is a technical question, which I will have to _____ our technical department.

(8) When you travel in an earthquake zone, there is _____ violence all around, a visible shattering.

Sentence structure

5. Rewrite the sentences by using the structure "despite + *n*.". Make changes where necessary.

> **Model**: In spite of the best laid plans and the best people, a project can still experience ruin and decay during its lifetime.
> → Despite the best laid plans and the best people, a project can still experience ruin and decay during its lifetime.

(1) In spite of this expenditure, they still do not know what ails their son or whether he is likely to get better.

_____

(2) In spite of the newly rediscovered friendship, there's no doubt that more difficulties lie ahead.

_____

(3) In spite of repeated assurances, he failed to repay the money he had borrowed.

_____

(4) For whatever odd reason, I was into him, in spite of the fact that all of my friends and family hated him.

_____

(5) In spite of the efforts of the United Nations, the problem of drug traffic continues to grow.

 Collocation

> Technology, which is not a static thing, is constantly evolving. In order to *stay relevant* (Text A) in the IT field, it is *perfectly natural* (Text B) for programmers to keep track of *diverse skills* (Text A) and new ideas. Professionalism and excellence do not come easily and cannot be achieved in a *comparatively short* (Text B) period of time. A lot of hard work and dedication is required for such achievement. All *professional programmers* (Text A) should realize that just writing good code is not enough. The more important thing is to strengthen their understanding and expertise in the business domain knowledge, and keep analyzing and practicing advanced skills and procedures by *working actively* (Text A) with others in the field.

6. Complete the following sentences by choosing the appropriate words provided in the box. Each word can be used only once.

purely	fresh	individual	obsolete
engineering	typical	vital	structural

(1) The construction of software should be a(n) _____ discipline. However, this doesn't preclude _____ craftsmanship. Think about the large cathedrals built in Europe during the Middle Ages. Each took thousands of people years of effort, spread over many decades. Lessons learned were passed down to the next set of builders, who advanced the state of _____ engineering with their accomplishments. But the carpenters, stonecutters, carvers, and glass workers were all craftspeople, interpreting the engineering requirements to produce a whole that transcended the _____ mechanical side of the construction. It was their belief in their individual contributions that sustained the projects.

(2) One of the most important skills a software developer can learn is the skill of self-teaching. Self-education is a(n) _____ skill in a world where new technologies are introduced every single day, and a(n) _____ web developer is expected to know at least three programming languages to even be eligible for a junior-level position.

(3) Many of us are drawn to the IT industry because things are always changing. It's an exciting and _____ work environment. There's always something new to learn. On the flip side, though, is the disheartening fact that our hard-earned investments in

technology-related knowledge depreciate faster than a new Chevy. Today's hot new item is tomorrow's _____ junk with a limited shelf life.

Translation

7. **Translate the following passage into English.**

中国的工匠精神有着悠久的历史和许多了不起的成就。早在原始社会，彩陶、玉器的形式和艺术手法已经成熟多样，代表了中华民族独特的审美追求。到了后来的朝代，青铜器、漆器、陶瓷、家具、纺织品和金银器也达到了很高的水准。工匠精神代代相传，并创造了许多杰作。现如今，工匠们继承和发展了中国传统的工匠精神，并融入了更多的创新元素，在现代工业文明中向工业化和市场化转变。

Unit project

Write a report on how to become a qualified IT professional.

> Based on this unit theme, you will be expected to engage in writing a report on how to become a qualified IT professional. To make sure the report is as reliable and profound as possible, follow these specific steps.

(1) Work in groups and design a survey on how to become a qualified IT professional. The following questions can be included in your survey. Add more questions if you can.

- What is an IT professional in your opinion?
- How long does it take to turn an entry-level software programmer into a senior one?
- What professional skills should an IT professional master?
- What should be an IT professional's attitude toward his career?

- Which is more important for an IT professional, keeping work smoothly or overcoming challenges bravely?

  …

(2) Each of your group members interviews 5–10 students on campus. Take down their answers to your questions.

(3) Write a report. Decide what findings should be included in the report and draw a conclusion.

(4) Report to the whole class about your conclusion.

Unit 3

How We Begin Matters

Learning objectives

In this unit you will:
- learn about the importance of a kickoff meeting;
- learn about the importance of making a good schedule in a project;
- learn how to write a comparison/contrast essay;
- learn how to identify topic sentences in paragraphs.

> By failing to prepare, you are preparing to fail.
>
> —*Benjamin Franklin*
>
> Give me six hours to chop down a tree and I will spend the first four sharpening the axe.
>
> —*Abraham Lincoln*

Preview

All projects start somewhere. As the old saying "a good beginning is half done" goes, a successful beginning, typically marked with a kickoff meeting and a proper schedule in the IT industry, will definitely guarantee the chances of success for the project. The project kickoff can work as a cornerstone—setting the tone, style and vision for the entire project. A well-organized schedule can elaborate on the team members' roles and responsibilities, functioning as a useful and accurate tool in the development processes. So how should people start a project perfectly? How can people run an effective kickoff meeting? What factors should people take into consideration when making an excellent schedule? How can people minimize future risks even before launching the project?

Section A

 Pre-reading activities

1. Match the halves of the quotations below.

A	When it's obvious that the goals cannot be reached, don't adjust the goals,	a	will affect its successful outcome.
B	A hard beginning makes	b	adjust the action steps.
C	The first step is	c	as good as half over.
D	A goal without a plan	d	a good ending.
E	It is our attitude at the beginning of a difficult task which, more than anything else,	e	but planning is indispensable.
F	In preparing for battle I have always found that plans are useless,	f	is just a wish.

2. Work in pairs and discuss the following questions, sharing your opinion.

   (1) Can you explain the quotations above in Chinese?

   (2) Do you agree with the sentences above?

Text A

The Importance of a Kickoff Meeting

1. In the life of every project there is a time before, when the project exists as a possibility. From this possibility, we **craft** our intentions for the project. We **envision** what

could be, and we dread what might happen. At some point, perhaps when a contract gets signed or a team comes together, the project transitions from a possibility to an **inevitability**.

2. We mark the project's official beginning with a project kickoff meeting. A kickoff meeting is the first meeting with the project team and the client of the project. It would follow the definition of the base elements for the project and other project planning activities. The kickoff meeting is more than just a business meeting for **solidifying** goals. It is an opportunity for the different members to get to know each other, to interact, and to **mingle**. **Fortifying** these bonds early on will make collaboration **agreeable** throughout the rest of the process. All the key players gather in the same room (often via teleconference) and unite under the same goal. The kickoff is a special meeting where everyone feels **invigorated** as the team sets the initial course for the best possible product.

3. We know that even if we have a **fabulous** beginning, the project can run into **adversity** later and fail. But when we bring a project to life without really preparing for its start, into a team that **bypasses** difficulties or simply doesn't know how to care for the project, the likelihood of failure is so much higher.

4. If you look for guidance on how to run a kickoff, you'll find they come in two distinct flavors. A lucky few projects start with a grand festival for their kickoff. The project teams reserve one or more days to come together, conducting workshops and games and **meticulous** investigations into how they can ensure the project starts out with the best possible resources and support available. These **correlative** kickoffs focus the collected experiences and skills of the whole team on the new project's success right from the start, greatly reducing the risk that the project will fail because a detail was **omitted** or an instruction was **misinterpreted**. Project kickoff workshops are a wonderful beginning.

5. For most projects, though, we can't afford this kind of **elaborate** beginning. And for some, the **pomp** is **overblown**. So rather than host an all-day workshop, many leaders of new projects pull together all the details they can find about the project requirements and scope and risks and timeline. For their kickoff, they gather the project team, walk them through everything they know and then send them off, hoping they didn't miss anything too important. Hoping the team paid attention.

6. Sometimes this works. Often, it's only **marginally** better than sending an email. It's sometimes interesting, but hardly **energizing**, because in this kind of kickoff, the teams do not work together to create anything and are not asked to do much more than nod along. These kickoffs result in teams that stay lightly connected and **accountable** for the project's success.

7. My team doesn't do high-end design and marketing projects. We don't build highways or plan space missions. Most of the projects we run take less than 6 months and have fewer

than 20 people actively working on them. But we still need a way to get these projects started with the whole team invested and contributing to the project's success right from the start. After fifteen years of running projects, we've found a consistent way to do just that.

8. Our project kickoff meeting must ensure everyone understands the project goals and **constraints**. We're talking about the basics: major deliverables and responsibilities. We discuss logistics, scope, and timeline at a high-level only—just enough to make sure we know the project's boundaries. Our projects run better when the people actually doing the work figure out the details together, which they'll do after we achieve a shared vision in the kickoff.

9. The kickoff must involve everyone, especially the project sponsors, in **discerning** and **embracing** what they need to do to make the project a success. When someone hires and **delegates** a job to you, they assume you're the expert and they don't have time to figure it out for themselves. Yet without the critical knowledge and support of the person in charge, the project can't succeed. Lots of project sponsors don't realize this. They expect you to take the requirements, maybe send the occasional status update, then emerge later with happy results. They don't know that you have no idea how their legal review process works, or that they hate the color orange. These are assumed facts for them, which it never occurs to them to mention. This kickoff brings those **hypotheses** out and gets everyone involved in adjusting the project plans to match.

10. The kickoff must be **engaging** and efficient. We don't run projects with kindergarteners, so no one should ever read out loud to the group. The format must emphasize dialogue over review. Ideally, the whole meeting should last approximately 1 hour. Sometimes we beat this time, sometimes we go a bit longer, but this meeting never runs more than 1 hour and a half.

11. The kickoff must work as an online meeting. Whenever possible, the kickoff should be a face-to-face meeting. Although much online meeting software has been developed and put into service, we still prefer face-to-face interaction to build trust and **empathize**. In reality, though, this isn't practical for most projects because of time and cost.

12. A project's kickoff meeting is like opening night for a new production. The stage has been set, scenes have been cast, the players are all in place, and the project story is ready to **unfold**. It's important to have a meeting that's well-organized, informative, and **uplifting**—something that addresses priorities, nurtures teamwork and generally **rallies** the troops. The project kickoff meeting is our greatest opportunity to set the tone for the entire project. If we can establish an atmosphere of communication, transparency, preparation and **momentum** building, we have more than met our goal for this first meeting.

13. Now let's kick that ball across the field, sending our project flying into **notional** glory and success!

(1,028 words)

英语读写教程 2（第二版）
Intermediate IT English Reading and Writing 2 (2nd Edition)

New words

craft	/krɑːft/	vt.	to make (sth.) skillfully, especially by hand 精工制作（某物）（尤指用手工）
envision	/ɪnˈvɪʒən/	vt.	to imagine sth. that you think might happen in the future, especially sth. that you think will be good 想象；预想
inevitability	/ɪnˌevɪtəˈbɪlɪtɪ/	n.	[U] the fact that something is certain to happen 必然性
solidify	/səˈlɪdɪˌfaɪ/	v.	~ (into sth.) (cause sth. to) become solid, hard or firm（使某物）变为固体；变硬；变得坚固
mingle	/ˈmɪŋgəl/	v.	1. ~ with sth./~ (together) to form a mixture with sth.; to combine 与某物混合；结合 2. to go about among sb./sth.; to associate with sb./sth. 混进某些人/某事物中；与某人/某事物交往或联系
fortify	/ˈfɔːtɪˌfaɪ/	vt.	~ sth. (against sth.) 1. to strengthen (a place) against attack, by building walls, etc. 防卫（某地）（筑围墙等）2. to support or strengthen (sb.) physically or morally（在物质或道义上）支持（某人）
agreeable	/əˈgriəbəl/	a.	pleasing; giving pleasure 令人喜悦的；令人愉快的；宜人的
invigorated	/ɪnˈvɪgəreɪtɪd/	a.	with restored energy 生气勃勃的；精力充沛的
fabulous	/ˈfæbjʊləs/	a.	wonderful; marvelous 极好的；绝妙的
adversity	/ədˈvɜːsɪtɪ/	n.	[U] unfavorable conditions; trouble 逆境；不幸；厄运
bypass	/ˈbaɪˌpɑːs/	vt.	1. to provide (a town, etc.) with a bypass 在（市镇等）外围辟一条旁道 2. to go around or avoid (sth.), using a bypass 走旁道以绕过或避开（某物）
meticulous	/mɪˈtɪkjʊləs/	a.	~ (in sth./doing sth.) giving or showing great precision and care; very attentive to detail 极精细的；极注意细节的
correlative	/kɒˈrelətɪv/	a.	(fml.) two or more facts, ideas, etc. that are closely related or dependent on each other 有相互关系的；相关的
		n.	either of two correlated variables 关联词；相关物
omit	/əʊˈmɪt/	vt.	to fail or neglect to do sth.; to leave sth. not done 忘记做某事物；不做某事物；忽略；疏忽
misinterpret	/ˌmɪsɪnˈtɜːprɪt/	vt.	to interpret (sb./sth.) wrongly; to make a wrong inference from (sth.) 误解某人/某事；误译
elaborate	/ɪˈlæbərət/	a.	very detailed and complicated; carefully prepared and finished 详尽而复杂的；精心制作的
elaborate	/ɪˈlæbəreɪt/	vt.	(fml.) to work sth. out in detail 详细制定某事物

68

pomp	/pɒmp/	n.	[U] splendid display or magnificence, especially at a public event 宏伟壮观的景象（尤指群众场面）；盛况
overblow	/ˌəʊvə'bləʊ/	v.	to blow into (a wind instrument) with greater force than normal 吹得过响；夸张；过分渲染
marginally	/'mɑːdʒɪnəlɪ/	ad.	not enough to make an important difference 少量地；在边缘；最低限度地
energizing	/'enəˌdʒaɪzɪŋ/	a.	supplying motive force 激励的
accountable	/ə'kaʊntəbəl/	a.	[pred.] ~ (to sb.) (for sth.) required or expected to give an explanation for one's actions, etc.; responsible（对自己的行为等）负责
constraint	/kən'streɪnt/	n.	[U] constraining or being constrained 约束；强制
discern	/dɪ'sɜːn/	vt.	to see (sth.) clearly (with the senses or the mind), esp. with an effort 看出；识别；辨认（某事物）（尤指需费力）
embrace	/ɪm'breɪs/	vt.	1. to take (a person, etc.) into one's arms as a sign of affection 拥抱（某人）2. (fml.) to accept or take (an idea, etc.) willingly 欣然接受或采取（某意见等）
delegate	/'delɪgeɪt/	vt.	~ (sth.) (to sb.) to entrust (duties, rights, etc.) to sb. in a lower position or grade 将（职责、权利等）委托给下级；授权给
hypothesis	/haɪ'pɒθɪsɪs/	n.	[C] (pl. hypotheses /-siːz/) idea or suggestion that is based on known facts and is used as a basis for reasoning or further investigation（根据已知事实提出有待于进一步论证或研究的）假说；假设
engaging	/ɪn'geɪdʒɪŋ/	a.	pleasant and attracting your interest 动人的；有魅力的；迷人的
empathize	/'empəˌθaɪz/	vi.	to be able to understand someone else's feelings, problems, etc., especially because you have had similar experiences 移情；产生情感共鸣
unfold	/ʌn'fəʊld/	v.	(cause sth. to) open or spread out from a folded state（使某物）展开；打开
uplifting	/ʌp'lɪftɪŋ/	a.	making you feel happier and more hopeful 令人振奋的；使人开心的
rally	/'rælɪ/	v.	to recover health, strength, etc.; to revive; to rouse（使某人/某事物）恢复健康、力量等；复苏；振作
momentum	/məʊ'mentəm/	n.	[U] force that increases the rate of development of a process; impetus 动力；冲力；势头
notional	/'nəʊʃənəl/	a.	[usu. before noun] existing only as an idea or plan, and not existing in reality 概念上的

New expressions

run into	to start to experience a difficult or unpleasant situation 遭遇（困难等）；偶然碰见
pull together	to improve something by organizing it more effectively 齐心协力；团结起来
result in	to lead to; to make something happen 导致
accountable for	responsible for 对……应付责任
contribute to	to help to make something happen 促成某事物
figure out	to think about a problem or situation until you find the answer or understand what has happened 想出；理解
in charge	in a position of having control or responsibility for a group of people or an activity 负责；主管
in place	in the usual or proper position 在平常的或应在的地方；准备就绪

Notes

a kickoff meeting（项目启动会）: the first meeting with the project team and the client of the project.

Reading comprehension

Understanding the text

1. Answer the following questions.

    (1) What is a kickoff meeting?

    (2) Does a good kickoff meeting guarantee the success of the project?

    (3) How do a few lucky projects start with?

    (4) What do most projects go through during the kickoff meeting?

    (5) Why should everyone understand the project goals and constraints?

    (6) How long should an ideal kickoff meeting last?

    (7) Why should a kickoff meeting be conducted as an online meeting?

(8) Why is it important to have a well-organized, informative, and motivating kickoff meeting?

Critical thinking

2. Work in pairs and discuss the following questions.

(1) Do you agree with the famous proverb in English "a good beginning is half done"? Why?

(2) What do you know about the kickoff meeting in an IT-related project?

(3) What preparation should people make in order to have a good kickoff meeting?

Word building

When the suffix *-ing* combines with the base forms of verbs to form adjectives, they are used to describe a continuing process or state.

Examples

Words learned	Add *-ing*	New words formed
energize	→	energizing
promise	→	promising
bore	→	boring
encourage	→	encouraging
amaze	→	amazing

The prefix *un-* combines with verbs to form new verbs. Verbs formed in this way express the idea that the process or state referred to by the original verb is reversed.

Examples

Words learned	Add *un-*	New words formed
fold	→	unfold
load	→	unload
cover	→	uncover
button	→	unbutton
dress	→	undress

3. **Add *-ing*, or *un-* to the following words to form new words.**

Words learned	New words formed
-ing	
frighten	
terrify	
astonish	
correspond	
embarrass	
un-	
fasten	
pack	
veil	
tie	
lock	

4. **Fill in the blanks with the newly-formed words in Activity 3. Change the form where necessary. Each word can be used only once.**

   (1) Do not _____ your safety belts until the plane has come to a complete stop.

   (2) His ability to absorb information was _____, but his concentration span was short.

   (3) President Obama said he would _____ an overall housing strategy in the next few weeks.

   (4) There is an increase in production of 20% above that of the _____ period of last year.

   (5) Mrs. Wang is the one who started it all. Whoever ties the bell around the tiger's neck must _____ it.

   (6) It is _____ to have someone looking over your shoulder while you're at work, as though you could not be trusted.

   (7) We made four trips to our new home with the small truck and it took us weeks to _____ everything.

   (8) She was possessed of a(n) _____ sensation that life was being squeezed slowly out of her.

(9) During their six-week voyage, researchers will employ a range of techniques to _____ some of the secrets of the giant marine mammals.

(10) A growing number of Americans are seeing the accumulation and distribution of computerized data as a(n) _____ invasion of their privacy.

Banked cloze

5. Fill in the blanks by selecting suitable words from the word bank. You may not use any of the words more than once.

A. circulate	B. structured	C. momentum	D. energize	E. supervision
F. advance	G. marginally	H. strategy	I. convey	J. freely
K. respective	L. opportunity	M. converted	N. open	O. invigorated

A project kickoff meeting is the best (1) _____ for a project manager to (2) _____ his or her team. During this meeting, the project management can establish a sense of a common goal and start understanding each individual. A strong and clear agenda is a must for a good project kickoff meeting. The agenda usually includes the purpose of the project, deliverables and goals, key success factors of the project, communication plan, and the project plan. Before the project kickoff meeting, make sure that you (3) _____ the meeting agenda to all the participants.

When the meeting starts, the project manager should take charge of the meeting by briefly taking the participants through the agenda while giving a brief introduction to each item in the agenda. Pay more attention to introducing the project roles and emphasize the reasons why the team members were assigned to (4) _____ roles.

Once the tone is set, present the agenda in a(n) (5) _____ manner. Talk about the project assumptions and how you develop the project plan. Present your reasoning behind the plan and (6) _____ the message that you are (7) _____ to suggestions when the project progresses.

Decide on a convenient time to hold regular meetings to talk about project progress. Emphasize the need for everyone's participation in the regular meetings. If the project requires working long hours, let them know in (8) _____. Showing them how you can help them to maintain the work-life balance is a good (9) _____.

At the end of the kickoff meeting, open up a Q&A session that allows the team members to (10) _____ express themselves. If the time is not enough to facilitate all the team members, ask them to send their queries and feedback via email.

Structured analysis and writing

Structure analysis

Write a comparison/contrast essay

Comparison and contrast essays are used to explore the similarities and differences between two subjects. Comparison essays focus on either similarities or similarities and differences, while contrast essays focus on only differences.

The comparison or contrast essays should make a point or serve a purpose. They usually clarify something unknown or not well understood, lead to a fresh insight or new way of viewing something, or bring one or both of the subjects into sharper focus. Two organizational patterns of such essays are block pattern and point-to-point. Comparison/contrast essays with a block pattern give all supporting details for one subject in one block and then give all supporting details for another subject in another block. A point-by-point pattern alternates the details from one side of the comparison or contrast to another.

Connectors that show comparison (similarities) are as follows:

| in addition | correspondingly | compared to | similarly | just as |
| as well as | likewise | same as | at the same time | |

Connectors that show contrast (differences) are as follows:

| however | on the contrary | conversely | meanwhile | in contrast |
| although | on the other hand | unlike | even though | |

Now let's take Paras. 4–5 from Text A as an example. Two kinds of kickoff meetings are contrasted in the two paragraphs. Para. 4 presents supporting details on how an elaborate kickoff meeting is held at the beginning of a project. Para. 5 then presents supporting details on how a poorly-organized kickoff meeting is started.

> *If you look for guidance on how to run a kickoff, you'll find they come in two distinct flavors. A lucky few projects start with a grand festival for their kickoff. The project teams reserve one or more days to come together, conducting workshops and games and meticulous investigations into how they can ensure the project starts out with the best possible resources and support available. These correlative kickoffs focus the collected experiences and skills of the whole team on the new project's success right from the start, greatly reducing the risk that the project will fail because a detail was omitted or*

> an instruction was misinterpreted. Project kickoff workshops are a wonderful beginning. (Para. 4, Text A)

> For most projects, **though**, we can't afford this kind of elaborate beginning. And for some, the pomp is overblown. **So rather than** host an all-day workshop, many leaders of new projects pull together all the details they can find about the project requirements and scope and risks and timeline. For their kickoff, they gather the project team, walk them through everything they know and then send them off, hoping they didn't miss anything too important. Hoping the team paid attention. (Para. 5, Text A)

Structured writing

Read the sample essay and see how a comparison / contrast essay is structured.

Topic
Traveling vacations or staycations
Introduction
Thesis statement
Body
Advantages of traveling vacations
Advantages of staycations
Conclusion

Sample essay

People are always looking forward to their vacation period. There are many options and plans as to how to spend the time. Some people would probably choose to travel to a new place, but there are still a certain number of people who prefer staycations. It's unfair to conclude which one is better because both can offer a lot of fun and relaxation.

Many people like to travel to a new place during the holiday simply because traveling is very rewarding. The first and the most foremost benefit of traveling is that it increases knowledge, and broadens people's horizons. Traveling to a new place enhances people's ability to understand different customs, cultures and values in the world and allows people to view things from a new perspective. People will become more and more open-minded as they learn to accept and appreciate the diversity of the world. Secondly, traveling means meeting new people. While on the road, people

can meet someone they would never get a chance to bump into if they stayed within their comfort zone. Traveling is a good chance to make new friends and change the cycle of the everyday routine that they have gotten trapped in over the years.

Compared to traveling, staycations also have a lot of advantages. First of all, staycations save money. Traveling usually involves a lot of expenses with accommodation, food and tickets. But when spending the holiday at home, people don't need to pay so much. Thus, the holiday budget is greatly reduced. Secondly, staycations save people a lot of trouble such as: booking the flight and the hotel, packing, catching the plane, jetlag, countless running and waiting. Instead, people can choose relaxing activities like joining a spa center or going to the local museum. This kind of holiday may not provide people with the opportunity to see the world, but it certainly helps them have a good rest and rid themselves of the post-holiday syndrome.

From the analysis above, it is obvious that both ways have their own respective advantages. So people can make decisions according to different situations. But one thing is certain that no matter what choice people make to enjoy their holiday, they will get plenty of joy and satisfaction.

6. **Write an essay of no less than 200 words on one of the following topics. One topic has an outline that you can follow.**

Topic
Differences between high school life and college life
Introduction
Body
Teaching method
Learning method
Student-teacher relationship
Conclusion

More topics:

- A high salary or career development
- More social practice or more certificates

Translation

7. Translate the following paragraph into Chinese.

Moral values in America are like those in any country. In fact, many aspects of morality are universal. But the stories and traditions that teach them are unique to each culture. Not only that, but culture influences how people show these virtues. One of the most basic moral values for Americans is honesty. The well-known legend about George Washington and the cherry tree teaches this value clearly. Little George cut down his father's favorite cherry tree, while trying out his new hatchet. When his father asked him about it, George said, "I cannot tell a lie, I did with my hatchet." Instead of punishment, George received praise for telling the truth. Sometimes American honesty—being open and direct, can offend people, but Americans do believe honesty is the best policy.

8. Translate the following paragraph into English.

人际关系就是一种善于听取别人的意见、体察别人的需要和虚心接受批评的能力。善于处理人际关系的人敢于承认错误，敢于承担自己的责任，这是对待错误的一种成熟和负责任的态度。人际关系差的人往往不能处理好批评。碰到错误，他们拒不承认自己有错，或情绪低落或大发雷霆，成为有刺的人，难以相处。

Section B

 Reading skills: *Identifying the topic sentence*

A topic sentence is a sentence in which the main idea of the paragraph is stated. It is composed of two parts: (a) the topic itself and (b) the controlling idea. The topic sentence gives a paragraph direction and purpose. Being able to identify the topic sentence in a paragraph will help readers quickly understand the main point the author makes.

Traditionally a topic sentence is the first sentence of a paragraph. In this lead position, it functions to introduce the examples or details that will explain the controlling idea. If the paragraph is meant as a freestanding unit of discourse and not part of a larger whole, the topic sentence, or rather the ideas it contains, is frequently restated at the end of the paragraph. In this position, the restated topic sentence serves as a concluding statement. Perhaps the least common placement for a topic sentence is in the medial position.

A topic sentence opens a paragraph and states or suggests what the body of the paragraph will discuss. To maintain clarity, topic sentences must be specific and focused, giving a clear introduction to the analysis or description that follows. Topic sentences can also be used as transitional devices, helping the author move from the information in prior paragraphs to a new or extended point.

Let's read the following paragraphs in Text A and see how to identify the topic sentences in them.

Example 1

<u>We mark the project's official beginning with a project kickoff meeting. A kickoff meeting is the first meeting with the project team and the client of the project.</u> It would follow the definition of the base elements for the project and other project planning activities. The kickoff meeting is more than just a business meeting for solidifying goals. It is an opportunity for the different members to get to know each other, to interact, and to mingle. Fortifying these bonds early on will make collaboration agreeable throughout the rest of the process. All the key players gather in the same room (often via teleconference) and unite under the same goal. The kickoff is a special meeting where everyone feels invigorated as the team sets the initial course for the best possible product. (Para. 2)

Example 2

<u>Our project kickoff meeting must ensure everyone understands the project goals and constraints</u>. We're talking about the basics: major deliverables and responsibilities. We discuss logistics, scope, and timeline at a high level only—just enough to make sure we know the project's boundaries. Our projects run better when the people actually doing the work figure out the details together, which they'll do after we achieve a shared vision in the kickoff. (Para. 8)

In example 1, the topic sentence is the first sentence. It states the fact that a project begins with a kickoff meeting. All the following sentences in the paragraph illustrate what a kickoff meeting involves. In example 2, the topic sentence is the first sentence. The first sentence states one important requirement of a good kickoff meeting—understanding project goals and constraints. And the following sentences in the paragraph explain the reasons in detail.

Read the following paragraphs from Text B and identify the topic sentence of each paragraph and its position.

(1) Before we can figure out how to make better schedules, we first have to understand what problems schedules solve. If they are so unreliable, why bother with them at all? Schedules serve several primary purposes, the first, and the most well-known of which is to make commitments about when things will be done. The schedule provides a form of contract between every person on a team or in an organization, confirming what each person is going to deliver over the next week, month, or year. Generally, when people think about project schedules, it's this first purpose that they're thinking about. Schedules are often focused externally, outside the project team rather than within, because they are used to help close a deal or comply with a customer's timeline. Often, the customer is explicitly paying for the timeline as well as for the service provided. In order to allow customers or partners to make plans based on a given project, a time has to be agreed upon for when specific things will happen. (Para. 3)

Topic sentence: _____

Position: _____

(2) The third purpose of schedules is to give the team a tool to track progress and to break work into manageable chunks. Breaking things down into one or two-day sizes actually helps people to understand what the work is that they need to do. Imagine if, when building a house, the architect gave one line item: "House: 120 days". With such low granularity, it's difficult for anyone, including the architect himself, to

understand which things need to be done first. But if the builder can provide a week-by-week subdivision of activities, everyone has a clearer understanding of what tasks will be done when, and each team member has a greater opportunity to ask good questions and clarify assumptions. (Para. 6)

Topic sentence: _____

Position: _____

Text B

The Truth About Making a Schedule

1. Some people tend to be late. It might be only a few minutes on occasion, or just a couple of times a week, but people are often behind on their daily schedules. High school students are late for class, adults are late for meetings at work, and friends arrive 10 minutes late at the bar for drinks. It seems that **subconsciously** we often believe that being on time isn't about **targeting** a specific moment but instead is about being within a range of moments, and for some people, that range is wider than for others. An interesting example is the many hostesses who greet us at restaurants. They tell us a table will be ready soon, but often we're made to wait quite a while. It's these experiences of delayed schedules, being put on hold on the telephone, or waiting in the doctor's office, that have caused us to become **cynical** about schedules. We have so much experience with life not working out according to them.

2. It isn't a surprise then that so many projects come in late. As human beings, most of us arrive at the task of scheduling projects with a **questionable** track record for delivering or receiving things on time. We tend to **estimate** based on weak **suppositions**, predict outcomes for work based on the best possible set of circumstances, and given our prior experiences simultaneously avoid placing too much confidence in any schedule we see or create. Why do we do this? And how does it impact project schedules?

3. Before we can figure out how to make better schedules, we first have to understand what problems schedules solve. If they are so **unreliable**, why bother with them at all? Schedules serve several primary purposes, the first, and the most well-known of which is

to make commitments about when things will be done. The schedule provides a form of **contract** between every person on a team or in an organization, **confirming** what each person is going to deliver over the next week, month, or year. Generally, when people think about project schedules, it's this first purpose that they're thinking about. Schedules are often focused **externally**, outside the project team rather than within, because they are used to help close a deal or **comply** with a customer's timeline. Often, the customer is **explicitly** paying for the timeline as well as for the service provided. In order to allow customers or partners to make plans based on a given project, a time has to be agreed upon for when specific things will happen.

4. The second purpose of a schedule is to encourage everyone who's contributing to a project to see his efforts as part of a whole, and invest in making his pieces work with the others. Until there is a **draft** schedule suggesting specific dates and times for when things have to be ready, it's unlikely that connections and dependencies across people or teams will be **scrutinized**. It's only when the details are written down, with people's names next to them that real **calculations** can be made and assumptions examined. There is psychological power in a schedule that **externalizes** and **amplifies** the commitment that is being made. Instead of dates and commitments existing only inside someone's mind, they are written down and exist in the universe all on their own. It is not as easy to forget or ignore something when it's posted on a whiteboard in the hallway, reminding you or the team of what needs to be done.

5. This psychological or pressure shift is what's called a forcing function. A forcing function is anything that when put in place naturally forces a change in perspective, attitude, or behavior. So, schedules are important forcing functions for projects. If used properly by a PM (project manager), schedules force everyone whose work appears on them to carefully think through the work they need to do and how it fits into what others are doing. This awareness of the relationship between parts is somewhat independent of the schedule itself. This forcing function is a critical step toward realizing the project's potential. Even if the schedule **slips**, is doubled, is **halved**, or goes through a variety of other **torturous permutations**, the commitments and connections everyone has made with each other will be maintained.

6. The third purpose of schedules is to give the team a tool to track progress and to break work into **manageable chunks**. Breaking things down into one or two-day sizes actually helps people to understand what the work is that they need to do. Imagine if, when building a house, the **architect** gave one line item: "House: 120 days". With such low **granularity**, it's difficult for anyone, including the architect himself, to understand which things need to be done first. But if the builder can provide a week-by-week **subdivision** of activities, everyone has a clearer understanding of what tasks will be done when, and each team member has a greater opportunity to ask good questions and **clarify** assumptions.

7. The larger and more complex the project, the more important schedules are. On larger projects, there are more dependencies between people, and decisions and timings have greater **odds** of impacting others. When you have a handful of people working on a small team, the odds of people recognizing problems in each other's work are much higher. Schedule slips on small teams aren't good news, but, in such a case, a half-day slip represents an additional half-day of energy for three people only, so recovery is possible. On a larger project, with dozens or hundreds of people and components, a one-day slip can quickly **cascade** and create problems in all sorts of **unforeseen** ways, which is often beyond a team's point of recovery. Either way, big teams or small, schedules give managers and bean counters the opportunity to ask questions, make adjustments, and help the team by **surfacing** and responding to issues as they **arise**.

8. Perfect schedules don't solve all of the problems that projects have. A schedule cannot **remedy** bad design or engineering practices, nor can it protect a project from weak leadership, unclear goals, and poor communication. But schedules can be good enough for the team and the leaders to believe in, provide a basis for tracking and making adjustments, and have a **probability** of success that satisfies the client, the business, or the overall project sponsor.

(1,056 words)

New words

subconsciously	/ˌsʌbˈkɒnʃəslɪ/	*ad.*	from the subconscious mind 潜意识地
target	/ˈtɑːgɪt/	*vt.*	[usu. passive] ~ sth. (at/on sth./sb.) to aim sth. 瞄准某物
		n.	[C] 1. object or mark that a person tries to hit in shooting, etc.; disc marked with concentric circles for this purpose in archery 目标；靶 2. person or thing against which criticism, etc. is directed 受批评等的人或事物；批评的目标、对象 3. result aimed at; objective 目的；目标
cynical	/ˈsɪnɪkəl/	*a.*	unwilling to believe that people have good, honest, or sincere reasons for doing 愤世嫉俗的；冷嘲的；讽刺的
questionable	/ˈkwestʃənəbəl/	*a.*	not likely to be true or correct 可疑的
estimate	/ˈestɪmeɪt/	*vt.*	to form an approximate idea of sth.; to calculate roughly the cost, size, value, etc. of sth. 估计
supposition	/ˌsʌpəˈzɪʃən/	*n.*	[C, U] sth. that you think is true, even though you are not certain and cannot prove it 假定；猜想；推测
unreliable	/ˌʌnrɪˈlaɪəbəl/	*a.*	unable to be trusted or depended on 不可靠的
contract	/ˈkɒntrækt/	*n.*	[C] legally binding agreement, usu. in writing 合同；契约

confirm	/kənˈfɜːm/	vt.	to provide evidence for the truth or correctness of (a report, an opinion, etc.); to establish the truth or correctness of (sth. previously believed, suspected, or feared to be the case) 证实；证明（报告、意见等）的正确性；确认
externally	/ɪkˈstɜːnəli/	ad.	on or from the outside 在（或从）外部；在（或从）外面；外表上
comply	/kəmˈplaɪ/	vi.	~ (with sth.) to do as one is requested, commanded, etc.; to obey 按要求、命令去做；依从；顺从；听从；服从
explicitly	/ɪkˈsplɪsɪtli/	ad.	in an explicit manner; clearly 清晰地；明确地
draft	/drɑːft/	n.	[C] rough preliminary written version of sth. 草稿；草案
		vt.	to make a preliminary version of (a document) 草拟；起草（文件）
scrutinize	/ˈskruːtɪˌnaɪz/	vt.	to look at or examine (sth.) carefully or thoroughly 仔细或彻底检查（某事物）
calculation	/ˌkælkjʊˈleɪʃən/	n.	[C, U] 1. problem solving that involves numbers or quantities 计算；盘算；估计 2. planning sth. carefully and intentionally 深思熟虑；慎重的计划
externalize	/ɪkˈstɜːnəˌlaɪz/	vt.	to make external or objective, or give reality to sth. 给……以外形；使客观化；使具体化
slip	/slɪp/	vi.	1. to become worse or lower than before 变差 2. ~ (over/ on/ sth.) (of a person, an animal, a car, etc.) to slide accidentally; to lose one's balance and fall or nearly fall in this way（指人、动物、汽车等）意外滑动；失去平衡跌倒或险些跌倒
halve	/hɑːv/	vt.	to divide (sth.) into two equal parts 把（某物）对半分
torturous	/ˈtɔːtʃərəs/	a.	very painful or unpleasant 拷问的；痛苦的
permutation	/ˌpɜːmjʊˈteɪʃən/	n.	[U] (fml.) variation in the order of a set of things 排列；置换
manageable	/ˈmænɪdʒəbəl/	a.	easy to control or deal with 易控制的；易管理的
chunk	/tʃʌŋk/	n.	[C] 1. thick solid piece cut or broken off sth.（从某物上切下或折下的）大块 2. (infml.) fairly large amount of sth. 某物相当大的部分
architect	/ˈɑːkɪˌtekt/	n.	[C] person who designs buildings and supervises their construction 建筑师；设计师
granularity	/ˌgrænjʊˈlærɪti/	n.	the quality of being composed of relatively large particles 间隔尺寸；粒度

subdivision	/ˈsʌbdɪˌvɪʒən/	n.	[C, U] (a part of which results from) the act of subdividing 再分；细分；再分成的部分
clarify	/ˈklærɪˌfaɪ/	vt.	(cause sth. to) become clear or easier to understand（使某事物）清楚易懂；澄清
odds	/ɒdz/	n.	[C] [pl.] probability or chance (that a certain thing will or will not happen) 可能性；机会
cascade	/kæsˈkeɪd/	vi.	to fall in or like a cascade 如瀑布落下；如瀑布状下垂；使串联
unforeseen	/ˌʌnfɔːˈsiːn/	a.	not known in advance; unexpected 未预见到的；意料之外的
surface	/ˈsɜːfɪs/	vi.	1. to appear or become visible; to make a showing 显露 2. (of a submarine, skin-diver, etc.) to come up to the surface of a body of water（指潜艇、赤身潜水者等）浮到水面
arise	/əˈraɪz/	vi.	to become evident; to appear; to originate 呈现；出现；发生
remedy	/ˈremɪdɪ/	n.	[C] (fml.) treatment, medicine, etc. that cures or relieves a disease or pain 祛除或减轻病痛的治疗（法）、药物等
		vt.	to provide a remedy for (sth. undesirable); to rectify 治理（不良事物）；纠正；补救
probability	/ˌprɒbəˈbɪlɪtɪ/	n.	[U] likelihood 可能性

 # New expressions

tend to do	to be likely to behave in a certain way or to have a certain characteristic or influence 倾向；趋向；趋于
agree upon	to have reached an agreement 达成协议；意见一致
invest in (doing) sth.	to give (time, effort, etc.) to a particular task, esp. in a way that involves commitment or self-sacrifice 为某任务付出（时间、精力等）（尤指涉及承诺或自我牺牲的）
instead of	as an alternative or replacement to (sb./sth.) 作为（某人/某事物）的替换
remind sb. of sth.	to cause sb. to remember or be newly aware of sb./sth. 使某人回想起或意识到某人/某事物
independent of	1. not dependent (on other people or things) 独立的；自主的 2. not connected with each other; separate 不相关联的；单独的；独自的；分开的

bean counter	sb. whose job is to examine the cost of doing sth., and who is concerned only with making a profit 会计；极善于计算的人
respond to	to act in answer to (sth.) or because of the action of another（对某事物或对他人的行动）反应；回应；响应
protect sth./sb. from	to keep sb. or sth. safe from harm, damage, or illness 保护、保卫某人／某事物免遭……

Reading comprehension

Understanding the text

1. Choose the best answer to each of the following questions.

(1) According to the passage, which experiences of delayed schedules have caused us to become cynical about schedules?

  A. Being put on hold on the telephone.

  B. Waiting in the doctor's office.

  C. Waiting for a table in the restaurant.

  D. All of the above.

(2) The first and the most well-known purpose of a schedule is _____.

  A. to make commitments about when things will be done

  B. to set a date for the kickoff meeting

  C. to make rules and regulations for the whole project

  D. to motivate the morale of employees

(3) The second purpose of a schedule is _____.

  A. to inform the employees of the deadline of the project

  B. to ensure the customer that calculations have been made and assumptions have been examined

  C. to encourage everyone in the project to see his efforts as part of a whole, and invest in making his pieces work with the others

  D. to write down the names on a whiteboard in the hallway

(4) Why does the writer consider schedules as an important function in a project?

   A. Because it is posted in the hallway and everyone can see it clearly.

   B. Because it motivates people to contribute to the whole project.

   C. Because it forces everyone whose work appears to them to carefully think through the work they need to do and how it fits into what others are doing.

   D. Because it reminds people of the deadline all the time.

(5) The third purpose of schedules is _____.

   A. to inform the team of how many conferences are to be held

   B. to give the team relevant training

   C. to provide the team with some project management lessons

   D. to give the team a tool to track progress and break work into manageable chunks

(6) Why are schedules more important for a larger and more complex project?

   A. Because it is time-consuming to make a schedule for a larger and more complex project.

   B. Because a one-day slip can quickly cascade and create problems in all sorts of unforeseen ways, which is often beyond a team's point of recovery.

   C. Because mistakes are not allowed to occur in a larger and more complex project.

   D. Because schedules of larger and more complex projects are difficult to make and usually involve many people and resources.

(7) According to the text, perfect schedules _____.

   A. don't solve all the problems in a project

   B. can remedy bad design and engineering practices

   C. protect a project from weak leadership

   D. save a project from unclear goals and poor communication

(8) The purpose of the text is _____.

   A. to prove to us that it is impossible to make a perfect schedule

   B. to demonstrate that schedules have three primary purposes

   C. to help us realize the importance of making a good schedule in completing a project

   D. to show the advantages and disadvantages of schedules

Critical thinking

2. Work in pairs and discuss the following questions.

(1) Do you think it is important to make a schedule in life?

(2) In your opinion, what factors are the main considerations in making a schedule?

(3) How can we stick to the schedule after we make it?

 Language focus

Words in use

3. Fill in the blanks with the words given below. Change the form where necessary. Each word can be used only once.

| cynical | questionable | estimate | comply | confirm |
| scrutinize | torturous | clarify | arise | remedy |

(1) She has told of her _____ ordeal in a new book written in German.

(2) He was so _____ that he sneered at everything that made life worth living.

(3) There are calls for his resignation, but there is no sign yet that he will _____.

(4) The research is _____ because the sample used was very small.

(5) There have been several tragic rail accidents. The government must act quickly to _____ this situation.

(6) These new statistics _____ our worst fears about the depth of the recession.

(7) Study the contract thoroughly and carefully, _____ your duties and what happens if you break the contract.

(8) Problems _____ because we did not know what data to capture and, after we captured it, how to analyze it.

(9) We were only able to make a rough _____ of how much fuel would be required.

(10) The Foreign Secretary's remarks this morning _____ an ambiguous statement issued earlier this week.

Expressions in use

4. Fill in the blanks with the expressions given below. Change the form where necessary. Each expression can be used only once.

| tend to do | agree upon | instead of | remind sb. of sth. |
| invest in | respond to | independent of | protect sth./sb. from |

(1) Your job is _____ your personal life and it should be treated as such.

(2) They encourage doctors to prescribe cheaper generic drugs _____ more expensive brand names.

(3) Now that you _____ this matter, I have a vague impression of it.

(4) People _____ be more aggressive when they're young and more conservative as they get older.

(5) The baby whale develops a thick layer of blubber to _____ the cold sea.

(6) In order to ensure competitiveness we will continue to _____ infrastructure projects such as building railways, roads, and most importantly education.

(7) It is something we can all _____ that Michael Jordan is the best basketball player in the world.

(8) By knowing the worth of their customers, employees can more appropriately _____ customers' special requests and needs.

Sentence structure

5. Rewrite the sentences by using the inverted sentence "Nor do/does/did/can sb. ...". Make changes where necessary.

| **Model:** | A schedule cannot remedy bad design or engineering practices. It cannot protect a project from weak leadership, unclear goals, and poor communication, either. |
| → | A schedule cannot remedy bad design or engineering practices, nor can it protect a project from weak leadership, unclear goals, and poor communication. |

(1) Her husband was not one to communicate his love to her through words, or demonstrate it through his actions. He did not express any desire to spend time with her.

(2) Mike didn't come to the party last night, and didn't even call me to give an explanation.

(3) Mr. Anderson performed no more miracles that night. He didn't trouble to see what had become of his flowering stick.

(4) The little girl's expression didn't change. She didn't move her eyes from my face.

(5) The official could not say whether the two criminals in Guangdong had been released. She didn't provide any additional details.

Collocation

> Kick-off meetings take place at the beginning of the project and at the beginning of major phases, for larger projects. A well-planned and ***interactive kickoff*** (Text A) meeting usually means a ***fabulous beginning*** (Text A) for a project. During the kickoff meeting, the core team may be involved in a one to three day or more workshops in which they seek ***a consistent way*** (Text A) to validate the project charter, begin the high-level planning, and ***nurture the teamwork*** (Text A) through discussions and exercises. Other groups may have kick-off meetings at which key people present project plans and schedules, seek feedback and ***amplify the commitment*** (Text B) regarding roles and responsibilities. These mini kick-off meetings may also be workshops to break complicated work into ***manageable chunks*** (Text B). The kickoff meeting is an enthusiasm generator for the whole team and displays a full summary of the project. By presenting a thorough knowledge of the goal and steps on how to reach it, the team members start work.

6. **Replace the underlined words in the following sentences with the words provided in the box to form collocations you have learned from this unit. Each word can be used only once.**

unachievable	adequately	absolutely	deliberate
appropriate	progressively	valuable	unrealistic

(1) After the initiation stage, the project is planned to a <u>suitable</u> level of detail. The main purpose is to plan time, cost and resources <u>sufficiently</u> to estimate the work needed and to effectively manage risk during project execution.

(2) Companies that offer above-average benefits, incentives, steadily increasing salaries, and comfortable working environments are doing so to attract a better breed of employees.

(3) As much as people loathe schedules, they still hold them up to a(n) unattainable standard.

(4) Some managers tend to set impractical goals in hopes of getting team members to work harder and more efficiently.

(5) Make sure you're completely clear on the objective of the meeting. Then ensure you're aligned with your client counterpart.

(6) Going into a kickoff with an informed team and a carefully-thought plan helps you get the most out of your discussion—learning as much as possible and making important project decisions without wasting precious hours, money, and face-to-face client time.

Translation

7. Translate the following passage into English.

　　大约 2400 年前，伟大的哲学家墨子用三年时间完成了一只木鸟，但这只鸟只在天上飞了一天就坏了。后来，他的徒弟采用较轻的竹子，使木鸟能飞得久一些。这就是最早的风筝。之后，人们在风筝上加入了布料和竹哨，使它们在天空中飞行时可以发出音乐声。当时，风筝被用来测试风向和距离，监视敌人，或传递信息。唐朝时期，纸张和更多吉祥图案和彩色装饰品应用于风筝制作中，放风筝成为了人们的一种娱乐方式。

Unit project

Make a schedule plan for a meeting.

> Based on this unit theme, you will be expected to engage in making a schedule plan for a meeting. To make sure the schedule is as reliable and profound as possible, you can follow the steps below.

(1) Work in groups and discuss what main factors should be included in making a schedule plan for the meeting. The following elements can work as some hints. Add more if you can.

- Goals and objectives of the meeting
- Specific time and place to hold the meeting
- Participants of the meeting
- Lasting time
- Agendas of the meeting
- Materials and devices needed

...

(2) Suppose you are the host of the meeting. Write an outline of a schedule plan for the meeting and present it in the form of a PPT.

Unit 4

Project Management

Learning objectives

In this unit you will:
- learn what a project manager is and how leadership can be cultivated;
- learn how to be a good project manager;
- learn how to further develop an expository essay;
- learn how to read for key ideas in sentences.

> Management is doing things right; leadership is doing the right things.
>
> —*Peter F. Drucker*
>
> Effective leaders help others to understand the necessity of change and to accept a common vision of the desired outcome.
>
> —*John Kotter*

Preview

Project management, as an idea, goes back a very long way. If you think about all of the things that have been built in the history of civilization, we have thousands of years of project management to learn from. The history of engineering projects reveals that most projects have strong similarities. They have requirements, designs, and constraints. They depend on communication, decision making, and combinations of creative and logical thought. Projects usually involve a schedule, a budget, and a customer. Most importantly, the central task of projects is to combine the works of different people into a singular coherent whole that will be useful to people or customers. Whether a project is built out of HTML, C++, or cement and steel, there is an undeniable core set of concepts that most projects share. So for software engineers who want to advance their careers in the IT industry, what management concepts and necessary skills are better recommended? What abilities should they have in order to manage and succeed? How can they become successful at working with teams and completing projects?

Section A

 Pre-reading activities

1. **Think of a group or organization in which you are a member. Visualize yourself in charge of a group discussion. As you lead the group, the following six problems arise. Read the problems and possible solutions. Choose the best of the possible solutions which matches that solution. Keep in mind that you are in charge of group discussion for a particular group.**

   (1) Your group is having trouble getting started. You have tried to make everyone feel comfortable. You have allowed time to get acquainted. Everyone seems interested and cooperative, but reluctant to speak up.

   A. Wait until they're ready to speak up.

   B. Suggest that the group vote on what to do next.

   C. Make some specific assignments for different people and help them complete their assignments.

   (2) The group is operating extremely well. Members get along well with each other. The discussion is lively. Everyone is contributing to the group. You want to ensure that this continues.

   A. Reduce your leadership. Let group members lead the group as much as possible.

   B. Make sure agreement is reached on each point before proceeding.

   C. Keep the group firmly under your control or the group will lose its momentum.

   (3) The group has been very productive. Two or three members have done most of the talking and all of the work. Everyone seems happy, but you would like to make some changes so that more members will get involved.

   A. Tell it like it is. Outline the changes and see that they are made.

   B. Propose the changes. Explain why they are needed, and then let the group decide what will be done.

   C. Don't do anything that might threaten group productivity.

(4) The group is working well and relations among members are very positive. You feel somewhat unsure about your lack of direction in the group.

  A. Leave the group alone.

  B. Slowly assert yourself to give the group more direction.

  C. Ask the group if you should provide more direction, then comply with their wishes.

(5) The group have been going great, but now it is falling apart. Members are beginning to bicker. It is hard to stay on the subject. Someone has just suggested that maybe the group should take a recess for two or three months.

  A. Let everyone have their say. Don't get involved.

  B. Take a vote on the suggested recess.

  C. Propose a new course of action for the group. If no one strongly disagrees, make assignments and see that they are carried out.

(6) Your group has completed an excellent discussion of a topic they chose, but no one wants to take any action although several activities would be appropriate and each activity has been discussed.

  A. Just keep quiet until the group arrives at a decision.

  B. Suggest that the group move on to another topic. If no one disagrees, list possible topics.

  C. Choose an activity for the group and make assignments.

2. Each of the three possible solutions to each problem in Activity 1 corresponds to one of the three styles of leadership: directing style, democratic style, and delegating style. Check your answers to see what kind of leadership style you have.

Text A

Develop Leadership Skills to Succeed as a Project Manager

1. Congratulations! You have one of the best jobs available anywhere in the world today.

You also have one of the most **demanding** jobs in existence. You've won the career **lottery**. Kind of. There are few roles that have the ability to positively impact a firm in more ways than the project manager (PM).

2. Project managers are at the **epicenter** of an organization's strategy execution. Strategy is executed in projects, and an organization's project management skills play a significant role in success or failure in the marketplace. PMs also **shepherd** new product development from the **fuzzy front-end** to market launch, establish expectations for the overall project, and facilitate the creation of IT and technology **groundwork** that enables a firm to serve clients and **wrestle** with opponents in the market.

3. Of course, you are making all of this magic happen without the benefit of a great deal of formal leadership authority. This would be the "Kind Of" part for winning the career lottery. Your job is important and importantly, your job is very difficult.

4. I've served as a project manager, managed, hired and acted as an executive sponsor for project managers for **consecutive** twenty years. I've concluded that the best ones are game changers for a firm's ability to execute. They are also **superb** leaders. The rest are administrators.

5. Don't get me wrong. There is nothing wrong with being a good administrator. Chances are, however, that you are not reading this to improve your administrative skills. Simply stated, if you want to climb the ladder, grow your career and your earnings, and increase your **visibility** as a senior, "go-to" project manager, you must master the very difficult skills of leading others.

6. And remember, leadership is not for the **faint** of heart.

7. It does not matter whether you are a functional manager, a **front-line** supervisor, a team leader, a project manager, a senior executive or the CEO. Leading others is hard work. There are no silver **bullets**. It does not get materially easier as you grow older. People are complex. Leading would be easy except for the people. Unfortunately or fortunately, people are all that we have.

8. A wise man once indicated to me that, "leadership is a profession with a body of knowledge waiting to be discovered." He was right. By **implication**, he was also **highlighting** that you cannot learn to be an effective leader by reading a book or taking a course. I agree, and I'm the book and course author.

9. Leadership is only learned by doing, and by the wisdom **imparted** to us through our own mistakes. Judging by the number of leadership mistakes I've made in my career, I should be at least as wise as **Solomon**.

10. The biggest project **fiascoes** that I've observed or participated in had little to do

with the typical items that we think of in our risk planning activities. With the **clarity** of **reminiscence** and hindsight, the big project failures were related to people issues and in all cases, the project manager failed as a leader.

11. You can spot these **real-time** disasters by learning to recognize the **symptoms** of poor leadership at work such as constant **bickering** and finger pointing, too many poorly managed meetings, no sense of purpose and no **camaraderie**, a **lousy** sponsor and poor collaboration.

12. Is this painful enough?

13. In one particularly impressive project **debacle**, I observed every one of these symptoms. The project manager in this case had excellent knowledge of the tools and techniques needed to structure and run a project. However, he dropped the ball on his leadership tasks, and the results were **catastrophic**.

14. The project died on the **vine** of leadership incompetence and in this instance, the organization **squandered** a great opportunity to **inflict** pain on a competitor. The competitor was not so incompetent, and succeeded where the other firm failed. The **ripple** effect of this project's failure was felt in the market for the next several years.

15. Successful project managers should possess four key qualities or attributes that senior **contributors** in all positions and high performance project management professionals consistently display as they **ply** their trades.

16. Leadership **Maturity**: When I look at the leadership maturity of project managers, I am looking to see how well they grasp this part of their role and what behaviors they exhibit in pursuit of developing teams and supporting team members.

17. Strategic Awareness: One of the critical failings of many organizations is failing to properly involve and educate project managers on the strategic importance of a project. While many projects may be internal in nature, linking the project to how the **outcome** will help the firm better serve customers or compete offers critical context for the project team.

18. Executive Presence: Many otherwise capable professionals **agonize** about developing executive presence. One individual that I worked with was so challenged in this regard that he refused to ride in elevators for fear of bumping into one of the executives and being put on the spot to answer a question. He was in great shape. To be competent project managers, people should constantly try to cultivate the ability to comfortably relate to senior managers and develop and deliver a message that is at the "right level of detail" and that is **crisp** and to the point.

19. Execution **Orientation**: The ability to work with others to get things done is of course a critical attribute for a high performer and for the project manager as leader.

Specifically, I'm looking for the project manager's ability to work outside of the project team with the broader organization and functional leaders to get things done. Qualified project managers have a big-picture view of what it takes to execute and implement within groups and across functional areas, work to develop meaningful performance indicators and trouble-shoot and problem solve with others to improve operational effectiveness.

20. Like so many things in life, improvement starts with awareness. Ideally, you work for an enlightened manager that pushes challenges and provides **feedback** in support of your development. However, real world experience indicates that most project managers are left to **sink** or swim when it comes to **strengthening** their skills outside of the science of project management. I vote for swimming.

21. Developing your capabilities in the areas identified above is **attained** mostly through time and experience, and is well **supplemented** by external study, select course-work and ideally, good feedback and coaching from someone in your professional world.

(1,062 words)

New words

demanding	/dɪˈmɑːndɪŋ/	*a.*	(of a task, etc.) needing much patience, skill, effort, etc.（指任务等）需要很大耐性、技巧、努力等的
lottery	/ˈlɒtərɪ/	*n.*	[C] way of raising money by selling numbered tickets and giving prizes to the holders of numbers selected at random（发行彩票）抽彩给奖（筹款法）
epicenter	/ˈepɪsentə(r)/	*n.*	[C] point at which an earthquake reaches the Earth's surface 震中；震央
shepherd	/ˈʃepəd/	*vt.*	to guide or direct (people) as if they were sheep 带领；引导
		n.	[C] a person who takes care of sheep 牧羊人
fuzzy	/ˈfʌzɪ/	*a.*	*(-ier, -iest)* blurred or indistinct, esp. in shape or outline 模糊的；不清楚的（尤指形状或轮廓）
front-end	/ˈfrʌnt end/	*n.*	the initial phase or part of a project, system, or device 项目、系统或设备的初始阶段或部分
groundwork	/ˈɡraʊndˌwɜːk/	*n.*	[U] sth. that has to happen before an activity or plan can be successful 地基；根据；基础
wrestle	/ˈresəl/	*v.*	1. ~ *(with sb.)* to fight (esp. as a sport) by grappling with sb. and trying to throw him to the ground 摔跤（尤指运动） 2. ~ *with sth.* to struggle to deal with or overcome sth. 奋力对付或制服某事物

consecutive	/kən'sekjʊtɪv/	*a.*	coming one after the other without interruption; following continuously 连续不断的
superb	/sʊ'pɜːb/	*a.*	excellent; splendid 卓越的；杰出的；极好的
visibility	/ˌvɪzɪ'bɪlɪtɪ/	*n.*	[U] fact or state of being visible 可见性；明显性
faint	/feɪnt/	*n.*	[sing.] act or state of fainting 昏厥；不省人事
front-line	/ˌfrʌnt 'laɪn/	*a.*	1. of, pertaining to, or involving the forefront in any action, activity, or field 第一线的 2. highly experienced or proficient in the performance of one's duties 第一流的；主力队员的
bullet	/'bʊlɪt/	*n.*	[C] small missile, usu. round or cylindrical with a pointed end, fired from a gun or rifle 子弹 *(silver bullet)* 银弹／奇迹般的解决方法
implication	/ˌɪmplɪ'keɪʃn/	*n.*	[U] *~ (for sb./sth.)* thing that is suggested or implied 含意；暗示；暗指
highlight	/'haɪlaɪt/	*vt.*	to emphasize 对（某事）予以特别的注意；强调
		n.	[C] best, most interesting or most exciting part of sth. 最有意思或最精彩的部分
impart	/ɪm'pɑːt/	*vt.*	*~ sth. (to sth.)* to give (a quality) to sth. 将（某性质）给予或赋予某事物
fiasco	/fɪ'æskəʊ/	*n.*	[C] (pl. ~s; US also ~es) complete and ridiculous failure 彻底的失败；惨败；大出丑
clarity	/'klærɪtɪ/	*n.*	[U] clearness; lucidity 清楚；明晰；清澈
reminiscence	/ˌremɪ'nɪsəns/	*n.*	[U] recalling of past events and experiences; reminiscing 回忆；话旧；怀旧
real-time	/ˌriːəl 'taɪm/	*a.*	实时的；接到指示立即执行的
symptom	/'sɪmptəm/	*n.*	[C] change in the body that indicates an illness 症状
bicker	/'bɪkə/	*vi.*	*~ (with sb.) (over/about sth.)* to quarrel about unimportant things （为小事）争吵
camaraderie	/ˌkæmə'rɑːdərɪ/	*n.*	[U] friendship and mutual trust; comradeship 友谊与互相信任；同志情谊
lousy	/'laʊzɪ/	*a.*	(informal) 1. very bad 非常糟的；极坏的；恶劣的 2. [only before noun] used to show that you feel annoyed or insulted because you do not think that sth. is worth very much（认为某物无太大价值而不满或感到受辱）讨厌的；倒霉的 3. *~ with sth./sb.* having too much of sth. or too many people（某事物或人）太多的
debacle	/deɪ'bɑːkəl/	*n.*	[C] (a) sudden and complete failure; fiasco 突然的大失败；惨败

Unit 4 Project Management

catastrophic	/ˌkætə'strɒfɪk/	*a.*	miserable; calamitous 灾难性的
vine	/vaɪn/	*n.*	[C] climbing or trailing plant with a woody stem whose fruit is the grape 葡萄藤
squander	/'skwɒndə/	*vt.*	~ *sth. (on sb./sth.)* to waste (time, money, etc.); to use sth. wastefully 浪费（时间、金钱等）；挥霍
inflict	/ɪn'flɪkt/	*vt.*	~ *sth. (on sb.)* to cause (a blow, penalty, etc.) to be suffered (by sb.) 使（某人）遭受（打击、惩罚等）
ripple	/'rɪpəl/	*n.*	[C] small wave or series of waves 波纹；涟漪
contributor	/kən'trɪbjʊtə/	*n.*	[C] sb. who gives money, help, ideas, etc. to sth. that a lot of other people are also involved in 捐赠者；贡献者；捐款人
ply	/plaɪ/	*v.*	1. to use or wield (a tool or weapon) 使用（工具或武器） 2. to ply one's trade 从事某（熟练）工作
maturity	/mə'tjʊərɪtɪ/	*n.*	[U] the quality of behaving in a sensible way like an adult 成熟
outcome	/'aʊtˌkʌm/	*n.*	[C] (usu. sing.) effect or result (of an event, circumstances, etc.) 结果；后果
agonize	/'ægəˌnaɪz/	*vi.*	*(~about/over sth.)* to suffer great anxiety or worry intensely (about sth.) （对某事物）极度忧虑或担心
crisp	/krɪsp/	*a.*	1. (of sb.'s manner, way of speaking, etc.) brisk, precise and decisive（指态度、说话方式等）干脆的；斩钉截铁的 2. (esp. of food) hard, dry and easily broken（尤指食品）脆的
orientation	/ˌɔːrɪen'teɪʃən/	*n.*	[U] activity of orientating oneself; state of being orientated 熟悉情况；认识环境；确定方位
feedback	/'fiːdˌbæk/	*n.*	[U] information about a product, etc. that a user gives back to its supplier, maker, etc. 反馈信息
sink	/sɪŋk/	*vi.*	(pt. sank; pp. sunk) to go down under the surface of a liquid or soft substance 下沉；沉没
strengthen	/'streŋθən/	*vt.*	to make an organization, army, etc. more powerful, especially by increasing the number or quality of the people in it 强化；加强
attain	/ə'teɪn/	*vt.*	to succeed in getting (sth.); to achieve 获得（某事物）；达到；实现
supplement	/'sʌplɪmənt/	*n.*	[C] thing added to sth. else to improve or complete it 增补的事物；补充

New expressions

faint of heart	fear of the heart, coward 心生畏惧；懦夫；胆小鬼
get sb. wrong	to misunderstand sb. 误会某人
silver bullet	new technology, especially some new technology of high hopes 喻指新技术，尤指人们寄予厚望的某种新科技；奇迹般的解决办法
impart to	to make information known to sb. 将（情况）通知或告知某人；透露某事物
finger pointing	the imputation of blame 相互指责
drop the ball	to screw up 搞砸
inflict on	to impose on 将……强加于……
ripple effect	chain reaction; halo effect 连锁反应；涟漪作用
in pursuit of	to go after 追求
bump into	to meet someone who you know when you were not expecting to 偶然间碰到

Reading comprehension

Understanding the text

1. Answer the following questions.

(1) What kind of job is a project manager according to the author?

(2) What do project managers do?

(3) Does leading get materially easier as a person grows older?

(4) How can leadership be learned?

(5) What are the symptoms of poor management?

(6) What qualities or attributes should successful project managers possess?

(7) What does the author mean when he says that most project managers are left to sink or swim?

(8) How can management capabilities be accomplished according to the writer?

Critical thinking

2. Work in pairs and discuss the following questions.

(1) What do you think are a project manager's responsibilities?

(2) How can people develop leadership capability?

Word building

The suffix *-ity* combines with adjectives to form nouns. New nouns formed in this way have the meaning of "the state or character of...".

Examples

Words learned	Add *-ity*	New words formed
curious	→	curiosity
public	→	publicity
visible	→	visibility
able	→	ability
responsible	→	responsibility

The suffix *-ize* combines with nouns or adjectives that refer to a state or conditions in order to form verbs. Verbs formed in this way describe the process by which that state or condition mentioned is brought about.

Examples

Words learned	Add *-ize*	New words formed
agony	→	agonize
modern	→	modernize
apology	→	apologize
familiar	→	familiarize

3. Add *-ity*, or *-ize* to the following words to form new words.

Words learned	New words formed
-ity	
rapid	

(continued)

Words learned	New words formed
mobile	
complex	
capable	
real	
-ize	
summary	
symbol	
computer	
colony	
normal	

4. **Fill in the blanks with the newly-formed words in Activity 3. Change the form where necessary. Each word can be used only once.**

   (1) The fall of the Berlin Wall _____ the end of the Cold War between East and West.

   (2) The _____ of the population's aging has made it more urgent for the adoption of countermeasures.

   (3) After a long war between England and Spain from 1588 to 1603, England renewed attempts to _____ North America.

   (4) There is increasing recognition of the _____ of the causes of poverty.

   (5) After a period of international tension, the two countries are now trying to _____ diplomatic relations with each other.

   (6) The fundamental problem lies in their inability to distinguish between _____ and invention.

   (7) Philosophy is the scientific knowledge that _____ the nature and society.

   (8) The accident which I suffered in the sports meeting last week greatly decreased my _____.

   (9) I'm trying to make a spreadsheet up to _____ everything that's done by hand at the moment.

(10) Their military _____ has been reduced because their air force has proved not to be effective.

Banked cloze

5. Fill in the blanks by selecting suitable words from the word bank. You may not use any of the words more than once.

A. impossible	B. literally	C. maintaining	D. particular	E. brilliantly
F. facilitate	G. responsibility	H. introverted	I. hindsight	J. dependent
K. extroverted	L. improvement	M. visibility	N. amplifying	O. symptom

One of the earliest engineering stories in Western history is the story of the Tower of Babel from Genesis. As the story goes, humanity was happily united in the desert. Things were going so well that, for no (1) _____ reason, they decided to build a tower into the sky. Things went along (2) _____ until the workers suddenly lost the ability to use the same language, at which point everything (3) _____ fell apart. It's suggested in the story that had they been able to continue to communicate well with each other, nothing would have been (4) _____.

These days, communication is still as important as in previous eras. Most software teams rely on peer-to-peer interaction and other, less hierarchically driven relationships. Although there are often clearly defined leaders, who sometimes give orders, projects are heavily (5) _____ on the team's ability to make use of each other's knowledge, to share ideas, and to work in synchronicity.

Because project managers spend a lot of time communicating with individuals and groups, they inevitably carry more (6) _____ for effective communication than other individuals on the team. Good project managers provide steady streams of good communication and healthy relations, (7) _____ the effectiveness of everyone they come into contact with. If it's the health of the social network of a team that prevents it from becoming another Tower of Babel, then it's the project manager who has the most natural role in building up and (8) _____ that network.

Doing this doesn't require a(n) (9) _____, game-show-host personality; nor does it demand a brilliant sense of humor or magical powers. Instead, it starts by admitting that communication and relationships are critical to success, and that there's room for (10) _____ for yourself and your team. If you admit it's important, then you'll want to understand where most communication problems occur and learn how to deal with them.

Structured analysis and writing

Structure analysis

Further develop an expository essay

In this unit, we will learn how to further develop an expository essay. Expository writing is also called informative writing because its purpose is to explain, inform, or clarify. This type of writing is often required of students when they are assigned to write essays explaining subject matter in various academic disciplines.

Exposition is explanatory communication, whether in speech or writing. So an expository essay is an organized piece of prose that explains a specific topic or set of ideas to a defined audience. Expository essays provide information and analysis. An expository essay may or may not have an overt central argument, though it does set forth points of view on the topic. It differs from the persuasive research paper in the level of research and argument it employs. While an expository essay should be focused on a particular topic and illustrate its points with specific examples, it doesn't usually have the depth of research or argument that you need in a major research assignment.

Usually, the expository essay is composed of five paragraphs. The introductory paragraph contains the thesis or main idea. The next three paragraphs, or the body of the essay, provide details in support of the thesis. The concluding paragraph restates the main idea and ties together the major points of the essay.

While the 5-paragraph structure gives you a helpful formula to work with, it's only one among many valid options, and its suitability will depend on other factors like the length and complexity of your essay. If you're writing a paper that's more than 3 or 4 pages long, it should be more than 5 paragraphs. In most cases, the structure of a longer essay will be similar to that of a 5-paragraph essay, with an introduction, a conclusion and body paragraphs performing the same basic functions—only the number of body paragraphs will increase. The length of the paragraphs may also increase slightly in proportion to the length of the essay.

A good expository essay should perform several of the following tasks that overlap and merge smoothly with each other:

1) Define your key terms or ideas;
2) Describe specific evidential examples;
3) Investigate the common thread among your examples;
4) Compare and contrast your examples and their relation to your thesis;

5) Analyze cause-and-effect relationships among your examples;

6) Connect your examples explicitly to your central idea and to each other;

7) Polish your essay through revision to make it artful, original, and interesting. Avoid clichéd language or the most obvious examples. You want your reader to learn something new and compelling, whether it's an unusual fact or a novel perspective on your topic.

Text A is an expository essay, explaining the importance of leadership ability in project management and how to develop such abilities. The author starts with a definition of the project manager in the IT industry. Then he clearly presents what challenges and difficulties a project manager will meet, illustrates the difference between a real project manager and an administrator, and gives examples of poor management. He then continues by informing the readers of 4 key qualities needed to develop leadership abilities. At the end of the essay, the author gives a restatement of his viewpoint, emphasizing that developing these capabilities in project management is accomplished mostly through time and experience, and is well supplemented by external study, good feedback and coaching.

Structured writing

Read the sample essay and see how an expository essay is structured.

> **Topic**
>
> Road rage
>
> **Introduction**
>
> A significant percentage of accidents are caused by a phenomenon widely known as road rage.
>
> **Body**
>
> What is the definition of road rage?
>
> What kind of drivers are prone to developing road rage?
>
> What are the symptoms of road rage?
>
> **Conclusion**
>
> What should you do if you meet a driver suffering from road rage?

Sample essay

Road Rage

Considering the ever-increasing pace of life across the globe, possessing a car and being able to drive it has become a necessity a long time ago. The number of car owners grows exponentially each year, and unfortunately, so does the amount of deaths and injuries related to driving. However, not all of these accidents are regular car crashes; a significant percentage of cases are caused by a phenomenon widely known as road rage.

Perhaps, the most suitable definition for this phenomenon is a driver's loss of emotional control and stability caused by traffic events, and leading to this driver's deviant or offensive behavior. Psychiatrists believe some drivers can be more prone to developing road rage than others. Usually, people who tend to fall into this condition are relatively young (in their late 20s or in the middle of 30s), male, and possibly suffering from a psychological condition called IED—intermittent emotional disorder. This condition can be generally characterized by sudden outbursts of anger accompanied by a decreased ability to control it, and to refrain from releasing it upon others. The factors responsible for such a behavior can be different, starting from chronic stress, and ending up with an intense emotional condition, such as losing a job or an important person.

If you have found yourself in a situation where another driver started behaving aggressively towards you, the most optimal reaction would be to avoid direct eye contact and not behave aggressively in response, regardless of whether it was your fault for causing road rage or not. This might seem a bit self-humiliating, as a refusal to stand for your own rights and dignity, but you should remember that drivers with road rage sometimes cannot handle their anger, and if they have firearms or other weapons with them, the situation might turn fatal.

6. Write an essay of no less than 200 words on one of the following topics. One topic has an outline that you can follow.

> **Topic**
>
> Why do teens smoke cigarettes?
>
> **Introduction**
>
> **Thesis statement:** Smoking cigarettes has become prevalent among teens nowadays and poses a threat both to their health and minds.

Body

Reason 1: Peer pressure. Young people smoke because their friends do it.

Reason 2: Portrayals of smoking in the media lure young people into imitating the coolness.

Conclusion

It's high time for us to prevent teens from getting rid of the bad behavior.

More topics:

- How music affects our life
- Some productive ways for students to spend leisure time

 Translation

7. Translate the following paragraph into Chinese.

Black Friday is the day after Thanksgiving Day in the USA and falls on the Friday after the fourth Thursday in November. It is one of the busiest shopping days in the USA. The term Black Friday comes from an old way of recording business accounts. In those days, losses were recorded in red ink and profits in black ink. Many businesses, particularly small businesses, started making profits prior to Christmas. Many hoped to start showing a profit, marked in black ink, on the day after Thanksgiving Day. Now people have a day off work or choose to take a day from their quota of annual leave on Black Friday. Some people make trips to see family members or friends who live in other areas or to go on vacation. Others start shopping for the Christmas season.

8. Translate the following paragraph into English.

"光棍节"是广泛流行于中国年轻人中的娱乐性节日，他们庆祝自己仍是单身贵族，并引以为傲。11月11日被选为"光棍节"是因为数字1象征单身。"光棍节"起源于

1993年的南京大学。在20世纪90年代,"光棍节"首先出现在南京各个高校中。随着一批批学子告别校园,这个节日被渐渐带入社会。在互联网时代的推广下,"光棍节"流行开来,国外其他区域的年轻人也开始追捧这个节日。这个节日现在已经演变成世界上最大的互联网购物节日。

Section B

 Reading skills: *Reading for the key ideas in sentences*

Although a sentence may give a great deal of information, it usually offers just one key idea. You should be able to find key ideas in sentences in order to understand them more clearly. You may ask the following questions to get the key ideas in different sentences:

1) Who or what is the sentence about?

2) What is the person or object doing or what is happening to the person or object?

3) What is the key idea and what are the minor details? Many words in a sentence describe things about the subject of the sentence but they merely add details to it. If you ask *when, what, where,* or *why,* you will easily find the details of a sentence, which also helps you to see the key idea.

Here is one example from Text A:

> *Simply stated, if you want to climb the ladder, grow your career and your earnings and increase your visibility as a senior, "go-to" project manager, you must master the very difficult skills of leading others.* (Para. 5)
>
> Key idea: As a senior; "go-to" project manager; master the skills of leading others

Why is it the key idea of the sentence? First of all, the sentence talks about the project manager, which answers the question of "who". Then we see all the advantages of being a senior, "go-to" manager: climb the ladder, grow your career and your earnings and increase your visibility. The whole sentence tells us if the manager wants to get the advantages, he must master the skills of leading others.

Of course, we cannot always easily decide which details are simply descriptive and which add much to the key idea. However, the starting point for determining the key idea in a sentence is to find who or what the sentence is about and what the person or object is doing.

Read the following paragraphs from Text B and write down the key idea of each sentence.

(1) Programmers and their bosses maintain schedules and engineering plans and a business analyst or marketing person does the planning or requirements work. Anything else that might qualify as project management simply gets distributed across the team. (Para. 1)

Key idea: _____

(2) If there is no clear owner for leading bug triage, or no one is dedicated to tracking the schedule and flagging problems, those tasks might lag dangerously behind individual, programming-centric activities. (Para. 2)

Key idea: _____

(3) But the hard truth is that it is hard to find good project managers because they need to maintain a balance of attitudes. (Para. 3)

Key idea: _____

(4) Project managers must be persuasive in getting the team to strive for simplicity and clarity in the work they do, without minimizing the complexities involved in writing good, reliable code. (Para. 7)

Key idea: _____

(5) Some political, cross-organizational, or bureaucratic activities are unavoidable time sinks: someone has to be in the room, or be on the conference call, and they have to be patient. (Para. 8)

Key idea: _____

Text B

The Art of Project Management

1. Project management can be a profession, a job, a role or an activity. Some companies

have project managers whose job is to **oversee** entire 200-person projects. Others use the title for line-level junior managers, each responsible for a small area of a large project. Sometimes the **absence** of a dedicated project manager works fine. Programmers and their bosses maintain schedules and engineering plans and a business **analyst** or marketing person does the planning or requirements work. Anything else that might **qualify** as project management simply gets **distributed** across the team. They might not mind early planning user **interface** design or business **strategy**. There can be significant **optimizations** in working this way.

2. But other times, the absence of a project manager creates **dysfunction**. Without a person whose primary job is to shepherd the overall effort, individual **biases** and interests can **derail** the direction of the team. Strong **adversarial factions** may develop around engineering and business roles, slowing progress and frustrating everyone involved. Consider that in hospital emergency rooms, one doctor takes the lead in deciding the course of action for a patient. This **expedites** many decisions and gives clarity to the roles that everyone on the **trauma** team is expected to play. Without that kind of clear **authority** for project management-type issues, development teams can run into trouble. If there is no clear owner for leading bug **triage**, or no one is dedicated to tracking the schedule and flagging problems, those tasks might lag dangerously behind individual, programming-centric activities.

3. But the hard truth is that it is hard to find good project managers because they need to maintain a balance of attitudes. Tom Peters, in his essay "Pursuing the Perfect Project Manager," calls these conflicting attitudes **paradoxes** or dilemmas. This name is appropriate because different situations require different behavior. This means that a project manager needs not only to be aware of these traits, but also to develop **instincts** for which ones are appropriate at which times. This contributes to the idea of project management as an art: it requires **intuition**, judgment, and experience to use these forces effectively. The following list of traits is roughly **derived** from Peters' essay.

4. **Ego/no-ego.** Because of how much responsibility project managers have they often derive great personal satisfaction from their work. It's understandable that they'd have a high emotional investment in what they're doing, and for many, this emotional connection is what enables them to maintain the intensity needed to be effective. But at the same time, project managers must avoid placing their own interests ahead of the project. They must be willing to delegate important or fun tasks and share **accolades** and rewards with the entire team. As much as the ego can be fuel, a good project manager has to recognize when his ego is getting in the way.

5. **Autocrat/delegator.** In some situations, the most important things are a clear line of authority and a quick response time. A project manager has to be confident and willful enough to take control and force certain actions onto a team. However, the general goal

should be to avoid the need for these extreme situations. A well-managed project should create an environment where work can be delegated and collaborated on effectively.

6. **Tolerate ambiguity/pursue perfection.** The early phases of any project are highly open and **fluid** experiences where the unknown heavily **outweighs** the known. Controlled ambiguity is essential for good ideas to surface, and a project manager must respect it, if not manage it. But at other moments, particularly in the later phases of a project, discipline and precision are **paramount**. It requires wisdom to discern when the quest for perfection is worthwhile, versus when a **mediocre** or quick-and-dirty solution is sufficient.

7. **Acknowledge complexity/champion simplicity.** Many people fall victim to complexity. When they face a complex organizational or engineering challenge, they get lost in the details and forget the big picture. Others stay in **denial** about complexity and make bad decisions because they don't fully understand the **subtleties** of what's involved. The balancing act here is to recognize which view of the project is most useful for the problem or decision at hand, and to comfortably switch between them or keep them both in mind at the same time. Project managers must be **persuasive** in getting the team to strive for simplicity and clarity in the work they do, without **minimizing** the complexities involved in writing good, reliable code.

8. **Impatient/patient.** Most of the time, the project manager is the person pushing for action, forcing others to keep work **lean** and focused. But in some situations, impatience works against the project. Some political, cross-organizational, or **bureaucratic** activities are unavoidable time sinks: someone has to be in the room, or be on the conference call, and they have to be patient. So, knowing when to force an issue, and when to back off and let things happen, is a sense project managers need to develop.

9. **Believer/skeptic.** There is nothing more powerful for team **morale** than a respected leader who believes in what he/she is doing. It's important for a project manager to have confidence in the work being done, and see true value in the goals that will be achieved. At the same time, there is a need for **skepticism** about how things are going and the ways in which they are being done. Someone has to probe and question, exposing **assumptions** and bringing difficult issues to light. The balancing act is to somehow vigorously ask questions and challenge the assumptions of others, without shaking the team's belief in what they are doing.

10. As Peters points out in his essay, it's very rare to find people capable of all of these skills, much less with the capacity to balance them properly. Many of the mistakes that any PM will make involve **miscalculations** in balancing one or more of these conflicting forces. However, anyone can get better at recognizing, understanding, and then improving his own ability to keep these forces in balance. So, looking at this list of conflicting but necessary

forces can help you step back, reconsider what you're doing and why, and make smarter decisions.

(1,019 words)

New words

oversee	/ˌəʊvə'siː/	vt.	to watch sb./sth. and make sure that a job or an activity is done correctly 监督；监视
absence	/'æbsəns/	n.	~ (from...) the fact of sb. being away from a place where they are usually expected to be; the occasion or period of time when sb. is away 缺席；不在
analyst	/'ænəlɪst/	n.	a person whose job involves examining facts or materials in order to give an opinion on them 分析者；化验员
qualify	/'kwɒlɪˌfaɪ/	vi.	~ (as sth.) to reach the standard of ability or knowledge needed to do a particular job, for example by completing a course of study or passing exams 取得资格（或学历）；合格
distribute	/dɪ'strɪbjuːt/	vt.	~ sth. (to/among sb./sth.) to give things to a large number of people; to share sth. between a number of people 分发；分配
interface	/'ɪntəfeɪs/	n.	the way a computer program presents information to a user or receives information from a user, in particular the layout of the screen and the menus（人机）界面（尤指屏幕布局和菜单）
strategy	/'strætɪdʒɪ/	n.	[C] ~ (for doing sth.) ~ (to do sth.) a plan that is intended to achieve a particular purpose 策略；计策；行动计划 [U] the process of planning sth. or putting a plan into operation in a skillful way 策划；规划；统筹安排
optimization	/ˌɒptɪmaɪ'zeɪʃən/	n.	making the best of anything 最佳化；最优化
dysfunction	/dɪs'fʌŋkʃən/	n.	malfunctioning, as of an organ or structure of the body 功能紊乱；机能障碍；机能不良
bias	/'baɪəs/	n.	1. [C] an interest in one thing more than others; a special ability 偏爱；特殊能力 2. [U] a strong feeling in favour of or against one group of people, or one side in an argument, often not based on fair judgment 偏见；偏心；偏向

derail	/dɪˈreɪl/	vt.	1. to obstruct (a process) by diverting it from its intended course 阻挠；破坏 2. (of a train) to leave the track（使）脱轨；出轨
adversarial	/ˌædvɜːˈseərɪəl/	a.	involving people who are in opposition and who make attacks on each other 对立的；敌对的
faction	/ˈfækʃən/	n.	[C] a small group of people within a larger one whose members have some different aims and beliefs to those of the larger group（大团体中的）派系；派别；小集团
expedite	/ˈekspɪdaɪt/	vt.	to make a process happen more quickly 加快；加速
trauma	/ˈtrɔːmə/	n.	[C, U] 1. (medical) an injury 损伤；外伤 2. an unpleasant experience that makes you feel upset and/or anxious 痛苦经历；挫折
authority	/ɔːˈθɒrɪti/	n.	[U] 1. the power to give orders to people 权力；威权；当权（地位）2. ~ (to do sth.) the power or right to do sth. 权；职权
triage	/ˈtriːɑːʒ/	n.	[U] the action of sorting according to quality 分类
paradox	/ˈpærəˌdɒks/	n.	[C, U] a statement containing two opposite ideas that make it seem impossible or unlikely, although it is probably true; the use of this in writing 似非而是的隽语；悖论；悖论修辞
instinct	/ˈɪnstɪŋkt/	n.	1. a feeling that makes you do sth. or believe that sth. is true, even though it is not based on facts or reason 直觉 2. ~ (for sth./for doing sth.) ~ (to do sth.) a natural tendency for people and animals to behave in a particular way using the knowledge and abilities that they were born with rather than thought or training 本能；天性
intuition	/ˌɪntjuˈɪʃən/	n.	[U] the ability to know sth. by using your feelings rather than considering the facts 直觉力
derive	/dɪˈraɪv/	vt.	to get sth. from sth.（从……中）得到；获得
		vi.	(~from) to come or develop from sth. 从……衍生出；起源于；来自
ego	/ˈiːɡəʊ/	n.	[C] the opinion that you have about yourself 自我；自我意识
accolade	/ˈækəˌleɪd/	n.	(fml.) praise or an award for an achievement that people admire 赞扬；表扬；奖励；奖赏；荣誉
autocrat	/ˈɔːtəˌkræt/	n.	a ruler who has complete power 独裁者；专制统治者；专制君主

delegator	/ˈdelɪgeɪtə/	n.	委托者；委托人；授权人
ambiguity	/ˌæmbɪˈgjuːɪtɪ/	n.	[C, U] the state of being difficult to understand or explain because of involving many different aspects 模棱两可；不明确
fluid	/ˈfluːɪd/	n.	[C, U] a liquid; a substance that can flow 液体；流体
outweigh	/ˌaʊtˈweɪ/	vt.	to be greater or more important than sth. 重于；大于；超过
paramount	/ˈpærəˌmaʊnt/	a.	more important than anything else 至为重要的；首要的
mediocre	/ˌmiːdɪˈəʊkə/	a.	not very good; of only average standard 平庸的；普通的；平常的
complexity	/kəmˈpleksɪtɪ/	n.	[U] the state of being formed of many parts; the state of being difficult to understand 复杂性；难懂
champion	/ˈtʃæmpɪən/	vt.	to fight for or speak in support of a group of people or a belief 为……而斗争；捍卫；声援
		n.	a person, team, etc. that has won a competition, esp. in a sport 冠军；第一名；优胜者
simplicity	/sɪmˈplɪsɪtɪ/	n.	[U] the quality of being easy to understand or use 简单（性）；容易（性）
denial	/dɪˈnaɪəl/	n.	[U] a refusal to accept that sth. unpleasant or painful is true 否认（令人不快、痛苦的事）
subtlety	/ˈsʌtəltɪ/	n.	1. [C] the small but important details or aspects of sth. 细小但重要的地方；微妙之处 2. [U] the quality of being subtle 细微；微妙；狡猾；巧妙；敏锐
persuasive	/pəˈsweɪsɪv/	a.	able to persuade sb. to do or believe sth. 有说服力的；令人信服的
minimize	/ˈmɪnɪˌmaɪz/	vt.	to reduce sth., especially sth. bad, to the lowest possible level 使减少到最低限度
lean	/liːn/	a.	strong and efficient because the number of employees has been reduced 精干的；效率高的
		vi.	(~ against/on sth.) to rest on or against sth. for support 倚靠；靠在；靠置
bureaucratic	/ˌbjʊərəˈkrætɪk/	a.	connected with a bureaucracy or bureaucrats and involving complicated official rules which may seem unnecessary 官僚的；官僚主义的
believer	/bɪˈliːvə/	n.	a person who believes in the existence or truth of sth., esp. sb. who believes in a god or religious faith 信徒

skeptic	/'skeptɪk/	n.	a person who questions the validity or authenticity of sth. purporting to be factual（对一切都）持怀疑态度的人；怀疑论者；不可知论者；无神论者
morale	/mɒ'rɑːl/	n.	[U] the amount of confidence and enthusiasm, etc. that a person or a group has at a particular time 士气
skepticism	/'skeptɪsɪzəm/	n.	skeptical attitude or temper 怀疑态度；怀疑论
assumption	/ə'sʌmpʃən/	n.	[C] a belief or feeling that sth. is true or that sth. will happen, although there is no proof 假定；假设
miscalculation	/ˌmɪskælkjʊ'leɪʃən/	n.	a mistake in calculating 算错；误算

 New expressions

run into	to be beset by 为……困扰；遭遇；陷入
lag behind	to fail to maintain a desired pace or to keep up; to fall or stay behind 落后；拖欠
aware of	knowing or realizing sth. 知道；意识到；明白
contribute to	to increase, improve or add to sth. 有助于；捐献
derive from	to come or develop from sth. 源出；来自；得自；衍生于
fall victim to	to become... the victim of 成为……的牺牲品；成为……的受害者；屈服于……；被……降服
strive for	to try very hard to achieve sth. 努力；奋斗；力争；力求
capable of	having the ability or qualities necessary for doing sth. 有能力；有才能
step back	to rein back; to back off 后退；退后

 Notes

Tom Peters（汤姆·彼得斯）: a well-known American management scientist and best-selling author. He is known as the "Pope of business". He received an MBA and Ph.D. from Stanford University and worked as a consultant for McKinsey & Company.

Reading comprehension

Understanding the text

1. Choose the best answer to each of the following questions.

(1) Sometimes the absence of a dedicated project manager works fine, because _____.

   A. the planning or requirements work gets distributed across the team

   B. early planning user interface design or business strategy is not important

   C. nobody likes to do the work

   D. the bosses can do the work by themselves

(2) According to the passage, what will happen if the project manager is absent?

   A. The absence of a project manager creates paradoxes.

   B. The absence of a project manager creates dysfunction.

   C. The absence of a project manager creates ambiguity.

   D. All of the above.

(3) Project managers must avoid _____.

   A. delegating important or fun tasks and sharing accolades and rewards with the entire team

   B. sharing accolades and rewards with the entire team

   C. placing their own interests ahead of the project

   D. motivating the morale of employees

(4) What are the early stages of any project like?

   A. Highly open experiences.

   B. Fluid experiences.

   C. The unknown heavily outweighs the known.

   D. All of the above.

(5) What are paramount in the later phases of a project?

   A. Interface design.

   B. Discipline and precision.

C. Business strategy.

D. A clear line of authority and a quick response time.

(6) A good project manager needs patience because _____.

A. the project manager is the person pushing for action, forcing others to keep work lean and focused

B. impatience works against the project

C. some political, cross-organizational, or bureaucratic activities are unavoidable time sinks

D. All of the above

(7) What can it help you to do after looking at this list of conflicting but necessary forces?

A. To ask questions and challenge the assumptions of others.

B. To step back, reconsider what you're doing and why, and make smarter decisions.

C. To probe and question, exposing assumptions and bringing difficult issues to light.

D. To strive for simplicity and clarity in the work they do.

(8) The purpose of the text is _____.

A. to prove to us that it is impossible to be a perfect project manager

B. to demonstrate that a perfect project manager should learn art

C. to help us realize the importance of being a perfect project manager

D. to show how to be a perfect project manager

Critical thinking

2. Work in pairs and discuss the following questions.

(1) Do you think it is important to be a perfect project manager?

(2) In your opinion, what factors are the main considerations in being a perfect project manager?

(3) What kind of people do you think are likely to become perfect project managers?

Language focus

Words in use

3. Fill in the blanks with the words given below. Change the form where necessary. Each word can be used only once.

| bias | oversee | outweigh | paradox | subtlety |
| derail | denial | minimize | champion | assumption |

(1) The government set up a state watchdog to _____ the country's alcohol production.

(2) He said he didn't know how many of the _____ cars had caught on fire.

(3) Peers working together _____ the pain of some schoolwork, while promoting learning and cooperation for both.

(4) It is a curious _____ that professional comedians often have unhappy personal lives.

(5) The terrorists issued a(n) _____ of responsibility for the attack.

(6) There are, inevitably, costs of globalization; but they are hugely _____ by the benefits.

(7) There's a common _____ that science is more difficult than other subjects.

(8) Some institutions still have a strong _____ against women.

(9) You learn how to understand your customers and the _____ of their needs.

(10) She held the title of world _____ for three years.

Expressions in use

4. Fill in the blanks with the expressions given below. Change the form where necessary. Each expression can be used only once.

| capable of | derive from | step back | strive for |
| contribute to | fall victim to | run into | lag behind |

(1) We must achieve modernization of science and technology, otherwise we will _____ other nations.

(2) Human beings differ from animals in that the former is _____ using language.

(3) The development of banking and other financial services _____ the expansion of trade.

(4) Many English words are _____ Latin and Greek words.

(5) Even the most positive, well-adjusted person in the world still _____ his or her own negative thoughts now and then.

(6) Building a worldwide famous fashion brand name has long been the goal that China's fashion industry_____.

(7) We are learning to _____ from ourselves and identify our strengths and weaknesses.

(8) She _____ the middle of the room, unable to utter one tone. She was so out of breath.

Sentence structure

5. Rewrite the sentences by using the structure "not only..., but also...". Make changes where necessary.

Model:	This means that a project manager needs to be aware of these traits. He also needs to develop instincts for which ones are appropriate at which times.
⟶	This means that a project manager needs not only to be aware of these traits, but also to develop instincts for which ones are appropriate at which times.

(1) We need to listen to what he says. We also need to watch what he does.

_____

(2) We need to be under various external pressures. We also need to be in the face of internal perplexities.

_____

(3) Self-driving vehicles will need to obey traffic laws. They also need to adapt to road conditions and implement driving strategies.

_____

(4) We need to build a strong body. We also need to keep a good mood in order to face the pressures or challenges of modern society.

_____

(5) It therefore presents an excellent opportunity to screen for HIV. It also presents an excellent opportunity to educate and advise about the dangers of the virus.

Collocation

> Project managers are at the epicenter of an organization's ***strategy execution*** (Text A). Successful project managers should possess four key qualities or attributes that senior contributors in all positions and high performance project management professionals ***consistently display*** (Text A) as they ply their trades: ***Leadership Maturity***, ***Strategic Awareness***, ***Executive Presence*** and ***Execution Orientation*** (Text A). Good project managers need to maintain a balance of attitudes. Tom Peters, in his essay "Pursuing the Perfect Project Manager", calls the ***conflicting attitudes*** (Text B) paradoxes or dilemmas. The conflicting but necessary forces include ego/no-ego, autocrat/delegator, tolerating ambiguity/pursuing perfection, acknowledging complexity/championing simplicity. Looking at the traits can help you step back, reconsider what you're doing and why, and make ***smarter decisions*** (Text B).

6. Replace the underlined words in the following sentences with the words provided in the box to form collocations you have learned from this unit. Each word can be used only once.

| vigorously | consecutive | adversarial | catastrophic |
| paramount | mediocre | paradox | reminiscence |

(1) While eye contact may be a sign of connection or trust in friendly situations, it's more likely to be associated with dominance or intimidation in <u>confrontational</u> situations.

(2) For Edison as an inventor, novelty was always <u>supreme</u>: the overriding goal of the business of innovation was simply to generate funding for new inventions.

(3) The <u>commonplace</u> design of many contemporary buildings can be traced to both clients and architects.

(4) The Party campaigned <u>spiritedly</u> in the north of the country.

(5) Call it the "learning <u>contradiction</u>": the more you struggle and even fail while you're trying to learn new information, the better you're likely to recall and apply that information later.

(6) You know that studying six <u>continuous</u> hours is not equivalent to studying one hour a day for six days.

(7) What you have left with me is a beautiful <u>memory</u> and what you have impressed in my mind is purity and friendship.

(8) The report describes the <u>calamitous</u> disintegration of the aircraft after the explosion.

Translation

7. Translate the following passage into English.

在管理方式上,儒家主张"以和为贵",通过"礼"与"德"两种手段,实现人性化管理。儒家"父子有亲,君臣有义,夫妇有别,长幼有序,朋友有信"的"五伦"道德规范和"仁、义、礼、智、信"的"五常"之道数千年来一直被奉为处理人际关系的基本准则和行为规范。

Unit project

Write a report on how to develop leadership ability for college students.

> This unit is about project management skills. Both texts emphasize the importance of leadership ability in project management. Based on this unit theme, you are asked to write a report on how to develop leadership ability for college students. To complete the project, you can follow the steps below.

(1) Work in groups of 4–5 and design a questionnaire on how to develop leadership ability for college students. The following questions can be included in your questionnaire. Add more questions if you can.

- Do you think leadership is important for college students?
- Is there a criterion for a good leader? What is it?
- What can college students do to improve their leadership ability?

- What is the biggest obstacle to developing leadership?

...

(2) Each of your group members interviews 8–10 students on campus. Take down their answers to your questions.

(3) Compare your answers with other group members'. Draw a conclusion from your questionnaire.

(4) Analyze your information and prepare a report presentation in class.

Unit 5

Reach out to Customers

Learning objectives

In this unit you will:
- learn how to make customer feedback actionable;
- learn about the importance of customer-centricity for IT organizations;
- learn how to write an example essay;
- learn about the conversion of one part of speech to another.

> We see our customers as invited guests to a party, and we are the hosts. It's our job every day to make every important aspect of the customer experience a little bit better.
>
> —*Jeff Bezos*
>
> When the customer comes first, the customer will last.
>
> —*Robert Half*

Preview

Customer feedback is paramount when determining a customer's needs and tastes, particularly when a business launches new products. Companies conduct focus groups, in-person research or customer phone surveys to determine the product features, flavors or styles that consumers want. Customer feedback helps companies determine what's important to their customers.

Without customer feedback, a company could not possibly meet the product needs of the consumers. Consequently, its products would likely fail in the marketplace. Companies that become truly customer-oriented create a sustainable competitive advantage, generate substantial shareholder value, and plant the seeds for future growth.

So what is the vital role customers perform in a company's further development? What strategies can a company employ to win a customer's business back in terms of customer feedback? How do the companies respond promptly and respectfully to consumer complaints and queries?

Section A

  Pre-reading activities

1. **Answer the following questions briefly based on the given pictures.**

   (1) How were surveys conducted traditionally? What are the limitations compared with the innovative ways in modern society with advanced Internet technology?

   (2) Can you offer some specific strategies that encourage customer feedback and provide you with insight into customers' attitudes toward your products and services?

   (3) Do you believe companies that launch products without researching and taking account of customer needs run a high risk of failure? Illustrate your points with specific reasons.

2. **Work in pairs and discuss the following questions.**

   (1) How do you ask the right questions in order to get actionable feedback from your customers? Please present one scenario simulation by asking some effective questions to get maximum exposure with your customers.

(2) What are the best ways you can use to make sure your customer feedback surveys actually get answered and that the feedback from your customers isn't just useless data?

Text A

Make Customer Feedback Actionable

1. We've probably all noticed that human beings are much more likely to give feedback if it's something negative. This is a far cry from that piece of **maternal** advice many of us grew up with: "If you don't have anything nice to say, don't say anything."

2. Negative feedback—or **constructive** criticism—is vitally important for businesses to take stock of what's going well and what isn't.

3. But the thing to remember is that simply receiving feedback isn't enough; the central question becomes how to make that feedback valuable and **actionable**.

4. For some industries, customer feedback doesn't seem to do much good. In the world of higher education, for example, it takes professional journalism and the threat of legal action to drag some of these problems into the light. And things aren't much better in the healthcare industry either, where it took **wide-ranging lawmaking** measures to bring change to an industry that's been borderline **hostile** toward its customers for decades.

5. But thanks to the Internet, we live in a more connected world than ever before; bad news travels pretty quickly, which also means companies are being more and more **obliged** to improve the quality of their service. Because of this, collecting and acting on feedback has never been more **acutely** important.

6. Above all, remember that feedback must result in a change that the customer can see and measure. To that end, it is important to know what you can do to make the feedback process easy and, more importantly, **contributive**.

7. When WebpageFX was in its infancy, we requested customer feedback **manually**. But as we've grown and taken on new work, we've learned to **streamline** the process while

keeping it as personable as possible. The "personable" part starts with making sure the request comes from a name within the company they already recognize. Some clients reply every six months like clockwork, while some might go five years between responses. Based on this alone, I'd guess that the **incentive** we offer, in the form of an Amazon gift card, is not the **draw** here. The real motivation lies in **fostering** productive conversation and maintaining a mutually beneficial working relationship.

8. The best feedback comes to us from clients we already have great relationships with. This means you need to have the element of trust already in place. And that brings me to probably the most important thing this process has taught us: surveys don't manufacture good will out of thin air. The foundation of mutual respect has to be there already. **Soliciting** feedback is a fantastic way to find out what you're doing well and what needs improvement, but it's not a **surrogate** for real relationships.

9. While we're really happy with our approach to customer feedback, and with our response rate, I'm not here to tell you that there's only one way to pick your customers' brains.

10. Our friends at Bortek Industries take a different, but no less effective, approach. **Whereas** we solicit customer **appraisals** on a **recurring** basis, Bortek has placed a feedback tool right on their homepage, inviting customers to speak their minds whenever the mood strikes them. I think this is a great **compromise** between our approach and what you've probably seen far too often on the Web, where a survey invitation pops up moments after you visit a site. Getting quality feedback means not **pestering** the people you serve.

11. I searched around for some really bad examples of customer feedback **machinery**, but the truth is there are far too many to name here. I'm sure most of us have dealt with **lackluster** customer service in our time, from contact info being either **deliberately** or **unintentionally** buried in their site, to a lack of communication **channels** altogether. In other words, if the only way your customers can provide feedback is by mailing in a survey or **maneuvering** a phone menu, you've **overlooked** some much simpler solutions.

12. One of our favorite tools at WebpageFX is the Net Promoter Score, which allows us to measure how likely our customers are to recommend us. In our experience, there is no better way to measure the impact you're having on the people you serve.

13. Client satisfaction might sound like a difficult thing to **quantify**, but there are ways to do so. In our brief client survey, we ask the usual questions: things like whether our clients feel we understand their business and their needs, and whether we communicate in a timely fashion. Client responses fall on a six-point scale, and thanks to the magic of spreadsheets and mathematics, we turn this into a Net Promoter Score for each of our clients.

14. We do this to let our clients' voices be heard, but also to remind ourselves that word of mouth is everything in a business like ours.

15. What is **collaborative** feedback? For us, it means making sure customer feedback is seen by more than one person. This lets us share responsibility for our **deficiencies**. What this does is help us reveal **lapses** in communication or specific areas or departments that could use improvement.

16. And collaboration works the other way around, too; sometimes we'll ask for feedback from multiple people in the organizations we work for, which helps to fine tune our response.

17. Finally, don't forget to follow up with your customers about their feedback. Nobody wants to feel as though they're not being taken seriously. If you can accommodate their requests or address their complaints, let them know you are to **swing** to action and what steps you're taking. And if you can't, politely explain that, too.

18. At the end of the day, feedback is a communication tool. And as it is in any other type of relationship, communication is vitally important in business. Just remember that giving and receiving feedback can be both fun and **instructive**—you just have to know how to ask for it, and what to do with it once it arrives.

(980 words)

New words

maternal	/mə'tɜːnəl/	a.	1. having feelings that are typical of a caring mother towards a child 母亲的；母亲般慈爱的 2. [attrib.] related through the mother's side of the family 母系的；母亲方面的
constructive	/kən'strʌktɪv/	a.	having a useful purpose; helpful 建设性的；有助益的
actionable	/'ækʃənəbəl/	a.	1. giving somebody a valid reason to bring a case to court 可予起诉的；可提起诉讼 2. that can be done or acted on 可行的；可执行的
wide-ranging	/ˌwaɪd 'reɪndʒɪŋ/	a.	including a wide variety of subjects, things, or people 范围或内容广泛的
lawmaking	/'lɔːˌmeɪkɪŋ/	n.	[U] the act of making or enacting laws 立法
hostile	/'hɒstaɪl/	a.	~ (to/towards sb./sth.) 1.very unfriendly or aggressive and ready to argue or fight 敌意的；敌对的 2. strongly rejecting sth. 坚决否定；强烈反对
oblige	/ə'blaɪdʒ/	vt.	[usu. passive] (be obliged to do sth.) to compel or require (sb.) by law, agreement or moral pressure to do sth.（按法律、协议或道义）强迫或要求（某人）做某事物
acutely	/ə'kjuːtli/	ad.	feeling or noticing sth. very strongly 尖锐地；剧烈地；敏锐地

contributive	/kən'trɪbjʊtɪv/	*a.*	helpful 有贡献的；有助的
manually	/'mænjʊəlɪ/	*ad.*	by hand rather than automatically or using electricity, etc. 手动地；手控地；用手操作地
streamline	/'striːmˌlaɪn/	*vt.*	to make a system, an organization, etc. work better, especially in a way that saves money 使（系统、机构等）效率更高；（尤指）使增产节约
incentive	/ɪn'sentɪv/	*n.*	[C, U] *~ (to do sth.)* something that encourages you to do sth. 激励；刺激；鼓励
draw	/drɔː/	*n.*	(usu. sing.) person or thing that attracts people 有吸引力的人或事物
foster	/'fɒstə/	*vt.*	1. to help the growth or development of (sth.); to encourage or promote 培养；培育（某物）；鼓励；促进 2. to take care of and bring up (a child that is not legally one's own) 照顾；抚养（法律上不属于自己的孩子）；领养；收养
solicit	/sə'lɪsɪt/	*v.*	*~ (sb.) (for sth.); ~ (sth.) (from sb.)* (fml.) to ask sb. for sth., such as support, money or information; to try to get sth. or persuade sb. to do sth. 索求；请求……给予（援助、钱或信息）；征求；筹集
surrogate	/'sʌrəgɪt/	*n.*	[C] *~ (for sb./sth.)* (fml.) person or thing that acts or is used instead of another; substitute 替代的人或事物；替代者；代理人；替代物
whereas	/weər'æz/	*conj.*	1. (esp. law) taking into consideration the fact that 尤用于法律考虑到……；鉴于 2. (fml.) but in contrast; while 然而
appraisal	/ə'preɪzəl/	*n.*	[C, U] 1. a judgment of the value, performance or nature of sb./sth. 评价；估价；估计 2. a meeting in which employees discuss with their manager how well they have been doing their job; the system of holding such meetings（上司对雇员的）工作鉴定会；工作表现评估
recur	/rɪ'kɜː/	*vi.*	1. to happen again or a number of times 再发生；反复出现 2. *~ to sb./sth.* (fml.) (of ideas, events, etc.) to come back into the mind（指想法、事情等）在头脑中重现
compromise	/'kɒmprəˌmaɪz/	*n.*	[C] an agreement made between two people or groups in which each side gives up some of the things they want so that both sides are happy at the end 妥协；折中；互让；和解

英语读写教程 2（第二版）
Intermediate IT English Reading and Writing 2 (2nd Edition)

pester	/'pestə/	vt.	~ sb. (for sth.); ~ sb. (with sth.) to annoy or disturb sb., esp. with frequent requests 打扰或纠缠某人（尤指不断提出要求）
machinery	/məˈʃiːnəri/	n.	[U] a system or set of processes for doing sth. 机器；结构；机制
lackluster	/ˈlækˌlʌstə/	a.	not interesting or exciting; dull 无趣味的；单调的；枯燥乏味的
deliberately	/dɪˈlɪbərətli/	ad.	done in a way that is intended or planned 慎重地；故意地；蓄意地
unintentionally	/ˌʌnɪnˈtenʃənəli/	ad.	not done deliberately 非故意地；非存心地
channel	/ˈtʃænəl/	n.	[C] a system or method that you use to send or obtain information, goods, permission, etc.（传递或获得信息、商品、许可等的）途径；手段；渠道
maneuver	/məˈnuːvə/	v.	to use cleverly planned and often dishonest methods to get the result that you want 用策略；操纵
overlook	/ˌəʊvəˈlʊk/	vt.	1. to take no (official) notice of sb./sth.; to ignore 忽视；忽略某人/某事物；不理会 2. to fail to see or notice sth.; to miss 未看到；未注意到某事物
quantify	/ˈkwɒntɪˌfaɪ/	v.	to describe or express sth. as an amount or a number 量化；以数量表述
collaborative	/kəˈlæbərətɪv/	a.	[only before noun] (fml.) involving, or done by, several people or groups of people working together 合作的；协作的；协力的
deficiency	/dɪˈfɪʃ(ə)nsi/	n.	1. [U] state of lacking sth. essential 缺乏；缺少 2. [C] lack of a necessary quality; fault 缺点；缺陷；毛病
lapse	/læps/	n.	[C] 1. a small mistake, especially one that is caused by forgetting sth. or by being careless（尤指）记错；过失；疏忽 2. ~ (from sth.) (into sth.) fall or departure from correct or usual standards; backsliding 堕落；失足
swing	/swɪŋ/	v.	1. (pt. pp. swung) (cause sb./sth. to) move to and from while hanging or supported（吊着或支着）摆动；摇摆 2. (~ into action) to act swiftly 迅速采取行动
instructive	/ɪnˈstrʌktɪv/	a.	(approv.) giving much useful information 提供丰富知识的；有益的

Unit 5 Reach out to Customers

New expressions

be a far cry from sth.	be very different from sth. 与某物大不相同；相差太远
take stock of sth.	to think carefully about the things that have happened in a situation in order to decide what to do next（对某事物）做出估计、估量
be hostile to/toward sb.	being very unfriendly or aggressive and ready to argue or fight 对某人充满敌意的
be obliged to do sth.	to compel or require (sb.) by law, agreement or moral pressure to do sth.（按法律、协议或道义）强迫或要求（某人）做某事
act on/upon sth.	to do sth. because of another person's advice or order, or because you have received information or had an idea 依据……行事
to that end	the aim or purpose you hope to achieve 为了到达那个目标
in one's infancy	the time when sth. is just starting to be developed 初期；初创期
like clockwork	happening at the same time and in the same way every time 非常准时的；极有规律的
in place	1. in the correct position; ready for sth. 在正确位置；准备妥当 2. working or ready to work 在工作；准备就绪
out of thin air	out of nowhere, as if by magic 凭空；无中生有
pick one's brains	to ask sb. who knows a lot about sth. for information and advice about it 向某人讨教（请教）
pop up	to appear, sometimes unexpectedly 突然出现；冒出来
in a ... fashion	in a particular way 以……方式
word of mouth	information you get by sb. telling you 口口相传；口头介绍
fine tune	to make small changes 微调；调整
follow up with	to find out more information about sth. and take action if necessary 跟进；追查（更多的信息）
at the end of the day	(spoken) used to give your final opinion after considering all the possibilities（口头语）最终；到头来；不管怎么说

Notes

1. WebpageFX（网络营销公司）: a full-service Internet marketing and SEO company offering innovative web marketing solutions to mid to large size companies across the globe.

2. Bortek Industries（美国能源清洁设备供应公司）: a locally owned, family company for over 50 years with a proud tradition of putting customer's needs first. Its purpose is to consistently provide the best possible solutions and support to solve customers' facilities maintenance, cleaning, and sanitation problems.

3. Net Promoter Score（净推荐值，亦可称口碑）: a management tool that can be used to gauge the loyalty of a firm's customer relationships.

Reading comprehension

Understanding the text

1. **Answer the following questions.**

    (1) What is the function of listening to the customer's feedback?

    (2) According to Paragraph 5, what does it indicate that collecting and acting on feedback has never been more important?

    (3) What does the saying that bad news travels pretty quickly indicate?

    (4) What is the real incentive for requesting customer feedback?

    (5) How did Bortek Industries advocate a different but effective approach in terms of customer feedback?

    (6) What function does collaborative feedback perform?

    (7) What is the purpose of following up with your customers about their feedback?

    (8) What strategies would you take to make customer feedback actionable?

Critical thinking

2. **Work in pairs and discuss the following questions.**

    (1) Why do companies have to gather customer feedback? Please offer some reasons to illustrate your point.

(2) Can you figure out the most typical means to find out the important needs of your customers?

(3) If you receive some negative responses in a customer survey, how would you deal with them effectively?

(4) How do you comment on the popular mantra that the customer is always right? What are the advantages and disadvantages of a customer-focused company?

Word building

The prefix *sub-* combines with nouns/verbs/adverbs/adjectives to form new words. Words formed in this way refer to "being below, less than; under or a smaller part of something".

Examples

Words learned	Add *sub-*	New words formed
marine	→	submarine
structure	→	substructure
urbanite	→	suburbanite
division	→	subdivision
title	→	subtitle

The suffix *-some* combines with verbs to form adjectives. Adjectives formed in this way refer to "behaving in a particular way, or having a particular quality".

Examples

Words learned	Add *-some*	New words formed
loath	→	loathsome
trouble	→	troublesome
meddle	→	meddlesome
fear	→	fearsome
adventure	→	adventuresome

3. Add *sub-* or *-some* to the following words to form new words.

Words learned	New words formed
sub-	
consciously	
standard	
tropical	
ordinate	
merge	
-some	
whole	
cumber	
toil	
quarrel	
awe	

4. Fill in the blanks with the newly-formed words in Activity 3. Change the form where necessary. Each word can be used only once.

(1) The submarine had had time to _____ before the warship could approach.

(2) Although the machine looks _____, it is actually easy to use.

(3) As the _____ country of old China, Siam offered most often and the most articles of tribute to the Ming Dynasty among all dependent countries.

(4) She has written good essays before, but this one is _____.

(5) The _____ climate of the Sunshine State means nighttime temperatures in the orange groves stay relatively high.

(6) _____, erratic and libidinous, Pushkin had affairs, fought duels and challenged authority wherever he went.

(7) I suppose that, _____, I was reacting against my unhappy childhood.

(8) The cold has made already _____ living conditions even worse.

(9) I know learning like this is _____ and ineffective, but I can't spare other time for study.

(10) In order to maintain physical well-being, a person should eat _____ food and get sufficient exercise.

Banked cloze

5. Fill in the blanks by selecting suitable words from the word bank. You may not use any of the words more than once.

A. totally	B. launching	C. qualify	D. scarce	E. actionable
F. strategically	G. identifying	H. participants	I. accountable	J. negative
K. quantify	L. solicit	M. prioritize	N. motivations	O. aspire

All entrepreneurs know that customer insights are invaluable to product design and continued improvement. However, acquiring and organizing useful feedback is easier said than done and developing a strategy can be a daunting task. Here are some tips to gain user feedback and uncover (1) _____ insights.

As simple as it sounds, the best way to acquire enough user feedback is simply to ask for it. At Travefy we (2) _____ comments in a variety of ways including automated "personal" emails to all trip organizers during the planning process as well as a Net Promoter Score (NPS) survey to all trip (3) _____.

Another way to improve both the quantity and overall quality of user comments is to reduce barriers by soliciting feedback at the moment. From a user's perspective, they feel heard, which can turn a(n) (4) _____ situation into a positive one.

No matter what your product is or company does, the bulk of user comments tend to be feature requests or product enhancements, not just bugs. As such, understanding general (5) _____ or "why" someone wants this feature is essential in (6) _____ the actual problem you need to solve.

Although most feedback tends to be qualitative in nature via emails or comments, a great way to better analyze these user thoughts is to somehow (7) _____ it. A simple way to do so is to simply tag all feedback by categories or request types.

When analyzing user feedback segmenting customers can be vital. There are many helpful ways to segment customers in order to (8) _____ suggestions, many of which depend on your goals and business.

No matter what business you run or how successful you are, time and resources are (9) _____ and a valuable commodity.

As a result, think (10) _____ about all feedback and when creating an action plan ask yourself, what enhancements will have the highest impact or reach the most users?

Structured analysis and writing

Structure analysis

Write an example essay

The example essay is an extended illustration of a point. In an example essay we may assemble a collection of facts or statistics to clarify a concept, to make an abstract idea concrete and familiar, and to show or support our points. With appropriate examples, ideas become specific, personal, and lively. In addition to clarifying, personalizing, and reinforcing the main ideas of an essay, examples often appeal powerfully to the readers' emotions. There are some tips on writing an example essay.

Firstly, cite enough examples to support your idea. The number of examples depends on the topic. Usually, three or four extended examples should suffice.

Secondly, state your examples accurately and effectively. The examples should represent the general idea you want to illustrate or support. Keep your examples as specific as possible.

Finally, put your examples in the best order. Examples and illustrations can be organized according to time, familiarity, and importance, usually in a least-to-most order, starting with the least interesting/significant and ending with the most interesting/significant.

Now let's look at the following paragraphs taken from Text A.

Examples	*For some industries, customer feedback doesn't seem to do much good. In the world of higher education, for example, it takes professional journalism and the threat of legal action to drag some of these problems into the light. And things aren't much better in the healthcare industry either, where it took wide-ranging lawmaking measures to bring change to an industry that's been borderline hostile toward its customers for decades.* (Para. 4)
Examples	*When WebpageFX was in its infancy, we requested customer feedback manually. But as we've grown and taken on new work, we've learned to streamline the process while keeping it as personable as possible.* (Para. 7) *Our friends at Bortek Industries take a different, but no less effective, approach. Whereas we solicit customer appraisals on a recurring basis, Bortek has placed a feedback tool right on their homepage, inviting customers to speak their minds whenever the mood strikes them.* (Para. 10)

As can be seen from the above paragraphs, examples are accurately and effectively used to support the author's point of view.

Structured writing

Read the sample essay and see how an example essay is structured.

> **Topic**
>
> Informal classroom learning sources
>
> **Introduction**
>
> Class learning is not sufficient for students who wish to become knowledgeable and open-minded.
>
> **Body**
>
> Write various kinds of non-classroom learning sources by making a list of examples.
>
> **Conclusion**
>
> Conclude the essay with a summary to emphasize the value of informal classroom learning sources.

Sample essay

Informal Classroom Learning Sources

For the students who wish to become knowledgeable and able men, class learning is not sufficient and the time is limited. Students with alert and curious minds may learn a great deal from sources other than their formal classes.

Informal learning sources can be of various kinds. First, students may learn much that will be valuable to them from working at a part-time job. For instance, they may learn how to manage their extra money. More important, they will find out what the society demands of their members. Second, they may discover many useful facts through reading non-classroom material. Both fiction and nonfiction books provide them with a wealth of useful information. Newspapers furnish them with information about current events that all educated people should be aware of. And many magazines provide articles that can be of practical use and interest to them. Third, even social clubs can have educational values. Certainly, being a successful member can teach a student skills in human relationships. Finally, students can spend a lot of time listening to the radio and watching the television because they can learn a great deal from broadcasts. From news programs, they can learn quickly what is happening at home and abroad. From talk shows, they can discover how others feel about issues. From entertainment shows such as soap operas and mysteries, they can glean information about the value systems of others.

To sum up, students should devote an adequate amount of time to their formal studies, but they should also take advantage of the non-traditional learning sources available to them in order to become learned men of vast scholarship.

6. Write an essay of no less than 200 words on one of the following topics. One topic has an outline that you can follow.

Topic

The spirit of the Olympic Games

Introduction

Many athletes in the Olympic Games have vividly interpreted the very spirit of the Games.

Body

Use a brief example or an extended example to illustrate the spirit.

Conclusion

Conclude the essay with a summary to emphasize the value of the spirit implied from the examples.

More topics:

- The great value of failure
- Worries about cell phone

 Translation

7. Translate the following paragraph into Chinese.

The attitudes and behavior of employees truly differentiate customer-driven companies. Leading companies create customer-driven cultures by clarifying and managing the attitudes and behaviors they want from their staff. One pragmatic approach to culture change currently in use by leading companies involves a simple two-step process. First, these companies list a few key staff attitudes and behaviors necessary to implement a customer-driven

strategy successfully. Embedded in these behaviors are the company-specific values by which the employees should deal with customers. Second, the company aligns and manages compensation and incentives, hiring/firing/promotion decisions, performance evaluation, and training to support and conspicuously reward the desired attitudes and behavior. Less than 20% of the companies we surveyed have their employee rewards aligned with their customer management objectives. In contrast, a full one-half of every Pizzahut store manager's quarterly bonus is tied to customer satisfaction levels, which are measured constantly by telephone surveys.

8. Translate the following paragraph into English.

中国是一个历史文化悠久的国度，也是一个礼仪之邦。每当客人来访，主人都会泡茶给客人喝。据说早在五六千年前，中国就有了茶树（tea-shrub），而且有关茶树的文明可以追溯到两千年前。中国的茶和丝绸、瓷器一样，在1000年前就为世界所知，而且一直是中国重要的出口产品。目前世界上40多个国家种植茶，其中亚洲国家的产量占世界总产量的90%。茶是世界三大饮料之一，茶的发现和利用是中国人对人类文化史的一大贡献。中国悠久的饮茶历史形成了颇有特色的中华茶文化。茶成为人们生活中不可缺少的一部分，它不仅是一种饮品，而且是文化的传播者，代表了中国人独特的哲学思想、美学观点和生活方式，体现了中国人的精神世界和处世之道。

Section B

 Reading skills: *Understanding conversion of one part of speech to another*

When readers enjoy reading English materials, particularly literary works, they usually come across many nouns or adjectives which can be vividly used as verbs without changing their inherent meanings. This phenomenon refers to the conversion of one part of speech to another. The examples of such words are countless in English, such as *coat, cover, house, mirror, author, father, voice, tip, bill, shoulder, stage, fault, survey, rank, weather, embrace, fuel, corner, doctor, picture, detail,* etc. The words mentioned above can be regarded both as nouns and verbs.

> **Example in Text A**:
>
> 1) *But as we've grown and taken on new work, we've learned to **streamline** the process while keeping it as personable as possible.* (Para. 7)
>
> 2) *Based on this alone, I'd guess that the incentive we offer, in the form of an Amazon gift card, is not the **draw** here.* (Para. 7)

The part of speech of the simple word "*streamline*" in English is usually seen as a noun, referring to the path of a particle in a fluid relative to a solid body past which the fluid is moving in smooth flow without turbulence. However, "*streamline*" in the first example is used as a verb which means to make a system, an organization, etc. work better, especially in a way that saves money (使系统、机构等效率更高；使增产节约).

The part of speech of the word "*draw*" in English is usually seen as a verb, meaning to make pictures, or a picture of sth. with a pencil, pen or chalk. But the word "*draw*" in the second example is used as a noun, referring to a person, a thing or an event that attracts a lot of people (有吸引力的人或事物).

Actually, the conversion of speech in English can be traced back to William Shakespeare, a prominent master of language in Britain, who innovatively wrote many sentences in his plays. For example, "*You can happy your friend, malice or foot your enemy, or fall an ax on his neck.*" Or "*He words me, girls, he words me.*" Shakespeare subtly used these simple words, enabling the readers to powerfully and vividly feel the deep emotions.

From the words with multiple parts of speech, readers are well aware of the rich and lively meanings in some specific context while doing extensive readings. What counts for them is to put the words into practice while they focus on writing, thus structuring vivid, dramatic and interesting sentences. In this way, they can appreciate the beauty and richness of the language of English.

Read the following sentences from Text B and try to interpret the meaning of the underlined words with a synonym. Then structure a sentence based on the usage of the same word.

(1) To understand the various customer constituencies, Gracy embraced a number of ethnography-based practices, including the day-in-the-life tow truck driver excursion.

_____

(2) The ride-along experience empowered the Agero team to deliver platform innovations keyed to solving the drivers' principal pain points—specifically, streamlining operations, providing better customer service, and achieving the work/life balance that was proving so elusive.

_____

Text B

What Customer-Centric IT Really Looks Like?

1. When Bernie Gracy took the tech leader **reins** at Agero, his first order of business was to take stock of the company's extensive technology **portfolio** and spend the day riding around in a tow truck.

2. Agero, a digital platform for connected vehicles and roadside assistance, claims management services, serves automotive OEMs, insurance companies, and an extensive network of roadside assistance companies. To understand the various customer **constituencies**, Gracy embraced a number of **ethnography**-based practices, including the day-in-the-life tow truck driver **excursion**. The ride-along experience **empowered** the Agero team to deliver platform innovations keyed to solving the drivers' **principal** pain points—specifically, streamlining operations, providing better customer service, and achieving the work/life balance that was proving so **elusive**.

3. "Living in your customers' shoes is the best way to inform the set of business strategies, offerings, and services a company can deliver," Gracy explains. "It's all about taking an outside-in role and living the experience of our service through the customers' **lens**."

4. CIOs have long had customer requirements in their sights, but leaders like Gracy are taking a broader view of customer **centricity**, promoting techniques and making cultural and organizational changes that create a direct line of engagement between IT and the end customer. Traditionally, IT organizations have primarily concentrated on delivering enterprise solutions and support strategies that meet the needs of internal employees. Customer-centric IT organizations are expanding that charter to account for the needs of external partners and consumers as they build out their digital product and service portfolios.

5. "Before it was about servicing the internal customers who were serving our external customers," Gracy says. "As we **digitize**, the internal gatekeeper role goes away and you engage straight through with customers. You have to link internal business processes to experiences those personas want to have."

6. IT's push towards customer centricity is important on a number of fronts. For one thing, it helps IT organizations build digital solutions that improve customers' lifetime value while driving new strategic **initiatives** that create competitive advantages. In addition, companies that prioritize customer needs and experiences tend to perform better: For example, Forrester found that customer experience leaders enjoyed a 17 percent compound average **revenue** growth rate compared to only 3 percent for companies slower to embrace customer-centric practices.

7. "Any line of business leader must understand what consumers want so they can manage the evolution of the products ahead of consumer expectations," Angela Yochem, the executive vice president and chief digital and technology officer for Novant Health, says. "It's the same sort of thing now with a technology focus. CIOs and tech leaders are the digital product and service leads now marketing digital services to end consumers. They must understand them."

Walking in the customer's shoes

8. While **courting** the customer is the ultimate end game, IT organizations need to cut their teeth on customer-centricity by **honing** best practices that start at home. Being recognized for **robust** service by internal customers is the **consummate** stepping stone for IT organizations making the leap to **cater** to outside customers. "You need to do the basic blocking and tackling and build **credibility** and trust with internal clients, then you can start talking about innovation and how to focus on external customers," says David Behen, vice president and CIO at La-Z-Boy.

9. IT people have a tendency to **complicate** and over engineer things, but when they start putting themselves in the shoes of a customer, they start to act and see things differently. Historically, when they evaluate a solution, they focus on the technical aspects like networks, databases, and code and don't pay as much attention to what it actually feels like when users are using it. But once walking in the customer's shoes, they will be much more in tune with the user interface and UX (User Experience) simplicity.

People, process, skills

10. In addition to tackling work from a new perspective, CIOs are also adding new positions such as product managers and business relationship managers to their **rosters** to create a closer connection to the customer. These roles are designed to engage with end customers and leverage their input to shape new workflows as opposed to viewing systems requirements through a purely technical lens. IT staffers that can translate business needs into technology requirements and explain how technology deployments solve critical pain points is another discipline customer-centric CIOs are cultivating.

11. Executive-level communication is also essential to promote, explain, and prepare the IT ranks for a turn towards customer centricity. Agero's Gracy is a big **proponent** of taking a **multidisciplinary** approach to get the message across, which in his case, includes internal blogging, town hall meetings, and inviting other members of the leadership team to speak on the benefits as well as the changing landscape.

12. At Vail Resorts, many of those initiatives have helped **infuse** a higher level of customer centricity in IT, and the results have been a widely-**heralded** series of innovations. Among the more popular: RFID (Radio frequency identification devices)-enabled lift tickets and passes to shorten wait times; mobile apps for tracking everything from vertical feet skied to actual lift line waits; and Emma, an AI-based digital mountain assistant that provides information on everything from current grooming and ski conditions to dining and **rental** recommendations.

13. While a formal methodology wasn't put in place, the changes have served to make Vail's IT team far more **responsive** to customer needs, including a desire to ensure their

digital innovations hit the mark throughout the entire lifecycle, from **ideation** through implementation in the field, says Tim April, the company's senior vice president and CIO. "We have a responsibility to think through IT operations as a guest experience," April says. "That changes the experience of being a technologist—you're not done when the technology is done and deployed, you have responsibility for the whole solution and that is a huge win."

(959 words)

New words

rein	/reɪn/	n.	[pl.] the reins, the state of being in control or the leader of sth. 控制；主宰；掌管
portfolio	/pɔːtˈfəʊlɪəʊ/	n.	a set of shares owned by a particular person or organization（个人或机构的）投资组合；有价证券组合
constituency	/kənˈstɪtjʊənsɪ/	n.	(esp. BrE) (pl. -ies) 1. [C] a district that elects its own representative to parliament（选举议会议员的）选区 2. [C + sing. / pl. v.] the people who live in and vote in a particular district 选区的选民 3. [C + sing./pl. v.] a particular group of people in society who are likely to support a person, an idea or a product（统称）支持者
ethnography	/eθˈnɒɡrəfɪ/	n.	[U] the scientific description of different races and cultures 人种志；人种论
excursion	/ɪkˈskɜːʃən/	n.	a short journey made for pleasure, especially one that has been organized for a group of people（尤指集体）远足；短途旅行
empower	/ɪmˈpaʊə/	vt.	to give sb. the power or authority to do sth. 授权；给（某人）……的权力
principal	/ˈprɪnsɪpəl/	a.	most important; main 最重要的；主要的
elusive	/ɪˈluːsɪv/	a.	difficult to find, define, or achieve 难找的；难以解释的；难以达到的
lens	/lenz/	n.	a curved piece of glass or plastic that makes things look larger, smaller or clearer when you look through it 透镜；镜片
centricity	/ˈsentrɪsɪtɪ/	n.	focus, hub 中心；中心性
digitize	/ˈdɪdʒɪˌtaɪz/	vt.	to change data into a digital form that can be easily read and processed by a computer（使数据）数字化
initiative	/ɪˈnɪʃɪətɪv, -ʃətɪv/	n.	[C] a new plan for dealing with a particular problem or for achieving a particular purpose 倡议；新方案

			[U] the ability to decide and act on your own without waiting for sb. to tell you what to do 主动性；积极性；自发性
revenue	/ˈrevɪˌnjuː/	n.	the money that a government receives from taxes or that an organization, etc. receives from its business 财政收入；税收收入；收益
court	/kɔːt/	vt.	to try to please sb. in order to get sth. you want, especially the support of a person, an organization, etc.（为有所求，尤指寻求支持而）试图取悦；讨好；争取
		n.	[C, U] the place where legal trials take place and where crimes, etc. are judged 法院；法庭；审判庭
hone	/həʊn/	vt.	to develop and improve sth., especially a skill, over a period of time 磨练；训练（尤指技艺）
robust	/rəʊˈbʌst/	a.	(of a system or an organization) strong and not likely to fail or become weak（体制或机构）强劲的；富有活力的
consummate	/ˈkɒnsəmət/	a.	extremely skilled; perfect 技艺高超的；完美的
cater	/ˈkeɪtə/	vi.	to provide the things that a particular type or person wants, especially things that you do not approve of 满足需要；迎合
credibility	/ˌkredɪˈbɪlɪti/	n.	[U] the quality that sb./sth. has that makes people believe or trust them 可信性；可靠性
complicate	/ˈkɒmplɪˌkeɪt/	vt.	to make sth. more difficult to do, understand or deal with 使复杂化
roster	/ˈrɒstə/	n.	a list of people's names and the jobs that they have to do at a particular time 花名册；值勤名单
proponent	/prəˈpəʊnənt/	n.	~ (of sth.) (fml.) a person who supports an idea or course of action 倡导者；支持者；拥护者
multidisciplinary	/ˌmʌltɪˈdɪsɪˌplɪnəri/	a.	involving several different subjects of study（涉及）多门学科的
infuse	/ɪnˈfjuːz/	vt.	~ A into B; ~ B with A (fml.) to make sb./sth. have a particular quality 使具有；注入（某特性）
herald	/ˈherəld/	vt.	1. ~ sb./sth. (as sth.) [often passive] to say in public that sb./sth. is good or important 宣布（好或重要）的事情 2. to be a sign that sth. is going to happen 是（某事）的前兆；预示
		n.	sth. that shows that sth. else is going to happen soon 预兆

rental	/ˈrentəl/	a.	of, relating to, or available to rent 与租借有关的；可供租用的
responsive	/rɪˈspɒnsɪv/	a.	reacting quickly and in a positive way 反应敏捷的；反应积极的
ideation	/ˌaɪdiˈeɪʃn/	n.	the process of forming ideas or images 观念形成；构思过程；构思能力

New expressions

take the reins	to be in charge; to take the leadership of 掌管；支配
take stock of	to stop and think carefully about the way in which a particular situation is developing in order to decide what to do next（对某情况）加以总结；作出评估；进行反思
in sb.'s shoes	in another person's position or situation 在某人的立场上
concentrate on	to focus energy, attention, etc. on sth. or an activity 集中注意力
account for	to be the explanation or cause of sth. 是……的说明（或原因）；对……负有责任
cut one's teeth on sth.	to gain experience from sth. 初获经验；初试牛刀
cater to	to provide the things that a particular type or person wants, especially things that you do not approve of 满足需要；迎合
as opposed to	used to make a contrast between two things（表示对比）与……截然相反；相对于
translate sth. into	to change sth., or to be changed, into a different form（使）转变；变为
get sth. across	to communicate successfully 通过；使……被理解

Notes

1. Agero: working with leading vehicle manufacturers and insurance carriers to drive the next generation of roadside assistance technology forward. Headquartered in Medford, MA, with an innovation center in San Francisco and operations throughout North America, it handles over 12 million roadside events annually and is trusted by dozens of leading corporations.

2. OEMs（原始设备制造商）: generally perceived as a company that produces non-aftermarket parts and equipment that may be marketed by another manufacturer. It is a common industry term recognized and used by many professional organizations such as SAE International, ISO,

and others. However, the term is also used in several other ways, which causes ambiguity. It sometimes means the maker of a system that includes other companies' subsystems, an end-product producer, an automotive part that is manufactured by the same company that produced the original part used in the automobile's assembly, or a value-added reseller.

3. CIO (首席信息官): chief digital information officer (CDIO) or information technology (IT) director, is a job title commonly given to the most senior executive in an enterprise who works with information technology and computer systems, in order to support enterprise goals. Normally, the CIO reports directly to the chief executive officer, but may also report to the chief operating officer or chief financial officer.

4. Novant Health: a four-state integrated network of physician clinics, outpatient centers and hospitals. Its network consists of more than 1,600 physicians and 29,000 employees at more than 640 locations, including 15 medical centers and hundreds of outpatient facilities and physician clinics. The organization was formed on 1 July 1997 by the merger of Carolina Medicorp of Winston-Salem, North Carolina and Presbyterian Health Services of Charlotte, North Carolina. Headquartered in Winston-Salem, North Carolina, Novant Health serves more than 4 million patients annually.

5. La-Z-Boy (乐至宝品牌): (pronounced "lazy boy") an American furniture manufacturer based in Monroe, Michigan, United States, that makes home furniture, including upholstered recliners, sofas, stationary chairs, lift chairs and sleeper sofas. The company employs more than 11,000 people. La-Z-Boy furniture is sold in retail residential outlets in the United States and Canada and is manufactured and distributed under license in other countries including the United Kingdom, Australia, Germany, Indonesia, Italy, Japan, Mexico, New Zealand, Turkey and South Africa. La-Z-Boy holds US and international patents on more than 200 different styles and mechanisms.

6. Vail Resorts (韦尔滑雪场): located in the town of Vail, Colorado, USA, and is one of the world's famous ski resorts. Built in the 1960s, Vail Ski Resort covers more than 5,000 acres and is one of the largest ski resorts in the United States at an elevation of more than 10,000 feet. Vail Ski Resort has more than 300 pistes, including four peaks, each with a different level of difficulty for skiers.

Reading comprehension

Understanding the text

1. **Choose the best answer to each of the following questions.**

    (1) What is Agero?

    A. A company that provides insurance services.

    B. A platform for connected vehicle and roadside assistance services.

C. A company that offers automotive OEMs.

D. A network of roadside assistance companies.

(2) What did Bernie Gracy do when he became the tech leader at Agero?

A. He created a new technology portfolio.

B. He rode around in a tow truck to understand the customer experience.

C. He embraced ethnography-based practices to improve operations.

D. He streamlined the internal business processes.

(3) What is the ultimate goal of customer-centric IT?

A. To deliver enterprise solutions that meet the needs of internal employees.

B. To build digital solutions that improve customers' lifetime value.

C. To create a direct line of engagement between IT and the end customer.

D. To promote techniques and make cultural and organizational changes.

(4) Why is customer-centricity important for IT organizations?

A. It helps drive new strategic initiatives that create competitive advantages.

B. It helps build credibility and trust with internal clients.

C. It helps focus on technical aspects like networks, databases, and code.

D. It helps cultivate disciplines that are not customer-centric.

(5) What is the role of product managers and business relationship managers in customer-centric IT?

A. To engage with end customers and leverage their input to shape new workflows.

B. To translate business needs into technology requirements.

C. To explain how technology deployments solve critical pain points.

D. To view systems requirements through a purely technical lens.

(6) What is the multidisciplinary approach recommended by Bernie Gracy to promote customer-centricity?

A. Internal blogging, town hall meetings, and inviting other members of the leadership team to speak on the benefits as well as the changing landscape.

B. Adding new positions such as product managers and business relationship managers.

C. Tackling work from a new perspective and cultivating IT staffers that can translate business needs into technology requirements.

D. Focusing on technical aspects like networks, databases, and code.

(7) How has customer-centricity changed the experience of being a technologist at Vail Resorts?

   A. Technologists are no longer responsible for the whole solution.

   B. Technologists are done when the technology is done and deployed.

   C. Technologists have a responsibility to think through IT operations as a guest experience.

   D. Technologists are not responsive to customer needs anymore.

(8) According to Tim April, the senior vice president and CIO of Vail Resorts, what is the responsibility of the IT team regarding IT operations?

   A. Ensuring that technology deployments are completed on time and within budget.

   B. Focusing on technical aspects like networks, databases, and code.

   C. Thinking through IT operations as a guest experience and taking responsibility for the whole solution.

   D. Managing customer complaints and feedback related to IT services.

Critical thinking

2. Work in pairs and discuss the following questions.

   (1) What is the importance of customer-centric IT in today's digital age?

   (2) How can IT organizations become more customer-centric?

   (3) Can you name some examples of companies that have successfully implemented customer-centric IT strategies?

 Language focus

Words in use

3. Fill in the blanks with the words given below. Change the form where necessary. Each word can be used only once.

excursion	empower	streamline	digitize	initiative
court	consummate	credibility	complicate	infuse

   (1) Not all business requirements are _____ and manual processes might co-exist alongside computer technology.

(2) She finally married a gentleman who had been _____ her for years.

(3) Cheap day _____ trains became popular and seaside resorts grew rapidly.

(4) He won the race with _____ ease.

(5) Far from helping the situation, the new regulations are likely to _____ matters.

(6) If you fail in one of your goals, it is important that you have others that will take over. So instead of sinking into depression, your _____ are gaining a new meaning.

(7) WHO should be _____ and supported to take a strong lead.

(8) You are inspiration-packed, wisdom-_____, made with love and blessed with talents.

(9) The scandal has ruined his _____ as a leader.

(10) Treatments were developed. Clinical schedules were _____ and standardized.

Expressions in use

4. Fill in the blanks with the expressions given below. Change the form where necessary. Each expression can be used only once.

| take stock of | in someone's shoes | concentrate on | account for |
| cut one's teeth on | cater to | take the reins | get across |

(1) This is a great opportunity to _____ what you absolutely love, things that work for you and will work in your new space.

(2) Recent pressure at work may _____ his behavior.

(3) In the contemporary western world, rapidly changing styles _____ a desire for novelty and individualism.

(4) David himself was not expected to _____ as CEO.

(5) If she would put herself _____, maybe she could understand why he felt so hurt by her behavior.

(6) Although the writer _____ his position and ideas, the language used is not very effective and the arguments have little depth.

(7) I _____ public speaking by participating in school debates and presentations from a young age.

(8) Water companies should _____ reducing waste instead of building new reservoirs.

Sentence structure

5. Rewrite the sentences by using the conjunction "while" at the beginning of a sentence or a clause to introduce information which contrasts or partly conflicts with the main statement, meaning "although, despite the fact that...". Make changes where necessary.

Model:	Despite the fact that a formal methodology wasn't put in place, the changes have served to make Vail's IT team far more responsive to customer needs.
→	While a formal methodology wasn't put in place, the changes have served to make Vail's IT team far more responsive to customer needs.

(1) Despite the fact that Tom is very good at science, his brother is absolutely hopeless.

(2) Even though I am willing to help, I do not have much time available.

(3) She is fascinated by algebra whereas he considers it meaningless nonsense.

(4) Although there was no conclusive evidence, most people thought he was guilty.

(5) Despite the fact that girls lack confidence, boys often overestimate their abilities.

 Collocation

Negative feedback—or *constructive criticism*—is *vitally important* (Text A) for businesses to take stock of what's going well and what isn't. Thanks to the Internet, we live in a more connected world than ever before, and collecting and acting on feedback has never been more *acutely important* (Text A). Living in your customers' shoes is the best way to inform the set of *business strategies* (Text B), offerings, and services a company can deliver. Any line of business leader must understand what consumers want so they can manage the evolution of the products ahead of *consumer expectations* (Text B). Executive-level communication is also essential to promote, explain, and prepare the IT ranks for a turn towards *customer centricity* (Text B).

6. **Replace the underlined words in the following sentences with the words provided in the box to form collocations you have learned from this unit. Each word can be used only once.**

principal	consummate	centricity	responsive
proponent	excursion	credibility	revenue

(1) The modern weapon system has demonstrated more and more network <u>centrality</u> characteristics.

(2) Harvard's Herbert Benson is probably the most persuasive <u>advocate</u> of this view.

(3) Ted supplemented his <u>income</u> by doing part-time work in the evenings.

(4) The <u>main</u> effect of the demand for new houses was to inflate prices.

(5) The common ancestor is, however, too recent for the new species to be a remnant of the first human <u>jaunt</u> from Africa.

(6) In accordance with the stress-triggering hypothesis, faults are unpredictably <u>reactive</u> to subtle stresses they obtain as neighboring faults shift.

(7) There is a(n) <u>reliability</u> gap developing between employers and employees.

(8) Therefore, it is necessary to extremely establish the <u>perfect</u> and effective logistics information management system.

 Translation

7. **Translate the following passage into English.**

中国的传统文化注重"以人为本",这也体现在商业领域中的"以客户为中心"理念中。中国哲学思想中,尤其是儒家思想,强调人际关系和社会责任。对待客户,就像对待朋友一样,需要真诚、尊重和关爱。企业应该从客户的需求出发,提供优质的产品和服务,让客户感受到自己被关注和重视。只有真正将客户放在心中,才能赢得客户的信任和忠诚。因此,"以客户为中心"的理念在中国商业文化中被广泛应用。

Unit project

Write a report on customer feedback based on a survey.

> This unit is focused on the critical importance of gathering and receiving customer feedback after the company has launched a new product. But what matters is how to make the customer feedback valuable and actionable. The two texts have expounded on the specific strategies that help to create customer-oriented companies. Text A focuses on the strategies to make the feedback process easy and useful, while Text B pinpoints what a real consumer-centric IT should look like.
>
> In this unit project, you are asked to write a report on a survey of customers in different ways and provide innovative strategies to make customer feedback actionable. Divide the class into 3–4 groups and assign each one with the task of conducting a survey on the customers of specific companies. To complete the project, you can follow the steps below.

(1) Work in groups and design a survey or interview on the critical importance of obtaining actionable customer feedback. The following questions can be included in your interview. Add more questions if you can.

- Would you mind if I asked a few questions about the product you purchased?
- What is your motive for buying the product at the beginning?
- What are the advantages of the product which appeal to you most?
- Could you offer some advice for further improvements to the product?
- What should I have asked you that I didn't?

...

(2) Each of your group members is required to sketch out a plan for conducting a survey of customers via telephone, email or face-to-face talks. Design some effective questions.

(3) Analyze and interpret the effectiveness and strategies of each means. Each group needs to prepare a 5-minute report presentation with PPT in class. Present the strengths and weaknesses of each means of conducting customer surveys.

(4) Compare your survey strategies with other group members'. Make a comparison among 3–4 means. Summarize the common characteristics of handling customers effectively and draw a conclusion from your comparative study, highlighting some common principles that contribute to making customer feedback valuable and actionable.

Unit 6

Gender Discrepancy in IT

Learning objectives

In this unit you will:

- learn about the obstacles and opportunities for women in the technology industry;
- learn about Grace Hopper, a pioneering programmer in history;
- learn how to write an advantage essay;
- learn how to use conjunctive connectives and sentence patterns.

> Recognize and embrace your uniqueness. Being a black woman, being a woman in general, on a team of all men, means that you are going to have a unique voice. It's important to embrace that.
>
> —*Erin Teague*
>
> Women belong in all places where decisions are being made. It shouldn't be that women are the exception.
>
> —*Ruth Bader Ginsburg*

Preview

Nowadays more and more women have begun to be drawn to the fast-moving, highly competitive and male-dominated IT industry. Some of them have even established great reputations for being successful executives and innovative entrepreneurs. But we still have to admit that in the tech world, women face certain discrimination. Although the number of them who enter the workplace is increasing, women are a small percentage of technical talent and executive positions. People therefore always question whether it is necessary for women to be involved in the tech world. If women do want to achieve great things in this field and believe that they can be better than their male colleagues, what should they do? What challenges await them on the road? What changes should they make psychologically? What efforts should males, companies and the whole society make?

Section A

 Pre-reading activities

1. **Listen to the talk by Sheryl Sandberg, the former COO (Chief Operating Officer) of Facebook, on why women are not making it to the top of any profession anywhere in the world and answer the following questions.**

   (1) Why does Sheryl Sandberg mention all the numbers at the beginning of her speech?

   (2) What suggestions does she offer to women who do want to stay in the workforce?

   (3) What is the implication of the first message Sandberg conveys in the talk?

2. **Listen to the talk again. Work in pairs and discuss the following questions.**

   (1) Do you think it's good for a woman to start a career in the tech world?

   (2) Are there any obstacles for women to conquer?

   (3) What should a female do in order to succeed in the tech-world dominated by men?

Text A

Women in Technology: A Brightening Outlook?

　　1. Is it almost **reverse** logic in some ways to call out "women in technology" as an issue that needs **addressing**? Surely it should just be people in technology, some of whom are women. It's obvious that women encounter many **obstacles** in the tech world, but we have to admit that there are both significant obstacles and emerging opportunities for women who

want to work in the technology industry, whether in a regular post or rising to become chief information officers. This is the **verdict** of several **high-profile** figures within the technology industry. They warn that there is simply not enough representation of women within the industry, but add that there are some clear signs of **amelioration**.

2. There are still two major issues: the number of women working in the industry, and the opportunities for them to advance their career and their pay. Industry body CompTIA warns that only 24% of US IT professionals are female, a figure "on a downward trend", according to Terry Erdle, executive vice president of skills at the organization. This **alarmingly** low figure is in spite of the "huge numbers of opportunities", he says, in areas such as cyber security, business continuity, data analysis, technology refresh, network and server management, web design and customer relationship management. Over 500,000 IT job openings were available in the US in the last quarter of 2013, according to Burning Glass Technologies Labor Insights.

3. As well as "an element of **sexism**" holding back women from these jobs, Erdle says, a real problem has been a **misperception** around the excitement of working in IT and just how essential it is to organizations running at their best.

4. To run at their best, companies should **maximize** the opportunities. It is in the interests of companies and governments to help women advance in the technology industry. Many professionals agree women offer a fresh perspective on product design, ways of working, risk-taking and many other aspects of business.

5. "The teams with the best results are those **comprising** professionals with different attitudes, methods and backgrounds; those who draw multiple approaches into one unified solution," adds Pamela Maynard, president for Europe, Africa and Latin America at IT **consultancy** Avanade. "There is also a connection between diverse leadership and financial success, as those diverse workforces see their **fiscal** success increase—there is tangible value to **diversifying** the **enterprise** and it is ultimately customers who win."

6. Maynard says any obstacles can in part be tackled if people **subscribe** to the **gospel** truth that women's participation is **advantageous** and fully recognize women's strengths, insights and skills to ensure that women are taking active steps in their careers early on, and the **pipeline** remains rich with female candidates.

7. Avanade itself has transformed its **recruitment** process to ensure female candidates are interviewed for all senior roles, with at least one woman on the **panel**. It has done the same for promotion reviews.

8. Bernadette Andrietti, a vice president at technology firm Intel, says she remains "positive" for the future of women in IT, as several factors are working in women's favor from early in their lives. She adds there is "definitely a **concerted** effort being made by

governments, education bodies, businesses and non-governmental organizations" to support an increase in Science, Technology, Engineering and Maths (STEM) careers and for women to take leadership in board positions across industries. The work needs to be done at an early age, she says, adding that as girls grow older, they should have the opportunity to listen to technology businesses talk at their schools, and to work as interns at those companies.

9. In developing economies, including Africa, "Businesses and governments are working together collaboratively to nurture technology talent to **bolster** the industry," Andrietti says. Intel launched its Explore and Learn program in this region, enabling people to access free or low cost locally relevant educational resources online. It should also be noted that in India, Intel's president is a woman—originally from Calcutta, Kumud Srinivasan being one of India's most high profile female technology executives.

10. The opportunities in an IT career are **unbounded**, and need to be properly **showcased**, the experts argue. Proper STEM education offers broad career options, both within traditional IT roles and also in other **disciplines** with a technology impact, including marketing, law, sales, project management and more. "We have to do a better job of **articulating** what a career in IT really **entails**," says Erdle at CompTIA. "You can combine your interest in technology with another passion—entertainment, fashion, sports, education, government, retail and many other industries. IT truly is one of those fields in which people can change the way we live, work, learn and play."

11. It is seen that modern society is now trying to provide women with more chances and channels to equip them with the required skills and knowledge. Women who want to make their voices sound in the IT industry are also trying to make a difference in a man's world, which can be reflected in the fact that so many successful women executives and entrepreneurs emerged as a voice for female **empowerment** in the tech culture.

12. In an interview with Time Magazine Hillary Clinton said "You have to think of ways to keep focus on what it is we (as women) are trying to convince the other person—**predominately** a man—to believe. On the outside, you have to find ways to raise these issues that are truly rooted in sexism or old-fashioned **irrelevant** expectations of women's lives. Not just to score a point, but to change a mind." As women start to emerge into high paying and high status jobs it's safe to say that workforce **inclinations** are starting to change and this starts with women's behaviors as well as **feats** in the workplace.

13. Of course some discrimination and **bigotry** towards women in certain workplaces—especially when it comes to wage inequality—still exists today. However, as women continue to prove themselves as a force to be **reckoned** with, workplace dynamics will hopefully change and old **mentalities** will fade away.

(1,003 words)

New words

reverse	/rɪˈvɜːs/	a.	contrary or opposite to what is expected（与预期的事）相反的；未料到的
address	/əˈdres/	v.	1. (usu. passive) ~ sth. (to sb./sth.) to write on an envelope, etc. the name and address of the person, company, etc. that you are sending it to by mail 写（收信人）姓名地址；致函 2. to make a formal speech to a group of people 演说；演讲 3. ~ (yourself to) sth. (fml.) to think about a problem or a situation and decide how you are going to deal with it 设法解决；处理；对付
obstacle	/ˈɒbstəkəl/	n.	[C] (usu. fig.) thing in the way that either stops progress or makes it difficult 障碍；妨害物
verdict	/ˈvɜːdɪkt/	n.	[C] decision reached by a jury on a question of fact in a law case（陪审团的）裁断；裁决；裁定
high-profile	/ˌhaɪ ˈprəʊfaɪl/	a.	[only before noun] attracting a lot of public attention, usually deliberately 高调的；备受瞩目的；知名度高的
amelioration	/əˌmiːljəˈreɪʃən/	n.	[U] making a bad situation better or less harmful 改善；改进；提高
alarmingly	/əˈlɑːmɪŋlɪ/	ad.	making you feel worried or frightened 令人挂虑地；惊人地
sexism	/ˈseksɪzəm/	n.	[U] (derog.) prejudice or discrimination against people (esp. women) because of their sex 性别偏见或歧视（尤指对女性）
misperception	/ˌmɪspəˈsepʃən/	n.	[U] (fml.) wrong understanding of the true nature of sth. 不正确的想法；不正确的推测
maximize	/ˈmæksɪˌmaɪz/	vt.	to increase (sth.) as much as possible 使（某事物）增至最大限度
comprise	/kəmˈpraɪz/	vt.	to have as parts or members; to be made up of 包括；包含；构成；组成
consultancy	/kənˈsʌltənsɪ/	n.	[C] a company that gives advice on a particular subject 咨询公司
fiscal	/ˈfɪskəl/	a.	of or related to government money or public money, usu. taxes 国库的；公款的；(通常指) 岁入的；财政的
diversify	/daɪˈvɜːsɪˌfaɪ/	vt.	to give variety to (sth.); to vary 使（某事物）多样化；使不同
enterprise	/ˈentəˌpraɪz/	n.	[C] a company or business 企业

Unit 6 Gender Discrepancy in IT

subscribe	/səbˈskraɪb/	vt.	~ (sth.) (to sth.) (agree to) contribute (a sum of money) 认捐；捐助（一笔款项）
		vi.	~ to sth. (fml.) to agree with (an opinion, a theory, etc.) 同意；赞成（某观点、理论等）
gospel	/ˈgɒspəl/	n.	1. (Bible) the Gospel [sing.] (the life and teaching of Jesus as recorded in) the first four books of the New Testament 圣经新约四福音书；福音 2. [C. usu. sing.] set of principles 原则；主义；信条
advantageous	/ˌædvənˈteɪdʒəs/	a.	helpful and likely to make you successful 有利的；有益的；有助的
pipeline	/ˈpaɪpˌlaɪn/	n.	[C] a line of connecting pipes, often under the ground, used for sending gas, oil, etc. over long distances 管道；管子
recruitment	/rɪˈkruːtmənt/	n.	[U] the process of finding possible candidates for a job or function, undertaken by recruiters 征召；招募
panel	/ˈpænəl/	n.	[C] a group of people with skills or specialist knowledge who have been chosen to give advice or opinions on a particular subject（进行公开讨论或做决策的）专门小组
concerted	/kənˈsɜːtɪd/	a.	[usu. attrib.] arranged or done in cooperation 共同筹划的；合作的
bolster	/ˈbəʊlstə/	vt.	~ sb./sth. (up) to give support to sb./sth.; to strengthen or reinforce sth. 支持某人/某事物；加强某事物
unbounded	/ʌnˈbaʊndɪd/	a.	without limits; boundless 无限的；无边际的
showcase	/ˈʃəʊˌkeɪs/	vt.	to show; to display 展示
		n.	[C] an event or situation that is designed to show the good qualities of a person, organization, product, etc. 供亮相的地方；显示优点的东西
discipline	/ˈdɪsɪplɪn/	n.	1. [U] training, esp. of the mind and character, aimed at producing self-control, obedience, etc. 训练；锻炼；磨炼（尤指在智力和品德方面）2. [C] branch of knowledge; a subject of instruction 学科；教学科目
articulate	/ɑːˈtɪkjuleɪt/	v.	to speak (sth.) clearly and distinctly 清楚明白地说（某事）
		a.	(of a person) able to express one's ideas clearly in words（指人）能用词语把意思表达清楚的
entail	/ɪnˈteɪl/	vt.	to make (sth.) necessary; to involve 使（某事物）必要；牵涉
empowerment	/ɪmˈpaʊəmənt/	n.	[U] the act of conferring legality or sanction or formal warrant 授权；许可

predominately	/prɪˈdɒmɪnətlɪ/	ad.	mostly; mainly 占多数地
irrelevant	/ɪˈreləvənt/	a.	not connected (with sth.); not relevant (to sth.)（与某事物）不相关的；无关系的；不切题的
inclination	/ˌɪnklɪˈneɪʃən/	n.	[C, U] ~ *(to/for/towards sth.)*; ~ *(to do sth.)* feeling that makes sb. want to behave in a particular way; disposition 倾向；意向；意愿
feat	/fiːt/	n.	[C] successful completion of sth. needing skill, strength or courage 技艺；武艺；功绩；伟业
bigotry	/ˈbɪɡətrɪ/	n.	[U] the possession or expression of strong, unreasonable prejudices or opinions 偏执；顽固
reckon	/ˈrekən/	vt.	to be of the opinion or consider that sb./sth. is as specified 认为某人／某事物是
mentality	/menˈtælɪtɪ/	n.	[C] characteristic attitude of mind; way of thinking 心态；精神状态；思想方法

New expressions

in spite of	despite 尽管
hold back	to prevent someone or something from making progress 阻止
at one's best	at a person's best situation 在最佳状态
in the interest of	for the benefit of 为了……的利益
keep one's focus on	to concentrate on 集中注意力
be rooted in...	to have developed from something and be strongly influenced by it 根植于……
reckon with	to take sb./sth. into account; to consider sb./sth. as important 考虑到或重视某人／某物
fade away	to gradually disappear; to lose color and brightness, or to make something do this 逐渐消失；慢慢减弱

1. Burning Glass Technologies（美国的劳动市场数据分析公司）: a company based in Boston, devoted to delivering job market analytics that empower employers, workers, and educators to make data-driven decisions.

2. Avanade (一家由埃森哲和微软共同出资的合资企业): a global professional services company providing IT consulting and services focused on the Microsoft platform with business analytics, business applications, cloud, digital marketing, technology and managed services offerings.
3. Intel (英特尔公司): an American multinational corporation and technology company headquartered in Santa Clara, California that was founded by Gordon Moore and Robert Noyce.
4. Calcutta (加尔各答): the capital of the Indian state of West Bengal.
5. Hillary Clinton (希拉里·克林顿): an American politician who was the 67th United States Secretary of State from 2009 to 2013, US Senator from New York from 2001 to 2009, First Lady of the United States from 1993 to 2001, and the Democratic Party's nominee for President of the United States in the 2016 election which she lost to Republican Party nominee Donald Trump.

Reading comprehension

Understanding the text

1. **Answer the following questions.**

   (1) What does the verdict of several high-profile figures within the technology industry mean?

   (2) What are the two major issues mentioned by the IT industry body CompTIA?

   (3) What do many professionals agree on women's particular strengths in IT development?

   (4) What changes has Avanade made to tackle the obstacles which women face in IT careers?

   (5) Is Andrietti positive for the future of women in the tech world?

   (6) What efforts should the government, education bodies and companies make collaboratively to improve the situations of women in the IT industry?

   (7) What does Hillary Clinton want to tell women from her interview with the *Time* Magazine?

   (8) According to the text, is there still discrimination against women in the tech world? Will it disappear in the future?

Critical thinking

2. Work in pairs and discuss the following questions.

(1) If you were a girl, do you want to participate in the IT industry after graduation?

(2) What do you think of the prospects of women in the IT industry?

(3) What obstacles may women face in the IT industry in your opinion?

Word building

The suffix *-ion* combines with verbs to form nouns. Nouns formed in this way refer to "the state or process described by the verb, or to an instance of that process".

Examples

Words learned	Add *-ion*	New words formed
represent	→	representation
accommodate	→	accommodation
combine	→	combination
classify	→	classification
consider	→	consideration

The suffix *-ment* combines with verbs to form nouns. Nouns formed in this way refer to "the process of making or doing something, or to the result of this process".

Examples

Words learned	Add *-ment*	New words formed
improve	→	improvement
govern	→	government
base	→	basement
replace	→	replacement
develop	→	development

3. Add *-ion* or *-ment* to the following words to form new words.

Words learned	New words formed
-ion	
corrupt	

continued

Words learned	New words formed
distribute	
vary	
react	
transmit	
-ment	
entertain	
establish	
judge	
resent	
punish	

4. Fill in the blanks with the newly-formed words in Activity 3. Change the form where necessary. Each word can be used only once.

(1) He got a six-year jail sentence, a harsh _____ for a first offense.

(2) A spokesman said the changes were not in _____ to the company's recent losses.

(3) While these commercial products may have been created to provide _____, in some countries they also supply an important window to the outside world.

(4) Electronic media make the potential for information _____ possible on a scale never before achieved.

(5) To further confuse the issue, there is an enormous _____ in the amount of sleep people feel happy with.

(6) The committee will work toward the _____ of a school for the handicapped.

(7) The accident was caused by an error of _____ on the part of the pilot.

(8) The chairman said _____, as a social and historical phenomenon, has existed in both ancient and modern times and in many societies.

(9) Government officials have assured WHO that all measures are being undertaken to prevent the _____ of the virus to human beings.

(10) We may have watched our parents suffer in silence and witnessed the _____ that characterized their relationship.

Banked cloze

5. Fill in the blanks by selecting suitable words from the word bank. You may not use any of the words more than once.

A. dramatically	B. assumption	C. depend	D. preparedness	E. adopted
F. irregular	G. reaction	H. adhere	I. virtue	J. deficient
K. limit	L. articulate	M. stereotyped	N. concerted	O. advantage

In recent years many countries in the world have (1) _____ policies for greater equality in Information Technology. However worldwide, female enrollment in tertiary level science and technology is less than male enrollment. In today's world of e-commerce and distance communication, companies (2) _____ on technological and computer expertise at all employment levels. Therefore, jobs in Information Technology and related fields increased (3) _____ in recent years and this trend is expected to continue well into the future.

Although women's participation is on the rise in some male-dominated occupational fields, the percentage of women in the IT field is actually declining. A widespread (4) _____ that hampers women's professional development is that by (5) _____ of being women, they cannot fully participate in work. For example, for women who have families, it's assumed they cannot travel or work (6) _____ hours. While it's true that women often shoulder more family responsibilities than men, and for some women, it's very important whether or not to accept or reject an assignment, but the presumption tends to (7) _____ women's advancement, with their outside responsibilities a foregone conclusion. Besides, some women are (8) _____ in nature, thinking that women are better at human skills of "nurturing, emotional expressiveness and communication activities", whereas men are better at "instrumental and task-oriented assignments".

In my opinion, education is the most important factor in improving women's ability to take (9) _____ of the opportunities offered by information technology. Stronger efforts are needed to develop women's skills and influence their (10) _____ to enter the market. What's more, relevant policies should be made to promote and guarantee their success in the industry.

Structured analysis and writing

Structure analysis

Write an advantage essay

An advantage essay is one whereby the writer chooses to look at the many good sides of a topic. By using facts, examples, or figures to illustrate the advantages of a particular topic, the writer comes to a conclusion that favors the good sides.

Advantage writing generally is composed of three parts: 1) introducing the topic and explaining why it is necessary to explore the topic; 2) using examples and figures to illustrate the advantages of your topic; 3) closing your essay with a brief summary of the advantages of your topic and reinforce your opinion at the very end of your essay.

Now let's start with a brief structure analysis of Text A.

Introduction	Points out the topic: The way people address "women in technology", not "people in technology, some of whom are women" demonstrates that women are a minority and hold low status in technology.
	Brings out the thesis statement: There are both significant obstacles and emerging opportunities for women who want to work in the technology industry. (Para. 1)
	Uses figures to further illustrate the topic. (Para. 2)
Body	Transitional paragraph: It's essential for companies to realize the importance of attracting women to technology. (Para. 3)
	Claims women's strengths and two ways companies and government should adopt to ensure more women's participation in the industry: maximizing the opportunity (Paras. 4–7) and beginning with education (Paras. 8–9).
Conclusion	Shows that opportunities in IT are immense. (Para.10)
	Quotes Hilary Clinton to tell women not just to score a point, but to change a mind. (Paras. 11–12)
	Concludes with a positive attitude about the future of women in tech. (Para. 13)

From the structure analysis above, we can see the writer analyzes in the body part the strengths and emerging opportunities of women in the technology industry and concludes the essay with a positive and optimistic view about the future of women in tech.

Structured writing

Read the sample essay and see how the advantages are introduced.

Topic

Advantages of online learning

Introduction

Thesis statement: Online learning has shown its giant advantages.

Body

Advantage 1: Being convenient and flexible.

Advantage 2: Changing passive study into initiative study.

Conclusion

Participating in online learning will raise people's interest and give them more opportunities for future career success.

Sample essay

With the development of computers and high technology, online learning has become more and more popular with the public. Compared with the traditional classroom, online learning has shown its giant advantages.

First of all, online learning is very convenient and flexible. Senior citizens, working professionals, young students, stay-at-home mothers, and others can seek varied online learning courses and degrees offered by different organizations. Online learning can be done in remote locations, from offices or homes as long as you have access to a computer and broadband Internet connectivity.

Secondly, online learning can change the passive study in the traditional teacher-centered classroom into the initiative study. People will be more motivated to learn because they can choose to take whatever courses they are interested in. With more enthusiasm and initiative, they will learn it better and go further.

In brief, more convenient and diverse choices are the major two advantages of online learning. With more participation in this new way of learning, people will be given more opportunities for future career success.

Unit 6 Gender Discrepancy in IT

6. **Write an essay of no less than 200 words on one of the following topics. One topic has an outline that you can follow.**

Topic
Advantages of mobile phones
Introduction
Thesis statement: Mobile phones are advantageous to modern people nowadays.
Body
Advantage 1: Mobile phones can promote convenient interpersonal communication.
Advantage 2: Mobile phones can provide a more wonderful life.
Conclusion
Using mobile phones benefits people a lot.

More topics:

- Advantages of choosing IT as a major
- Advantages of traveling

Translation

7. **Translate the following paragraph into Chinese.**

As China is rising as a political and economic world power, thanks to its three-decade reform and opening up, more and more people in overseas countries start to learn Chinese and turn to a Confucius Institute in their own countries as their first choice for learning Chinese language and Chinese culture. During the learning process, the learners concurrently develop their interest in this ancient land, whose civilization is so vastly different from theirs. And the learners have opportunities to learn about Chinese philosophy, art, architecture, medicine and catering culture and experience first-hand the splendors of this venerable civilization.

8. Translate the following paragraph into English.

"文房四宝"（Four Treasures of the Study）是对中国书法传统书写工具的统称，包括笔、墨、纸、砚（ink stone）。"文房"指的是学者的书房。除了这四宝，书房里的工具还有笔筒、笔架、墨盒、腕托、笔洗、墨块（inkpad），这些都是书房的必备品。唐宋是书法的繁荣时期，当时著名的生产商制造的经典文房四宝被后世学者高度赞扬。中国传统文化及艺术的发明和发展与文房四宝密切相关。在某种程度上，文房四宝代表了中国传统文化的重要元素。

Section B

Reading skills: *Conjunctive connectives and sentence patterns*

When doing reading comprehension, readers are supposed to use conjunctive connectives and sentence patterns to gain a better understanding of the logical relationship implied in the passage. On the other hand, if readers correctly use conjunctive connectives and sentence patterns, their writing skills will be improved as well.

Actually, there are a variety of conjunctive connectives in English that indicate coordinative, progressive and causal relationships. Meanwhile, these connectives are also indicative of adversative and contrast relations between two sentences or paragraphs, or denote spatial location, purpose, emphases, examples, conditions or summaries, etc. In addition to connectives, sentence patterns such as emphatic sentences, inverted sentences, and noun clauses make English articles more logical, coherent, and meaningful.

Example 1

Yet this biological approach ignores the histories of the body, and emotions. It overlooks the fact that loneliness is not a universal human condition, but a historically specific one. Before 1800, loneliness wasn't even a word in regular use in the English language. Where it was used, it meant the same as a much more common term: loneliness, the state of being alone. Trees were lonely, roads were lonely, even clouds—as William Wordsworth noted in his famous poem. But that loneliness was not the same as today's loneliness, that disconnect between the relationships we have and those we want to have. (July 2020, *English Digest*)

Example 2

One of the greatest technology pioneers of the 20th century is someone most people have never heard of. Yet without this genius, there might not be smartphones and apps, a video games industry, or even the internet. We now take it for granted that a computer can be operated by anyone with no special training, and that anyone can learn to code if they want to, but it was a brilliant woman, Rear Admiral Grace Hopper, who struggled for 15 years in the middle of the 20th century to make that vision a reality. (Para. 1, Text B)

Apparently, in example 1, connectives such as "*yet*", and "*but*" are used several times to indicate the adversative relation while in example 2, the sentence pattern of subjunctive mood such as "*without... there might not be...*" and the emphatic sentence "*it was... who...*" both implicitly or explicitly emphasize the importance of the genius, Grace Hopper.

1. Read the following paragraph and choose the appropriate conjunctive connectives to complete the paragraph.

| but | or | and | such as | but also |

Artificial Intelligence (AI) is getting better all the time, (1) _____ stands poised to transform a host of industries. (2) _____ in order to learn to drive a car or recognize a face, the algorithms that make clever machines tick must usually be trained on massive amounts of data. Internet firms gather these data from users every time they click on a Google search result, say, (3) _____ issue a command to Alexa. They also hoover up valuable data from users through the use of tools like reCAPTCHA, which ask visitors to solve problems that are easy for humans (4) _____ hard for AIs, (5) _____ deciphering text from books that machines are unable to parse. That does not just screen out malicious bots, (6) _____ helps digitize books.

2. Read the following paragraph and modify the given paragraph by using conjunctive connectives given in the box.

Original version:

Admission fees may become the barrier stopping people from entering museums. They encourage people to be better prepared before they get inside for a deep visit. Imagine that you are entering the Picasso Museum without knowing anything about him, what kind of impact could this museum have on you? You will definitely walk out of it with regret and wish you could have known him more. Such a rare opportunity could be missed when live history is brought out in front of you and you could benefit a lot by asking a lot of questions and exchanging ideas with the people around. Museums were initially established for the increase and diffusion of knowledge.

Modified version:

| Yet | quite paradoxically | because | if | Admittedly |

(1) _____, admission fees may become the barrier that stops people from entering the museum. (2) _____, (3) _____, the money visitors pay can actually improve their experience in the museum because they will make more preparations before their visit. (4) _____ the visitors do not have to spend a penny, they will more often than not enter the Picasso Museum and then walk out of it without learning anything. This is, of course,

a great shame (5) _____ the visitors take the free admission for granted and have not checked for more information about Picasso and when they do get in, they cannot benefit from exchanging ideas with people around.

Text B

Grace Hopper: A Pioneering Programmer in History

1. One of the greatest technology pioneers of the 20th century is someone most people have never heard of. Yet without this genius, there might not be smartphones and apps, a video games industry, or even the internet. We now take it for granted that a computer can be operated by anyone with no special training, and that anyone can learn to code if they want to, but it was a brilliant woman, Rear Admiral Grace Hopper, who struggled for 15 years in the middle of the 20th century to make that **vision** a reality.

2. During the Second World War, the Harvard Computation Laboratory housed early computers used to solve problems in **ballistics**. In 1944, Grace Hopper, a 37-year-old math Ph.D., joined the Navy as a **lieutenant** and was assigned to that lab. Her group also included the soon-to-be-famous mathematician John von Neumann, and together they laid down some of the fundamental principles of computation.

3. But it was after the war that Hopper had her big idea. By then computers were programmed in machine code, which to the untrained eye looks like **hexadecimal gibberish**—B0 61 E3 79, that sort of thing—but which was still an improvement on a forest of plugs. Hopper wanted to make programming even easier. What if you could use normal English words like "if" and "stop"? And what if a program then automatically performed the **tedious** work of translating those instructions into a language the machine could understand? That would be a kind of automatic programming. Then, Hopper dreamed, programmers would be freed from the hundreds of hours of **banal arithmetical** manipulations required to write machine code, and they could concentrate on a more high-level, creative view of what the program was intended to do.

4. Hopper didn't just dream: She made it happen. In 1951, she created the first "compiler", a program that would translate a new, more human-friendly set of instructions into machine code automatically. This was a vastly more efficient system. In one test, the old-fashioned way of writing a program to solve a simple **geometrical** equation took three people more than 14 hours, of which a full eight hours was spent just on translating the program **laboriously** into machine-readable instructions using a code manual. The same equation was turned into a functional program using Hopper's compiler by a single person in less than one hour.

5. Did the programming world fall over itself to **hail** Grace Hopper for her brilliant revolution? No. Quite the opposite, in fact. The head of computer operations at General Electric, Herb Grosch, led a **vocal** resistance movement for more than a decade. They argued that programming was far too delicate and **ingenious** an activity for any part of it to be left to the computer itself. It was clear to Hopper that programmers regarded themselves as "high priests", jealously guarding their status as **intermediaries** between ordinary people and the **occult** computer brain. They felt that her compiler was a threat to their status.

6. Hopper spent a decade writing papers and giving conference talks while the computing **priesthood** tried to smack her down, but the tide only really began to turn when she appealed directly to business executives, the potential users of her product. To them, she promised greater speed, efficiency, and ease. One of her early compilers was called "Business Language Version 0", which reflected her idea that programming could be made **transparent** and simple enough for office workers to understand. Her strategy finally worked. By the end of the decade, **payroll** and inventory applications were being written at various military departments and industrial corporations with Hopper's own language, FLOW-MATIC—a system that hardcore programmers still mocked because it was too easy for ordinary people to understand.

7. Another source of resistance to Grace Hopper's innovations is still all too recognizable today—sexism. In 1960, Hopper participated in the development of the computing language COBOL. The majority of the elite computing "priesthood" predicted its rapid **demise**. According to one historian of technology, many of the skeptics had "concluded that the fruits of such an unstructured, female-dominated process could not be expected to survive, let alone flourish". Yet things improved rapidly, in part thanks to Hopper's own example. By 1968, according to an article in *Cosmopolitan* titled "The Computer Girls", there were more than 20,000 women programmers working in the US, and there was a demand for as many more: In this field, it said, sex **discrimination** was rare, and a woman could be "fully accepted as a professional". Hopper told the magazine that programming was like planning a dinner: "You have to plan ahead and schedule everything so it's ready when you need it. Programming requires patience and the ability to handle detail. Women are naturals at computer programming."

8. In the face of incomprehension and jealous anger from most of her colleagues in the industry, Grace Hopper spent a decade-and-a-half predicting a coming "computer age". Of course, she eventually won. The world of smartphones and social media has **vindicated** her totally. Yet the modern tech world arguably has more of a problem with women now than it did in the 1960s: A 2016 study found that code written by women was more likely to be approved by other coders than code written by men—but only if their peers didn't know that the code came from women. And even though she didn't live to see it **materialize**, our **visionary** heroine still had deeper thoughts about the world we live in now than most of today's high-profile Silicon Valley **entrepreneurs**. "We're flooding people with information. We need to feed it through a **processor**," she once said. "A human must turn information into intelligence or knowledge. We've tended to forget that no computer will ever ask a new question." When we consider the age of Big Data and increasing automation, it's clear that Grace Hopper still has much to teach us.

(981 words)

New words

vision	/ˈvɪʒən/	n.	1. an idea or a picture in your imagination 想象；幻想 2. the ability to think about or plan the future with great imagination and intelligence 想象力；眼力；远见卓识
ballistics	/bəˈlɪstɪks/	n.	[U] the scientific study of things that are shot or fired through the air, such as bullets and missiles 发射学；弹道学
lieutenant	/lefˈtenənt/	n.	an officer of middle rank in the army, navy, or air force （陆军）中尉；（海军或空军）上尉
hexadecimal	/ˌheksəˈdesɪml/	a.	a system for representing pieces of data using the numbers 0–9 and the letters A–F 十六进制的
gibberish	/ˈdʒɪbərɪʃ/	n.	(infml.) words that have no meaning or are impossible to understand 莫名其妙的话；胡话；令人费解的话
tedious	/ˈtiːdɪəs/	a.	lasting or taking too long and not interesting 冗长的；单调乏味的；令人厌烦的
banal	/bəˈnɑːl/	a.	very ordinary and containing nothing that is interesting or important 平庸的；平淡乏味的；无关紧要的
arithmetical	/ˌærɪθˈmetɪkəl/	a.	relating to arithmetic 算术的
geometrical	/ˌdʒɪəˈmetrɪkl/	a.	of geometry; of or like the lines, shapes, etc. used in geometry, especially because of having regular shapes or lines 几何学的；（似）几何图形的 ~ equation 几何方程

laboriously	/ləˈbɔːrɪəslɪ/	*ad.*	taking a lot of time and effort 耗时费力地；辛苦地
hail	/heɪl/	*vt.*	to describe sb./sth. as being very good or special, especially in newspapers, etc. 赞扬（或称颂）……为……
vocal	/ˈvəʊkəl/	*a.*	telling people your opinions or protesting about sth. loudly and with confidence 大声表达的；直言不讳的
ingenious	/ɪnˈdʒiːnjəs/	*a.*	1. (of an object, a plan, an idea, etc.) very suitable for a particular purpose and resulting from clever new ideas（物体、计划、思想等）精巧的；新颖独特的；巧妙的 2. (of a person) having a lot of clever new ideas and good at inventing things 心灵手巧的；机敏的；善于创造发明的
intermediary	/ˌɪntəˈmiːdɪərɪ/	*n.*	a person or an organization that helps other people or organizations to make an agreement by being a means of communication between them 中间人；调解人
occult	/ɒˈkʌlt/	*a.*	[only before noun] connected with magic powers and things that cannot be explained by reason or science 神秘的；玄妙的；超自然的；不可思议的
priesthood	/ˈpriːsthʊd/	*n.*	the job or position of being a priest 牧师（或教士、神父）的职位；司祭品
transparent	/trænsˈpærənt/	*a.*	(of language, information, etc.) easy to understand（语言、信息等）易懂的
payroll	/ˈpeɪˌrəʊl/	*n.*	1. a list of people employed by a company showing the amount of money to be paid to each of them（公司员工的）工资名单 2. the total amount paid in wages by a company（公司的）工资总支出
demise	/dɪˈmaɪz/	*n.*	the end or failure of an institution, an idea, a company, etc. 终止；失败；倒闭
discrimination	/dɪˌskrɪmɪˈneɪʃən/	*n.*	the practice of treating sb. or a particular group in society less fairly than others 区别对待；歧视；偏袒
vindicate	/ˈvɪndɪˌkeɪt/	*vt.*	(infml.) 1. to prove that sth. is true or that you were right to do sth., especially when other people had a different opinion 证实；证明有理 2. to prove that sb. is not guilty when they have been accused of doing sth. wrong or illegal 澄清（责难或嫌疑）；证明（某人）无罪
materialize	/məˈtɪərɪəˌlaɪz/	*vt.*	to take place or start to exist as expected or planned 实现；发生；成为现实

visionary	/ˈvɪʒənəri/	*a.*	original and showing the ability to think about or plan the future with great imagination and intelligence 有眼力的；有远见卓识的
entrepreneur	/ˌɒntrəprəˈnɜː/	*n.*	a person who makes money by starting or running businesses, especially when this involves taking financial risks 创业者；企业家（尤指涉及财务风险的）
processor	/ˈprəʊsesə/	*n.*	1. a machine or person that processes things 加工机（或工人）2. (computing) a part of a computer that controls all the other parts of the system（计算机的）处理器；处理机

New expressions

take it for granted	to believe sth. is true without first making sure that it is 认为……是理所当然
lay sth. down	to officially state sth. or say that rules, principles, etc. must be obeyed（正式或坚决地）阐述；声明；规定
to the untrained eye	to sb. without the skill or knowledge to judge what they see 对不知情的人／外行人来说
be intended to do sth.	to have a plan, result or purpose in your mind when you do sth. 打算；计划；想要做某事
translate sth. into sth.	to change sth., or to be changed into a different form（使）转变；变为
fall over oneself to do sth.	to be very eager to do sth., especially sth. you do not usually do 忙不迭地做某事；急着做某事（尤指一般不做的事）
threat to sth.	a person or thing that is likely to cause trouble, danger, etc. 构成威胁的人；形成威胁的事物
free sb. from/of sth.	to allow sb. to say and do what they want, after controlling or restricting them in the past 解放；使摆脱
appeal to sb.	to attract or interest sb. 对某人有吸引力；引起兴趣
let alone	used after a statement to emphasize that because the first thing is not true or possible, the next thing cannot be true or possible either 更不用说
be a natural at/for sth.	to become a person who is very good at sth. without having to learn how to do it, or who is perfectly suited for a particular job 有天赋的人；擅长做某事的人

| tend to do sth. | if sth. tends to happen, it happens often and is likely to happen again 易于做某事；往往会发生某事 |

Notes

1. Grace Hopper (葛丽丝·霍普, 1906–1992): a remarkable woman who grandly rose to the challenges of programming the first computers. During her lifetime as a leader in the field of software development concepts, she contributed to the transition from primitive programming techniques to the use of sophisticated compilers.

2. The Harvard Computation Laboratory (哈佛计算机实验室): founded by Howard Hathaway Aiken in 1944, was the first establishment of an academic center for computer research.

3. John von Neumann (约翰·冯·诺依曼): was a mathematician, physicist, computer scientist and engineer. In the 1940s, his interest in self-replicating natural processes in the physical universe led von Neumann, in collaboration with Stanislaw Ulam, to consider self-replicating machines. In 1952 he developed the concept of cellular automata. With pencil and graph paper, he constructed the first self-replicating 2-D automaton.

4. Herb Grosch (赫伯·格罗施): a computer pioneer who managed important space and technology projects. Grosch is respected for discovering and describing the relationship between speed and cost of computers.

5. COBOL (Common Business Oriented Language, 面向商业的通用语言): (Computer Science) a high-level computer programming language designed for general commercial use.

6. Silicon Valley (硅谷): a region in California to the south of San Francisco that is noted for its concentration of high-technology industries.

7. Big Data (大数据): a field that extracts and analyzes information from a huge amount of data that grows exponentially with time.

Reading comprehension

Understanding the text

1. Choose the best answer to each of the following questions.

   (1) According to the text, but for the innovation of Grace Hopper, the following things could not be probably invented EXCEPT _____.

   A. apps   B. smartphones   C. color TV   D. the Internet

(2) What did Grace Hopper do together with John von Neumann during the Second World War?

   A. They both served in the Navy.

   B. They established mathematical principles.

   C. They founded the Harvard Computation Laboratory.

   D. They officially stated the basic computation rules.

(3) What is the key role that automatic programming plays according to the passage?

   A. An improvement on a forest of plugs.

   B. Freeing programmers from heavy tedious work.

   C. Making programming easier and more accessible to all people.

   D. Translating those instructions into a language without any bugs.

(4) Which of the following statements is **NOT** true in terms of Hopper's ambition?

   A. Hopper not only had an ambition, but also made that vision a reality.

   B. She successfully created a more efficient system which can liberate engineers from laborious work.

   C. She created the first "compiler" which can automatically translate a set of instructions into machine code.

   D. All equations could be turned into a functional program by using Hopper's compiler single-handedly.

(5) The programming world's attitude towards Grace Hopper's brilliant revolution was _____.

   A. opposed   B. controversial   C. supportive   D. unclear

(6) Hopper's strategy embodies the following features **EXCEPT** _____.

   A. transparency   B. flawlessness

   C. simplicity   D. efficiency

(7) In terms of the source of resistance to Grace Hopper's innovations—sexism, which of the following statements is **NOT** true?

   A. Grace Hopper's innovations meet the expectations of most elite computing researchers.

   B. An article in *Cosmopolitan* said that a woman could be fully accepted as a professional.

   C. Many skeptics concluded that female-dominated innovations in computing could not be expected to survive and flourish.

D. Hopper's own example, to a large extent, contributed to the improvement of women's participation in the field of programming.

(8) What can be inferred from a 2016 study which found that code written by women was more likely to be approved by other coders than code written by men—but only if their peers didn't know that the code came from women?

A. Women are more innovative than their peers in the programming world.

B. Visionary heroines still had deeper thoughts and more innovation than most of today's high-profile Silicon Valley entrepreneurs.

C. People are still potentially prejudiced against women in the programming world.

D. Both women and men could exert great influence in the programming world.

Critical thinking

2. Work in pairs and discuss the following questions.

(1) Why is Grace Hopper considered as one of the greatest technology pioneers of the 20th century?

(2) What is Hopper's ambitious dream in terms of automatic programming?

(3) What did Hopper do to make her dream a reality?

(4) What is the programming world's attitude to Hopper's brilliant revolution?

(5) When and why did the tide begin to turn?

(6) What is the attitude toward women in terms of computer programming?

(7) What is the finding of a 2016 study? And what does the conclusion imply?

(8) What does the author mean by maintaining that Hopper still has much to teach us?

 # Language focus

Words in use

3. Fill in the blanks with the words given below. Change the form where necessary. Each word can be used only once.

gibberish	vocal	hail	ingenious	vindicate
materialize	demise	visionary	processor	intermediary

(1) The book titled *Deng Xiaoping and the Transformation of China* was a National Book Critics Circle Award finalist and _____ as a definitive account of Deng.

(2) Financial institutions act as _____ between lenders and borrowers.

(3) I have every confidence that this decision will be fully _____.

(4) His combination of intellect and empathy made him a truly unique and _____ individual.

(5) You can download the file and edit it on your word _____.

(6) Foley has been particularly _____ in his criticism of the government.

(7) Most analysts believe that some kind of environmental degradation underlies the _____ of many extinct salmon populations.

(8) When he was talking to a girl he could hardly speak, and when he did speak he talked _____.

(9) Many fish have _____ ways of protecting their eggs from predators.

(10) The promotion he had been promised failed to _____.

Expressions in use

4. Fill in the blanks with the expressions given below. Change the form where necessary. Each expression can be used only once.

| lay down | appeal to | free... from... | let alone |
| tend to (do) | intend to do | take it for granted | translate into |

(1) Recent studies show that girls _____ be better at languages than boys.

(2) He seemed to _____ that he should speak as a representative.

(3) It is _____ that all candidates must submit three copies of their dissertation.

(4) We _____ all we can to ensure that they have a fair environment for competition.

(5) Others are skeptical that AI will ever reach human levels of intelligence and cognition, _____ surpass it.

(6) Reforming the stagnant economy requires harsh measures that would _____ job losses.

(7) The design has to _____ all ages and social groups.

(8) They need someone to lead them out of the maze and _____ them _____ confusion and illusion.

Sentence structure

5. Rewrite the sentences by using the pattern of subjunctive mood "but for/without..., sb. would/should/might (not) have done...; If sb. had done..., sb. would/should/could (not) have done...". Make changes where necessary.

> Model: I was interrupted by the endless cellphones. As a result, I didn't finish my homework.
> → But for the endless interruptions of cellphones, I would have finished my homework.

(1) The general was agile and alert, so he wasn't smashed beneath the huge dead tree.

(2) He didn't see the doctor in time, so he has not recovered from his illness.

(3) I didn't catch the train yesterday, because I was ten minutes late when I arrived at the station.

(4) It is your article that makes it possible for me to know that there exists such a quiet and picturesque village.

(5) John Bodman's wife was so persistent in forcing her presence upon him at all times and on all occasions that the idea of murder occurred to him.

 Collocation

> It is, therefore, not so much the content of scientific discoveries that should *be highlighted*, but the understanding of the scientific process itself that must *be enhanced*. No one expects the public at large to fully understand all discoveries or be able to arbitrate between possible treatments. But what must *be reaffirmed* is that in science, doubt is not a vulnerability but a strength.

6. Complete the following sentences with the correct words provided in the box to form collocations you have learned from this unit. Each word can be used only once.

| detected | programmed | utilized | maintained | instilled | operated |

(1) We now take it for granted that a computer can be _____ by anyone with no special training.

(2) By then computers were _____ in machine code.

(3) To restore economies to health quickly, connections between workers and firms needed to be _____, so that activity could pick up from where it had left off.

(4) Right now, deepfake videos have subtle imperfections that can be readily _____ by automated systems, if not by the naked eye.

(5) The mindset of military service excellence is _____ in every citizen from children in Israel.

(6) Many completed plants are not yet fully _____ and still have decades of life in them.

Translation

7. Translate the following passage into English.

当前，世界迎来新一轮科技革命和产业变革，信息技术创新成为驱动这一轮科技革命和产业变革的基础动力。超级计算机是信息技术创新的代表性成果之一，历经多年积累，银河、曙光、天河、神威等我国系列超级计算机一个接一个迈上世界舞台，成为创新关键驱动力。中国已启动了新一代百亿亿次超级计算机系统的研制工作，它将继续推动国家的科技创新、战略性新兴产业快速发展,推动大数据、人工智能、物联网的快速发展,共同为解决人类发展面临的重大挑战发挥重要作用。

Unit project

Write a report on women's importance in the IT industry.

> This unit is about women's role in the IT industry. The two texts hold basically the same opinion that it is good and necessary for women to participate in the tech world. Even though there are still many obstacles materially and psychologically, women's future in the IT world will become better with more effort. In this unit project, you are asked to write a report on women's importance in the IT industry. To complete the project, you can follow the steps below.

(1) Work in groups and design a questionnaire on women's importance in the IT industry. The following questions can be included in your questionnaire. Add more questions if you can.

- Do you want to apply for a job in an IT company after graduation?
- Do you think it is good for a girl to work in an IT company?
- What are the advantages?
- What are the disadvantages?

…

(2) Each of your group members interviews 5–10 girls on campus. Take down their answers to your questions.

(3) Compare your answers with other group members'. Draw a conclusion from your questionnaire.

(4) Analyze your information and prepare a report presentation in class.

Unit 7

Get Advancement in IT

Learning objectives

In this unit you will:
- learn to think about career choices in the IT industry;
- learn how to build your career without becoming a manager;
- learn how to write a process analysis essay;
- learn how to use synonyms and synonymous expressions.

> Your career is like a garden. It can hold an assortment of life's energy that yields a bounty for you. You do not need to grow just one thing in your garden. You do not need to do just one thing in your career.
>
> —*Jennifer Ritchie Payette*
>
> No one can discover you until you do. Exploit your talents, skills and strengths and make the world sit up and take notice.
>
> —*Rob Liano*

Preview

Few people actively manage their careers. But the most successful ones don't arrive at success by chance. They have a goal in mind and they create a solid and well-thought-out plan to achieve that goal. If you really want to succeed in the competitive world, you need to do more than just polish your resume and take whatever job you happen to get. You need to think things through and decide what actions you should take, when you should take them, and how you should go forward with them. As a software engineer, you should thoroughly analyze your interests, knowledge, qualities and attitudes before making your occupational planning. It is your career's navigation that can bring you what you want and let you continue to learn.

So as a new software engineering graduate, what kind of career development plan should be developed? What factors should you take into consideration before making career choices? What kind of skills should be mastered in order to make a suitable occupational plan?

Section A

Pre-reading activities

1. **Answer the following questions briefly based on the given pictures.**

   (1) What kind of job do you want to do in the future?

   (2) As a computer science major, how would you choose your first job? What are the most important factors in determining your choice?

2. **Work in pairs and discuss the following questions.**

   (1) Can you show us how to be the most successful software developer we could be—not just in writing code—but in life in general?

   (2) If you are a software developer, what occupational plan will you make? Visualize a five-year career plan with your partners.

Text A

Getting Started with a "BANG"

1. Imagine sitting in a field in the middle of summer enjoying a nice **fireworks** show. All around you **creaming** rockets burst into explosions of blue, red, purple, and yellow. You watch as one particular rocket **soars** high up into the sky and then… nothing. No **bang**, no explosion, just a **fizzle**. Which firework do you want your software development career to be like? The one that explodes high in the air with a loud bang, or the one that reaches **altitude** and then quietly falls back to the ground?

2. Most software developers starting out in their careers make a few huge mistakes. The biggest of those mistakes, by far, is not treating their software development career as a business. Don't be **beguiled**, when you set out into the world to write code for a living, you're no different than the **blacksmith** of old times setting up shop in a **medieval** town. Times may have changed, and most of us work for a company, but our skills and our trade belong to us and we can always choose to set up shops somewhere else.

3. This kind of mindset is crucial to managing your career, because when you start to think of yourself as a business, you start to make good business decisions. When you're used to getting a regular paycheck that isn't really **dependent** on your performance, it can be easy to develop a mindset that you're just an employee of a company. While it's true that you may be an employee of a particular company at any given time in your career, it's important not to let that particular role **confine** you and your career.

4. It's better to think of an employer as a customer for your business of developing software. Sure, you might only have a single customer, and all of your revenue may be coming from that single customer, but viewing the relationship this way moves you from a position of powerlessness and dependency to one of **autonomy** and self-direction.

5. This is the first thing you must do in your career: **convert** your mindset from that of an **indentured** servant to a business person who is running his own business. Just having

this mindset at the start will change the way you think about your career and cause you to be mindful and present in the active management of it.

6. Now, just thinking of yourself as a business doesn't really do you much good. You have to understand what it is to think in this fashion if you want to get any benefit from it.

7. We can start off by thinking about what makes up a business. Most businesses **necessitate** a few things to be successful. First, you need to have a product or a service. A business without something to make available doesn't have a way to make money, because they have nothing to sell. What do you have to sell? What is your product or service?

8. You may very well have an actual digital product to sell as a software developer, but most software developers are selling the service of developing software. Developing software is a wide term that can cover a variety of different activities and individual services, but in general, software developers are selling their ability to take an idea and make it into a **digitized** reality.

9. Just thinking about what you offer as a business in this way has a **forceful** impact on how you view your career. Businesses are constantly **revising** their products and improving them. You should too. The service you provide as a software developer has a **phenomenal** value, and it's your job to **acquaint** the customers with not only what that value is, but what makes it different from the offerings of thousands of other software developers out there.

10. It's important to at least realize that having a product or service by itself is not enough. You've actually got to be able to let potential customers know about that product or service if you want it to **yield** a return. Companies all over the world realize this key truth about business and that's why they spend a big sum of money and effort on marketing. As a software developer offering your service, you also have to **exert** yourself on marketing. The better you market your offerings, the higher price you'll be able to charge for your services and the more customers you'll **potentially** be able to attract.

11. You can imagine that most software developers starting out don't think about their careers in this way. Instead of starting out with a bang, they enter the scene with a barely **audible** pop. So don't do what they do. Instead, focus on what service you're providing and how to market that service, **ponder** on ways you can improve your offering, about how you can tailor the service you're providing to **avail** yourself of the needs of a particular type of client or industry. Focus on being a **specialist** who provides a very specialized set of services to a very particular type of client. Remember, as a software developer hunting for a good job, you only really need to land one client.

12. Also, think about how best to spread the word about your service and find your customers. Most software developers create a resume and **blast** it out to companies and

recruiters. But, when you think about your career as a business, do you really think that is the best and only way to prospect potential clients? Of course not. Most successful companies figure out how to get customers to come to them to buy their products or services; they don't go out chasing customers one by one.

13. You can do the same thing by making yourself a more **marketable** software developer through many techniques. Even without getting into the **specifics**, the point is to think outside of the box and start thinking like a business. What is the best way you can attract customers and how can you tell them about the service you have to offer? If you can answer this simple question, you'll start off your career with a bang.

(1,019 words)

New words

firework	/ˈfaɪəˌwɜːk/	n.	[C, usu. pl.] a small container filled with powder that burns or explodes to produce colored lights and noise in the sky 烟火
creaming	/ˈkriːmɪŋ/	n.	[U] a process of separation of an emulsion 分层
soar	/sɔː/	vi.	to go up high in the air quickly 急速升入
bang	/bæŋ/	n.	[C] sudden loud noise 突然的巨响
		v.	to strike (sth.) deliberately and violently, often in order to make a loud noise 故意猛砸（常为产生巨响）
fizzle	/ˈfɪzəl/	vi.	to make a weak fizzing sound 发出微弱的嘶嘶声
altitude	/ˈæltɪˌtjuːd/	n.	[C] height above sea-level 海拔；高度
beguile	/bɪˈɡaɪl/	vt.	(fml.) 1. ~ sb. (into doing sth.) to deceive sb. 欺骗某人 2. to charm (sb.) 迷住（某人）
blacksmith	/ˈblækˌsmɪθ/	n.	[C] person whose job is to make and repair things made of iron, esp. horseshoes 铁匠（尤指马蹄铁匠）
medieval	/ˌmedɪˈiːvəl/	a.	of the Middle Ages, about AD 1100–1400 中古的；中世纪的（约公元 1100—1400 年）
dependent	/dɪˈpendənt/	a.	~ (on/upon sb./sth.) needing support from sb. 需要某人支持的；依靠的；依赖的
confine	/kənˈfaɪn/	v.	to keep sb. or sth. within the limits of a particular activity or subject 限制；束缚
autonomy	/ɔːˈtɒnəmi/	n.	[U] the ability or opportunity to make your own decisions without being controlled by anyone else 独立自主；自主权

convert	/kən'vɜːt/	v.	1. ~ (sth.) (from sth.) (into/to sth.) to change (sth.) from one form or use to another 改变（某事物）的形式或用途 2. ~ (sb.) (from sth.) (to sth.) to change one's beliefs, esp. one's religion; to persuade sb. to change his beliefs （使）改变信仰（尤指宗教信仰）
indentured	/ɪn'dentʃəd/	a.	bound by contract 契约的
necessitate	/nɪ'sesɪteɪt/	vt.	(fml.) to make (sth.) necessary 使（某事物）成为必要
digitized	/'dɪdʒɪtaɪzd/	a.	recorded or stored in digital form 数字化的
forceful	/'fɔːsfʊl/	a.	strong and assertive 强有力的
revise	/rɪ'vaɪz/	vt.	1. to re-examine (sth.), esp. in order to correct or improve it 复查（某事物）；（尤指）复核；校订；修正 2. to go over (work already done) in preparation for an examination 复习（功课）
phenomenal	/fɪ'nɒmɪnəl/	a.	very remarkable; extraordinary 非凡的；格外的；了不起的
acquaint	/ə'kweɪnt/	vt.	(~sb./oneself with sth.) to make sb./oneself familiar with or aware of sth. 使某人/自己熟悉或了解某事物
yield	/jiːld/	vt.	to bear, produce or provide (a natural product, a result or profit) 生出、产生或提供（自然产物、结果或利润）
exert	/ɪɡ'zɜːt/	vt.	1. ~ sth. (on sb./sth.) to bring (a quality, skill, pressure, etc.) into use; to apply sth. 用（某特质、技巧、压力等）；应用（某物）2. [不用于被动语态] ~ oneself: to make an effort 努力；尽力
potentially	/pə'tenʃəli/	ad.	with a possibility of becoming actual 潜在地；可能地
audible	/'ɔːdɪbəl/	a.	that can be heard clearly 听得见的
ponder	/'pɒndə/	vi.	~ (on/over sth.) to think about (sth.) carefully and for a long time, esp. in trying to reach a decision; to consider （长时间地仔细）考虑（某事物）（尤指以便作出决定）；深思
avail	/ə'veɪl/	vt.	~ oneself of sth. (fml.) to make use of sth.; to take advantage of sth. 使用某事物；利用某事物
specialist	/'speʃəlɪst/	n.	[C] an expert who is devoted to one occupation or branch of learning 专家；专科医生；行家
blast	/blɑːst/	v.	to destroy or break apart (esp. rocks) using explosives 用炸药炸开（尤指石头）
		n.	[C, U] explosion; destructive wave of air from an explosion 爆炸；（由爆炸所引起具有破坏力的）气浪；冲击波

recruiter	/rɪˈkruːtə(r)/	n.	[C] sb. who supplies members or employees 招聘人员
marketable	/ˈmɑːkɪtəbəl/	a.	capable of being marketed 市场的；可销售的；有销路的；市场买卖的
specific	/spɪˈsɪfɪk/	n.	[usu. pl.] particular aspect or precise detail 具体的方面；详情；细节
		a.	1. detailed, precise and exact 详细的；精确的；确切的
			2. relating to one particular thing, etc.; not general 特定的；具体的

 New expressions

burst into	to suddenly begin (sth.) 突然开始（某事）
start out	to set out; to take steps in carrying out an action 开始着手做
treat sth./sb. as	to regard sth./sb. as 当作；看成
be dependent on	to rely on 依靠；依赖
in this fashion	in this manner 照这样
have an impact on	to have an influence on 对……有影响
charge for	to collect fees for 要价；收费
figure out	to think out 想出
start off with	to start from 从……开始

Notes

John Z. Sonmez (约翰·森梅兹): the founder of Simple Programmer where he tirelessly pursues his vision of transforming complex issues into simple solutions. John is a life coach for software developers, and helps software engineers, programmers and other technical professionals boost their careers and live a more fulfilled life. He empowers them to accomplish their goals by making the complex simple.

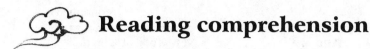 Reading comprehension

Understanding the text

1. Answer the following questions.

(1) Which two kinds of fireworks does the writer describe in the first paragraph? What are their implied meanings?

(2) What biggest mistake do most software developers make?

(3) Why is it crucial to start to think of oneself as a business in managing one's career?

(4) What should a software developer think of his/her employer as? Why?

(5) What is the first thing a software developer should do in his/her career?

(6) What makes up a business? How does a business make money?

(7) Is a software developer a business? What does he/she sell?

(8) What question needs to be answered before a software developer starts off his/her career with a bang?

Critical thinking

2. Work in pairs and discuss the following questions.

(1) Where do you envision yourself as being in your profession in five years?

(2) What are the goals you want to achieve in five years? What will you do to achieve your career goals?

Word building

The suffix *-cy* combines with adjectives to form nouns. Nouns formed in this way refer to "the state or quality of being...".

Examples

Words learned	Add *-cy*	New words formed
pregnant	→	pregnancy
accurate	→	accuracy
secret	→	secrecy

(continued)

Words learned	Add -cy	New words formed
fluent	→	fluency
frequent	→	frequency

The suffix -ist combines with nouns or adjectives to form nouns. Nouns formed in this way refer to "a person believing or practicing, concerned with, or doing the specified action".

Examples

Words learned	Add -ist	New words formed
capital	→	capitalist
social	→	socialist
art	→	artist
real	→	realist
ideal	→	idealist

3. Add -cy, or -ist to the following words to form new words.

Words learned	New words formed
-cy	
dependent	
intimate	
private	
urgent	
consistent	
-ist	
biology	
terror	
special	
novel	
tour	

4. **Fill in the blanks with the newly-formed words in Activity 3. Change the form where necessary. Each word can be used only once.**

(1) It's not preferable to do a lot of work one day and none the next—we need some _____.

(2) Increasing disability with age means a growing _____ on others, as made clear in the article.

(3) Parental love is generally recognized by _____ to be a very precious natural asset.

(4) Though they are well apart, there is a sense of _____ between them.

(5) The _____ who carried out the brain scan thought Tim's chances of survival were still slim.

(6) The scientist believes that it is a matter of _____ to weaken conventional notions of race that cause racial prejudice.

(7) Yesterday, the Italian prime minister expressed indignation and worry about the _____ attack two days ago.

(8) Dublin has rocketed up the charts to become one of Europe's most popular _____ destinations for city breaks.

(9) The idea of keeping personal information on the Internet immediately raises concerns about _____.

(10) Anne Tyler is an American _____ who is famous for her humorous language and life-like characters.

Banked cloze

5. **Fill in the blanks by selecting suitable words from the word bank. You may not use any of the words more than once.**

A. creatures	B. imperative	C. disagreement	D. emotions	E. rattlesnakes
F. prowess	G. conclusion	H. logical	I. accrue	J. tantrum
K. determine	L. compel	M. particular	N. convince	O. redeemed

As software developers, we sometimes tend to think that all people think about things from a(n) (1) _____ perspective. It's easy to fall into the trap of falsely believing that solid reasoning is enough to (2) _____ another person to accept your way of thinking. The truth of the matter is that even though we like to pride ourselves on our intellectual (3) _____, we're all very emotional (4) _____. We like little babies who are walking around wearing suits and ties and pretending to be all grown up. A slight injury is just as likely to cause us to cry or throw a(n) (5) _____, but we've learned to control and hide those (6) _____ out of sight. For this reason, it's (7) _____ to avoid arguments at all costs. Logic and pure reason do little to (8) _____ a screaming toddler that it indeed makes sense for him to go to sleep so that he'll be well rested for the day ahead, and it will do just about as much good in convincing a slighted coworker that your way of doing things is best. I have come to the (9) _____ that there is only one way under high heaven to get the best of an argument—and that is to avoid it. Avoid it as you would avoid (10) _____ and earthquakes.

Structured analysis and writing

Structure analysis

Write a process analysis essay

A process analysis essay tells the reader how to perform a task or accomplish a goal. To write this type of essay, break down the task you are trying to teach into a series of individual, easy-to-digest steps. Keeping your language clear, precise and unambiguous will help ensure that your reader fully understands the process.

1) Choose a teachable process

Before you begin writing your essay, choose the process you want to teach, so you can focus on the details that matter to achieving that process. Choose a topic that is complex enough to warrant instructions and simple enough that you can break it down into a few paragraph-long steps.

2) Explain the process

Begin with an introductory paragraph that tells your reader what you are going to teach and describes why it might be useful or important.

3) Break it down

Each paragraph of your essay will describe one of the steps in your process. Arrange your steps in the order they should be performed. Splitting your essay into a different section, for each step will help your reader comprehend them without becoming confused.

4) Keep it simple

While writing, avoid vague pronouns like "it" and ambiguous phrasing. Tell the reader directly such as "check if a survey is peer reviewed" rather than "you should check if a survey is peer reviewed". While you should begin your sentences with temporal phrases such as "once" and "then" to locate your steps in relation to each other, avoid beginning multiple sentences in a row with the same phrasing, as this will make your essay repetitive and mechanical.

5) Describe the results

End your paper with a conclusion paragraph describing the result of your process. Tell your readers what they should have produced or achieved by following your steps—this will allow them to check if they have been successful.

Now let's read the following sentences taken from Text A, and pay attention to how to make a software development career successful.

Topic

Which firework do you want your software development career to be like? The one that explodes high in the air with a loud bang, or the one that reaches altitude and then quietly falls back to the ground? (Para. 1)

↓

Explain the process

1) Having a business mindset (Paras. 2–5)

This is the first thing you must do in your career: convert your mindset from that of an indentured servant to a business person who is running his own business. (Para. 5)

2) How to think like a business (Paras. 6–12)

We can start off by thinking about what makes up a business. (Para. 7)

Software developers are selling their ability to take an idea and make it into a digitized reality. (Para. 8)

The better you market your offerings, the higher price you'll be able to charge for your services and the more customers you'll potentially be able to attract. (Para. 10)

Also think about how best to spread the word about your service and find your customers. (Para. 12)

↓

3) Describe the results

You can do the same thing by making yourself a more marketable software developer through many techniques. Even without getting into the specifics, the point is to think outside of the box and start thinking like a business. What is the best way you can attract customers and how can you tell them about the service you have to offer? If you can answer this simple question, you'll start off your career with a bang. (Para. 13)

As can be seen from the above sentences, the techniques are used to introduce how to be a successful software developer.

Structured writing

Read the sample essay and see how a process analysis essay is structured.

> **Topic**
>
> How to succeed in college?
>
> **Introduction**
>
> Without a clear goal, deep motivation and a well-thought-out plan, some college students may gradually idle away their time and fail to achieve any success during their four-year study.
>
> **Body**
>
> Set goals.
>
> Develop a sense of curiosity and good reading habits.
>
> Remember to learn outside of the classroom.
>
> **Conclusion**
>
> Success in college requires hard work, determination and the ability to persevere.

Sample essay

How to Succeed in College

College can be considered as one of the most precious periods in a person's life. But without a clear goal, deep motivation and a well-thought-out plan, some college students may gradually idle away their time and fail to achieve any success during the four-year study. There is no secret recipe for success in college. However, most students who succeed in college share certain characteristics.

First of all, set goals. A list of short and long-term goals serves as a road map for achievement in college. But when you set goals, try to be realistic about them and balance them out with other personal goals you may have. Getting through college isn't always about getting Straight As or graduating summa cum laude. It's about doing the best you're capable of, given your resources.

Secondly, develop a sense of curiosity and good reading habits. Read about the world in a way to which you are not accustomed. For example, if you're majoring in humanities, read Scientific American from time to time to learn about the intersection of language and music or the science of sleep loss. The more curious you are in seeking new kinds of knowledge, the more creative you will be at synthesizing the complexities of our world.

Thirdly, remember to learn outside of the classroom. Take some time to join clubs and participate in meaningful extracurricular activities. Try to meet as many interesting people as possible during your time at college. Experiencing all these new things in life enhances your interpersonal communication ability and explores your interests and passion.

Success in college requires hard work, determination, and the ability to persevere. Academic achievement will help you prepare for your career and become more sure of yourself as you consider your life goals. Think about your strengths and weaknesses as a student. If you're ambitious, committed to seeking help, and willing to invest time in your work, you'll achieve success in college.

6. Write an essay of no less than 200 words on one of the following topics. One topic has an outline that you can follow.

Topic

How to overcome fear?

Introduction

Fear is one of the greatest limitations that we will ever face in our lives. Many people will never experience the true joy of living just because they are afraid.

Body

Acknowledge fear and reflect on the traumatic events.

Face the fear by identifying false beliefs and practicing engaging with it.

Learn relaxation techniques.

Conclusion

Once you overcome fear and discover that you are in control of your life, the possibilities become endless.

More topics:

- How to be a skilled software developer?
- How to solve the problem of heavy traffic?

Translation

7. Translate the following paragraph into Chinese.

Yellowstone was the first National Park in the US and is also widely held to be the first national park in the world. It is located primarily in the US state of Wyoming, although it also extends into Montana and Idaho. It spans an area of 3,468.4 square miles, comprising lakes, canyons, rivers and mountain ranges. Hundreds of species of mammals, birds, fish and reptiles have been documented, including several that are either endangered or threatened. The vast forests and grasslands also include unique species of plants. The park is the centerpiece of the Greater Yellowstone Ecosystem, the largest remaining, nearly intact ecosystem in the Earth's northern temperate zone.

8. Translate the following paragraph into English.

故宫是明清两代的皇宫，又称紫禁城。它始建于1406年，1420年建成。故宫规模宏大，气势磅礴，布局严谨，是世界是上现存的皇宫中历史最悠久、建筑面积最大、保存最完整的一座封建皇宫，是"世界五大宫"之一。目前故宫内陈列了我国各个朝代的艺术珍品，是中国最丰富的文化和艺术宝库。1987年故宫被联合国教科文组织列为"世界文化遗产"。

Section B

 Reading skills: *Using synonyms and synonymous expressions*

Synonyms are different words that have the same or similar meanings. They come in every part of speech, including nouns, verbs, adjectives, adverbs, and prepositions. The usage of synonyms and synonymous expressions in English follows certain rules and guidelines to ensure effective communication and clarity. Here are some key rules to keep in mind:

1) Context: Always consider the context in which you are using synonymous expressions. Different synonyms may be suitable in different situations, depending on the tone, formality, and subject matter.

2) Register: Pay attention to the register or level of formality required in your communication. Some synonyms may be more appropriate for formal writing or professional settings, while others are better suited for casual conversations or informal writing.

3) Connotation: Be aware of the connotations associated with each synonym. Some words may have positive, negative, or neutral connotations, which can impact the overall tone and meaning of your message.

4) Precision: Choose synonyms that accurately convey your intended meaning. While two words may have similar meanings, they may not be interchangeable in all contexts.

5) Collocations: Consider the typical word combinations or collocations associated with each synonym. Certain words naturally go together, and using the wrong combination might sound awkward or unnatural.

6) Nuance: Pay attention to subtle differences in meaning between synonyms. While they may have similar core meanings, there could be nuances that make one more suitable than the other in a particular context.

7) Avoid overuse: Resist the temptation to excessively use synonyms, especially in rapid succession. Repeating the same idea using different words can make your writing or speech less clear and more cumbersome.

8) Proofreading: Always proofread your writing to ensure that the synonymous

expressions you've used are appropriate and do not alter the intended message.

Overall, the key to using synonyms and synonymous expressions effectively is to understand their nuances and choose the most appropriate word or phrase based on the specific context and purpose of your communication. Reading extensively and paying attention to how native speakers use language can help you develop a better sense of synonymous expression usage in English.

Read some examples of synonymous expressions and how they can be used differently based on context, connotation, and register:

1) Happy, Content, Joyful:

"She was happy with her test results." (Neutral)

"After receiving the promotion, he felt content with his career." (Formal)

"The children were joyful when they saw the presents under the tree." (Informal)

2) Skillful, Proficient, Expert:

"He is a skillful guitar player." (Neutral)

"She became proficient in using the software after months of practice." (Formal)

"The company hired an expert to handle the complex project." (Informal)

3) Help, Assist, Aid:

"The volunteers will help clean up the park." (Neutral)

"The organization is dedicated to assisting refugees in need." (Formal)

"They provided aid to the victims of the natural disaster." (Informal)

Remember, these examples showcase how synonymous expressions can be used differently based on the context and level of formality. Always consider the nuances and appropriateness of each synonym to effectively convey your intended message.

Now read the following paragraphs in Text B and learn how to identify the synonyms which signify the same meaning in a given context.

Example 1

1) *That's what engineers recently wondered on Quora, and it's an important question worth addressing, particularly for those not psyched about managing people.* (Para. 1)

2) *You identify and solve problems that are core to the business, or you enable those around you to more effectively solve those core business problems.* (Para. 9)

3) *If ten or twenty years from now, you're still solving the same scale and scope of problems as you're tackling today, then you haven't increased your ability to create impact.* (Para. 5)

Unit 7 Get Advancement in IT

Example 2

1) *Your ability to decide where to spend your efforts to <u>maximize your impact</u>—what code to write, what software to build, and which business problems to tackle—is unbounded.* (Para. 8)

2) *How do you <u>grow your impact</u> as a software engineer without becoming a manager?* (Para. 9)

3) *Here are some examples of how you might <u>amplify your impact</u> without going into management.* (Para. 10)

4) *These are just a few examples of how you can <u>increase your impact</u>, but the possible paths are limitless.* (Para. 17)

Example 3

1) *You build tools and abstractions that <u>multiply the output of</u> the engineering teams around you.* (Para. 11)

2) *Jeff Dean, through his contributions to Protocol Buffers, MapReduce, BigTable, Spanner, and other systems infrastructure, has <u>increased the output of</u> other engineers at Google by over an order of magnitude.* (Para. 11)

In the abovementioned examples, synonyms such as "*address the need, or solve the problems*", "*maximize, increase, grow, or amplify your impact*", and "*multiply or increase the output*" make expressions in the passage more unique and diverse. On the other hand, the conversion of one part of speech to another is also a striking feature in English articles.

1. Read the following sentences and try to interpret the meaning of the underlined words with a synonym. Then form a new sentence based on using the same word in a different part of speech.

(1) Japan has announced it will release more than 1 m tonnes of contaminated water from the wrecked Fukushima nuclear power plant into the sea, a decision that has <u>angered</u> neighboring countries, including China, and local fishers.

(2) The accord is also a coup for China, by far the biggest market in the region with more than 1.3 billion people, allowing Beijing to cast itself as a <u>champion</u> of globalization and multilateral cooperation and giving it greater influence over rules governing regional trade.

(3) In Thursday's statement, officials pledged to stick to the strategy of <u>boosting</u> domestic demand and opening up the economy over the next five years.

(4) Relativism develops when science is <u>divorced</u> from method and viewed as just another claim in the market place of ideas.

(5) The communique published by state media following a four-day closed-door meeting didn't specify the pace of growth policy makers would <u>target</u>.

(6) China is aiming to <u>halt</u> the rise in its carbon dioxide emissions before 2030 and to achieve carbon neutrality before 2060.

Text B

What If You Don't Want to Manage in Tech?

1. Is staying a software engineer your whole life a good career choice? Or must you transition into management to continue climbing the engineering ladder? That's what engineers recently wondered on Quora, and it's an important question worth addressing, particularly for those not psyched about managing people.

2. The good news is that staying a software engineer and **opting** out of management is a fine career choice. If you want to **bypass** the glass ceiling, however, don't expect years of technical experience alone to carry you up the career ladder. As a rough model, your career success and growth are **proportional** to the value you create.

3. One of the biggest career mistakes that engineers—particularly those who opt out of management—make is to **equate** technical ability plus experience with increased impact.

They hold onto a belief that if they continue to do good work, they'll eventually be rewarded with a promotion. That mental model is **flawed** for two reasons.

4. First, your technical ability to write code and build software **plateaus** over time. As time goes on, you become more proficient at coding and software design and make fewer mistakes. Your early promotions up the initial **rungs** of the career ladder reflect your early technical learning. By year 10, you'll still learn—and you might still be picking up new programming frameworks and languages—but your progress and improvement aren't going to be as **dramatic** as it was in year 1.

5. Second, experience doesn't directly translate into impact. If ten or twenty years from now, you're still solving the same scale and scope of problems as you're tackling today, then you haven't increased your ability to create impact. And if you're not creating more value, why would any employer pay you more than someone without that experience?

6. It can be easy, comfortable, and even fun to keep doing what you've been doing—and it can be a reasonable lifestyle decision if you'd rather spend your energy elsewhere —but you shouldn't then also expect your career to grow on its own. What matters isn't the number of years of experience but how much value you create. To keep growing your career, you have to keep finding new ways to increase your impact.

7. Transitioning into management is one way—but not the only way—to grow a successful career. Many engineers become managers because management provides an obvious and well-defined **leverage** point to scale impact. Management, however, is not the only path for career growth, nor is every strong engineer well-suited to becoming a manager. As long as you can find other leverage points to **amplify** your impact, your career will continue to grow. Most large companies where technology plays a strong role, such as Google, Amazon, Microsoft, etc., will also have a well-defined technical career track to recognize that other leverage points exist besides management. Climbing that ladder to become a staff or principal engineer, however, is where many engineers struggle.

8. So what's the secret to growing your career without becoming a manager? The key observation is that while your technical programming ability may plateau, the impact of your technical contributions doesn't have to. Your ability to decide where to spend your efforts to maximize your impact—what code to write, what software to build, and which business problems to tackle—is unbounded.

9. So how do you grow your impact as a software engineer without becoming a manager? You identify and solve problems that are core to the business, or you enable those around you to more effectively solve those core business problems. When the hours you put in directly translate into meaningful and **measurable** results, when your efforts directly move growth and revenue metrics, your employer is **incentivized** to give you more resources and

flexibility so that you can achieve bigger results faster.

10. Here are some examples of how you might amplify your impact without going into management, based on software engineers I know.

11. You build tools and **abstractions** that **multiply** the output of the engineering teams around you. For example, Jeff Dean, through his contributions to Protocol Buffers, MapReduce, BigTable, Spanner, and other systems **infrastructure**, has increased the output of other engineers at Google by over an order of **magnitude**. It's no wonder why Google created the engineering level of Senior Google Fellow essentially for him.

12. You develop sufficient **expertise** to consult on software or experiment designs from other engineering teams, and your feedback is valuable enough that it **shaves** days' or weeks' worth of work or turns key projects from failures into successes.

13. You become an expert in a deep, technical field that is material to a growing company. For example, you become a machine learning expert and then work on news feed ranking at Facebook, ads ranking at Google, or search ranking at Airbnb. The projects you ship directly translate into growth and revenue for the company.

14. You identify a critical business opportunity, perhaps by working with the sales and business teams, and you become part of the founding team within the company to build out a product to address that need.

15. You build out **onboarding** and **mentoring** programs to teach and train other engineers, and you make them significantly more valuable members of the team.

16. You make significant contributions to building the engineering brand for your company. For example, if diversity is a strong part of your engineering brand, you may move forward with the state of diversity in hiring in the industry.

17. These are just a few examples of how you can increase your impact, but the possible paths are **limitless**. Notice that in none of these paths, is building software an end goal—rather, it is a means of helping the team and the business succeed.

18. Focus on what creates the most value. Your career success and growth will follow.

(964 words)

New words

| opt | /ɒpt/ | v. | to choose one thing or do one thing instead of another 选择；挑选 |
| bypass | /ˈbaɪˌpɑːs/ | v. | 1. to go around a town or other busy place rather than through it 避开；绕……而行 2. to avoid obeying a rule, |

system, or sb. in an official position 绕过（规定、制度或某个官员）

proportional	/prəˈpɔːʃənəl/	a.	sth. is in the correct or most suitable relationship to it in size, amount, importance, etc. 成比例的；相称的
equate	/ɪˈkweɪt/	v.	to consider that two things are similar or connected 等同
flaw	/flɔː/	n.	1. ~ *(in sth.)* a mistake in sth. that means that it is not correct or does not work correctly 错误；缺点 2. ~ *(in sth.)* a crack or fault in sth. that makes it less attractive or valuable 裂痕；裂隙；瑕疵 3. ~ *(in sb./sth.)* a weakness in sb.'s character（性格上的）弱点；缺点
		v.	to add a flaw or blemish to 使有缺陷
plateau	/ˈplætəʊ/	n.	1. a large area of flat land that is higher than the land around it 高原 2. a period during which the level of sth. does not change, especially after a period when it was increasing 平稳时期（尤指增长后的）稳定期
		vi.	if sth. plateaus, it reaches and then stays at a particular level 达到稳定水平（或时期、状态）
rung	/rʌŋ/	n.	1. one of the bars that form the steps of a ladder 梯子的横档；梯级 2. (*infml.*) a particular level of position in an organization or system（组织或体制中的）等级、地位
dramatic	/drəˈmætɪk/	a.	1. great and sudden 巨大而突然的；急剧的 2. intended to be impressive, so that people notice 引人注目的；给人深刻印象的
leverage	/ˈliːvərɪdʒ/	n.	1. influence that you can use to make people do what you want 影响 2. the action, power, or use of a lever 杠杆作用；杠杆力量；杠杆的使用
amplify	/ˈæmplɪˌfaɪ/	v.	1. to increase the effects or strength of sth. 增强 2. to explain sth. that you have said by giving more information about it 详述；（进一步）阐述
measurable	/ˈmeʒərəbəl/	a.	1. that can be measured 可测量的；可度量的 2. [usually before noun] large enough to be noticed or to have a clear and noticeable effect 显著的；有明显影响的
incentivize	/ɪnˈsentɪvaɪz/	v.	to encourage sb. to work harder, start a new activity, etc. 刺激；鼓励
abstraction	/æbˈstrækʃən/	n.	1. a general idea about a type of situation, thing, or person rather than a specific example from real life 抽象概念 2. when you do not notice what is happening around you

			because you are thinking carefully about sth. else 心不在焉；出神
multiply	/'mʌltɪˌplaɪ/	v.	to increase by a large amount or number, or to make sth. do this （使）大大增加；（使）倍增
infrastructure	/'ɪnfrəˌstrʌktʃə/	n.	the basic systems and structures that a country or organization needs in order to work properly, for example, roads, railways, banks, etc. 基础设施（如公路、铁路、银行等）；基础结构
magnitude	/'mægnɪˌtjuːd/	n.	the great size or importance of sth. 巨大；庞大；重要性
expertise	/ˌekspɜːˈtiːz/	n.	special skills or knowledge in a particular subject, that you learn by experience or training 专门技能（知识）
shave	/ʃeɪv/	v.	to make the price slightly smaller or the record time slightly shorter 减去；削减；略降（价格等）
onboarding	/ɒnˈbɔːdɪŋ/	a.	the mechanism through which new employees acquire the necessary knowledge, skills, and behaviors to become effective organizational members and insiders 新员工入职培训
mentoring	/'mentərɪŋ/	n.	a system where people with a lot of experience, knowledge, etc. advise and help other people at work or young people preparing for work 职业辅导制度
limitless	/'lɪmɪtləs/	a.	without end, limit or boundary 无限制的；无界限的；无限度的；无止境的

New expressions

be worth doing sth.	used to say that sth. is interesting, useful or helpful 值得做某事
opt out of sth.	1. to avoid doing a duty 躲避尽责 2. to decide not to be part of a group or system 决定不参与；决定退出
glass ceiling	the attitudes and practices that prevent women or particular groups from getting high level jobs, even though there are no actual laws or rules to stop them （指妇女或某一群体的人在职务晋升上遇到的）无形障碍；无形顶障
career ladder	a series of levels which sb. moves ups and down within a profession （职业中逐渐晋升的）阶梯；途径
equate sth. with sth.	to consider that two things are similar or connected 把……和……等同起来

be rewarded with sth.	to achieve sth. through hard work and effort 酬谢；奖赏某人
order of magnitude	a degree in a continuum of size or quantity 程度；规模
it is little/no wonder that...	it is not surprising 不足为奇；难怪
consult sb. about sth.	to ask for information or advice from someone because it is their job to know sth. 向某人咨询；请教
shave sth. off sth.	if you shave a small amount off sth. such as a price or a record, you make the price slightly smaller or the record time slightly shorter 略减；削减

Notes

1. Quora (知乎网): a question-and-answer website where questions are created, answered, edited and organized by its community of users. The company was founded in June 2009, and the website was made available to the public on June 21, 2010. Quora aggregates questions and answers to topics. Users can collaborate by editing questions and suggesting edits to other users' answers.

2. Protocol Buffers: Google's language-neutral, platform-neutral, extensible mechanism for serializing structured data.

3. MapReduce: a patented software framework introduced by Google to support distributed computing on large data sets on clusters of computers.

4. BigTable: a compressed, high performance, and proprietary database system built on Google File System (GFS), Chubby Lock Service, SSTable and a few other Google programs; it is currently not distributed or used outside of Google, although Google offers access to it as part of their Google App Engine.

5. Spanner: Google's scalable, multiversion, globally distributed, and synchronously replicated database. It is the first system to distribute data at a global scale and support externally-consistent distributed transactions.

6. Airbnb: a website for people to rent out lodging. Founded in August 2008 and headquartered in San Francisco, California, the company is privately owned and operated by Airbnb, Inc. Every property is associated with a host whose profile includes recommendations by other users, reviews by previous guests, as well as a response rating and private messaging system.

Reading comprehension

Understanding the text

1. **Identify whether the following statements are true (T) or false (F).**

   (1) The main idea of the passage is to offer suggestions on how employees amplify their impact without going into management.

   (2) Technical experience alone is enough to bypass the glass ceiling and climb the career ladder in software engineering.

   (3) As time goes on, a software engineer's technical ability and proficiency in coding and software design will continue to improve dramatically.

   (4) The secret to growing employees' careers without becoming a manager lies in identifying and solving problems that are core to the business.

   (5) Both employees' technical programming ability and the impact of their technical contributions may plateau over time.

   (6) Google's creation of the engineering level of Senior Google Fellow was dedicated to Jeff Dean's great contributions.

   (7) Employees have to identify a critical business opportunity instead of working with the sales and business teams.

   (8) Although a few examples demonstrate how employees can increase their impact, the possible paths are unbounded.

Critical thinking

2. **Work in pairs and discuss the following questions.**

   (1) To your knowledge, what's the secret to growing your career without becoming a manager?

   (2) How do you amplify your impact without going into management?

   (3) How do you interpret the conclusion that the possible paths of increasing the impact are limitless?

Unit 7 Get Advancement in IT

 **Language focus**

Words in use

3. Fill in the blanks with the words given below. Change the form where necessary. Each word can be used only once.

infrastructure	proportional	dramatic	plateau	bypass
incentivize	magnitude	amplify	leverage	expertise

(1) A new road now _____ the town.

(2) COVID-19 has accelerated the growth in the digital economy through a(n) _____ increase in working from home, online shopping, digital entertainment, and online services, among other areas.

(3) The fee charged by the realtor is directly _____ to the price of the property.

(4) The problem is of the same order of _____ for all concerned.

(5) Years of civil war have wrecked the country's _____ and destroyed its social fabric.

(6) Inflation rates have reached a(n) _____ after the economic recession.

(7) While there is no doubt that the pandemic has _____ the adoption of new technologies, technological advancements have already changed the world over the last two decades.

(8) His position as mayor gives him _____ to get things done.

(9) All the applicants for the post had the relevant _____ to do the job.

(10) The chance of promotion is supposed to _____ many employees.

Expressions in use

4. Fill in the blanks with the expressions given below. Change the form where necessary. Each expression can be used only once.

equate... with...	order of magnitude	transition into	worth doing
consult... about...	shave... off...	opt out of	be rewarded with...

(1) An increasing number of people are _____ their accountants _____ the tax laws.

(2) This bill is an important step towards helping those veterans _____ the workforce.

(3) Some parents _____ education _____ exam success.

(4) The team has worked hard and their efforts have _____ success.

(5) The beautiful scenic spot is _____ an appointment before you go.

(6) Today there is a growing tendency for people to _____ politics.

(7) That was a problem but this crisis is of a different _____.

(8) She _____ half a second _____ the world record.

Sentence structure

5. **Analyze the sentences by means of learning the predicative clause: "subject + be + that...; this may be because...; it is/was as if...; it looked as though...". Then translate each sentence into Chinese.**

Model:	His argument is that the unusual history of these people has subjected them to unique evolutionary pressures that have resulted in this paradoxical state of affairs.
Analysis:	The main structure of the sentence is "subject be predicative", that is, "his argument is that...". In the clause, the main structure is "the history has subjected them to pressures...". An attributive clause is included in the predicative clause with the antecedent "pressures" serving as the subject in the clause.
Translation:	他认为这些人群不同寻常的历史使得他们承受了独特的进化压力，从而导致了这种矛盾的状态。

(1) The trouble is that part of the recent acceleration is due to the usual rebound that occurs at this point in a business cycle, and so is not conclusive evidence of a revival in the underlying trend.

   Analysis: _____

   Translation: _____

(2) This may be because some people do not have the genes necessary to generate particular smell receptors in the nose.

   Analysis: _____

   Translation: _____

Unit 7 Get Advancement in IT

(3) For a while, it looked as though the making of semiconductors, which America had invented and which sat at the heart of the new computer age, was going to be the next casualty.

Analysis: _____

Translation: _____

(4) The reality of life in the present world is that although most American women now have an equal say in the decisions affecting the family, they sometimes earn less than men for the same work.

Analysis: _____

Translation: _____

(5) However, the difficulty with the evidence produced by these studies, fascinating as they are in collecting together anecdotes and apparent similarities and exceptions, is that they are not what we would today call norm-referenced.

Analysis: _____

Translation: _____

(6) One reason why it is hard to design and teach such courses is that they cut across the insistence that liberal-arts education and professional education should be kept separate, and taught in different schools.

Analysis: _____

Translation: _____

 # Collocation

> The cholera *pandemic* of the early 1830s hit France hard. It wiped out nearly 3% of Parisians in a month, and hospitals were overwhelmed by patients whose *ailments* doctors could not explain. The end of the *plague* prompted an economic revival, with France following Britain into an industrial revolution. (*English Digest*, September 2021)
>
> China can and should be involved as a full partner in *tackling* these challenges. Europe is right to engage actively, deeply and constructively with China, while also *attending to* its abiding and admirable concerns about human rights around the world. (*English Digest*, March 2021)

> Your ability to decide where to spend your efforts to *maximize* your impact—what code to write, what software to build, and which business problems to tackle—is *unbounded*. These are just a few examples of how you can *increase* your impact, but the possible paths are *limitless*. (Text B)

6. **Choose the correct words of synonyms in the following sentences with the words provided in the box to form collocations you have learned from this unit.**

| highlight | vulnerable | accelerate | harbor |
| amplify | jeopardize | credit | foretell |

(1) As he predicted, wireless communications have had world-changing effects.

(2) In fashion folklore, Gabrielle Chanel is famously acclaimed as the designer who popularized trousers, making them a key piece in women's wardrobes.

(3) While there is no doubt that the pandemic is growing the adoption of new technologies, technological advancements have already changed the world over the past two decades, from living standards to the very nature of our work.

(4) Medical and scientific responses to past crises suggest that urgency may also result in compromised research quality and ethics, which may in turn undermine public faith in government and science, waste precious resources and lead to the loss of human life.

(5) What must be reaffirmed is that in science, doubt is not a(n) frailty but a strength.

(6) *Bookshop.org*, which launched in the US earlier this year, has promoted UK plans and goes online this week in partnership with more than 130 shops.

(7) China unveiled the first glimpses of its economic plans for the next five years, promising to build the nation into a technological powerhouse as it emphasized quality growth over speed.

(8) Utopia Planitia is a rather bland expanse of rock-strewn sand—decent for spacecraft landings but decidedly subpar for addressing cutting-edge research questions, such as whether Mars shelters past or present life.

Translation

7. Translate the following passage into English.

华为的 5G 设备物美价廉，目前领先于许多竞争对手。华为产品的高性能得益于多年来在研发上的巨额投入、规模经济效应以及在中国数字市场上的边干边学。用一名美国联邦通信委员会成员的话来说，"拥有 5G 的国家将拥有相关创新并为世界其他国家设定标准，而那个国家目前不太可能是美国。"

Unit project

Make a career plan.

> This unit is about how to make a proper career plan for IT engineers, especially for those who have worked in this field for a period of time. Based on this theme, you are now asked to make a career plan. To complete the project, you can follow the steps below.

(1) Try to understand the major considerations in career planning.

- Make a self-assessment
  - ✓ interest
  - ✓ ability
  - ✓ personal quality
  - ✓ occupational value
  - ✓ advantage and disadvantage

- Make a career analysis
  - ✓ economic condition
  - ✓ family expectation
  - ✓ industry analysis
  - ✓ career outlook
  - ✓ opportunity and threat in the external environment
- Set your goals
  - ✓ short-term goal
  - ✓ mid-term goal
  - ✓ long-term goal
- Adjust the plan and check
  - ✓ Assessment
  - ✓ Feedback

(2) Work in groups or pairs discussing the definition, function and importance of career planning. Summarize the main points and make a presentation of them.

(3) Suppose you have just started your job as an entry-level software engineer in an IT company, and make a five-year career plan. Talk about your plan with your classmates and present it to the whole class.

Unit 8

Why Corporate Culture Counts

Learning objectives

In this unit you will:

- learn about the importance of corporate culture;
- learn how to read corporate culture;
- learn how to write an essay with paragraph coherence and unity;
- learn how to use passive voice.

> Being a great place to work is the difference between being a good company and a great company.
>
> —Brian Kristofek
>
> Corporate culture is the only sustainable competitive advantage that is completely within the control of the entrepreneur.
>
> —David Cummings

Preview

Corporate culture encompasses the beliefs and behaviors that determine how a company and its employees interact and how they work with customers. Successful companies have distinct cultures that reflect the values of their founders and the focus of the business they're building. A healthy culture empowers employees to view themselves as part of a team and their work as integral to that team's success, while signs of a bad culture can include high turnover, tardiness and indifferent or unmotivated employees. Many corporate cultures are implied rather than defined. They develop over time from the cumulative traits of employees. Understanding why its culture works enables a corporation to hire the right people—and to avoid the wrong ones.

So what rites or rituals does corporate culture include? What role does corporate culture play in a great company's development? Why do successful corporations in the world tend to prioritize maintaining culture? If you are to work in an international company after graduation, how will you prepare yourself to attach importance to the potential value of corporate culture? What specific advice or effective strategies will you offer to the top leaders to help your company build a winning culture?

Section A

 Pre-reading activities

1. **Listen to the interviews of the staff in Apple Inc. on the critical role that company culture played in Apple's success and answer the following questions.**

    (1) According to the interview, what difference does Apple Inc. make compared to other companies in the world?

    (2) What core values have been deeply instilled into the culture of Apple Inc.?

    (3) From the interviews, can you summarize the fundamental traits that hold the secret to entrepreneurial success?

2. **Work in pairs and discuss the following questions.**

    (1) What are the essential ingredients that constitute a great corporate culture?

    (2) A strong company culture can propel a business from the verge of bankruptcy to breathtaking heights in just a few years. Do you agree or disagree with this idea? And why?

    (3) What is the subtle relationship between corporate culture and the leadership of the company? Please illustrate your points with a specific example such as Microsoft, Dell, Lenovo, etc.

Text A

Five Dangerous Myths About Corporate Culture

1. It is a great thing that corporate and **institutional** leaders are starting to talk about culture. The next step is to stop thinking about culture as an object, something they can **manipulate** with an email message or an employee lunch.

2. Organizational culture is the fuel that drives any team's success. It reflects the **implicit** values, norms and behaviors of an organization. It doesn't matter whether the team is trying

to reach the **summit** of a mountain in the Himalayas or put on a Broadway show. The team energy is the whole **enchilada**. If people don't care about you or their work, you can't **flog** them to care or even reward them enough to care.

3. The good news is that people naturally care about their work, if they feel that they are part of the mission. If they are respected and listened to and given the **latitude** to do their jobs their own way, they will care. Your job as a leader is to take away the **hindrances** that keep people from feeling connected to their own power sources.

4. If you want a great culture, your team members have to trust you. You have to win their trust. You can't "policy" your way to a healthy culture. You can't measure your way there, either. Policies and **yardsticks** hurt your culture.

5. Here are five dangerous myths about corporate culture. These myths get in the way of your organization. You can push a button and change the price on an SKU or **shift** the load on your server. But you can't press a button and change your culture.

6. You have to **soften** and be honest to get your employees to trust you. You have to trust them. That is a hard thing for a lot of leaders to do. We get lazy when we don't have to live in the **gritty**, human world—when we can stay locked away in the halls of made-up management theory. We think that our policies and **forecasts** will protect us from having to deal with **sticky** human topics, but sticky human topics are the very things that make or break a culture.

7. The first dangerous myth about corporate culture is the myth that culture is a nice thing to have, but **incidental** to your success in the marketplace. Until your culture is front and center for your leaders at every level, you can expect the exact same result you're getting now.

8. Secondly, when you **delude** yourself that you can control your culture through pay and benefits policies, you **misapprehend** the nature of culture. The **carrot-and-stick** mindset comes from the Machine Age idea that employers can get employees to do whatever they want them to do through rewards and punishments. The mindset itself is **insulting** and anti-human.

9. People are not donkeys. You can push and **prod** them and give them cupcakes when

they do a good job but doing so **demeans** them, and you. If you believe in yourself enough to believe in your people, take away whatever is **impeding** your team from charging down the field as fast as they want to go. It might be stupid rules or a **moribund** decision-making process that is in their way.

10. It might be the **undercurrent** of fear that keeps people from sharing their good ideas. Figure out which energy blocker is in your team's way and remove it. Pay people fairly and then forget about pay and focus on the energy in your shop.

11. The third dangerous myth lies in the fact that we think we can manage our company's culture from on high. We send out insulting Employee Engagement Surveys when we should be interacting with team members personally every chance we get, and many times every day. If you believe in the power of corporate culture, you start by living your own values.

12. You ease up on the yardsticks and punishments for insignificant **infractions**. You back off on fear-based policies that treat your employees like children or criminals. You don't manage corporate culture—you allow it to **flourish** by removing the artificial barriers that keep your teammates from bringing themselves to work.

13. Fourthly, HR programs don't make your culture great. HR programs are **nifty**, but they sit on top of a healthy, trusting culture. They can't create it. You have to start by telling the truth about what's not working in your organization right now. You have to get the elephants out on the table and talk about them, no matter how sticky or uncomfortable they are. You have to give up the idea that the company is in charge and the employees are **interchangeable** parts of the machine. That is an outdated idea that will keep your organization locked down and **stuck** and unhappy as long as you **cling** to it.

14. Finally, the point of your culture-building activities, words and actions is not to please your investors next quarter. The point of creating a great culture is to build a healthy organization that will bend and **flex** with the market and keep responding faster than your competitors can do.

15. You will feel the great culture in your company when you walk in the door and your customers will talk about it. You will see it in your financial reports, but your cultural awakening won't be a project about "improving productivity" unless we expand our definition of "productivity" to mean "creating healthy and **sustainable** growth".

16. The notion of "employee performance" is itself a dangerous myth. Passion on your team **resembles** an energy field made of **subatomic particles** of goodwill and creativity. The energy field is all around us but if you try to measure the individual particles, the reading makes no sense. Culture is an energy field. If you want to create a great culture, you have to focus on the waves **swelling** and crashing around you and ignore the particles.

(974 words)

New words

institutional	/ˌɪnstɪˈtjuːʃənəl/	a.	[usu. before noun] connected with an institution 机构的；慈善机构的
manipulate	/məˈnɪpjʊˌleɪt/	vt.	to control or influence sb./sth., often in a dishonest way so that they do not realize it（暗中）控制；操纵；影响
implicit	/ɪmˈplɪsɪt/	a.	1. suggested or understood without being stated directly 含蓄的；未言明的 2. (fml.) forming a central part of something, but without being openly stated 隐含其中的；不明言的
summit	/ˈsʌmɪt/	n.	[C] 1. the highest point of sth., especially the top of a mountain 最高点；（尤指）山顶 2. an official meeting or series of meetings between the leaders of two or more governments at which they discuss important matters（政府间的）首脑会议；峰会
enchilada	/ˌentʃɪˈlɑːdə/	n.	[C] 1. *the big ~*: (infml.) sth. that is the most important or biggest of its type 头等大事 2. *the whole ~*: (infml.) all of sth. 整件事情；全部细节
flog	/flɒɡ/	vt.	1. to punish sb. by hitting them many times with a whip or stick 鞭笞；棒打（作为惩罚） 2. *~ sth. (to sb.)* (Brit. infml.) to sell sth. (to sb.) 卖（给某人）某物
latitude	/ˈlætɪˌtjuːd/	n.	[U] 1. the distance of a place north or south of the equator (= the line around the world dividing north and south), measured in degrees 纬度 2. (fml.) freedom to choose what you do or the way that you do it（选择做什么事情或做事方式的）自由
hindrance	/ˈhɪndrəns/	n.	[C, U] *~ (to sth./sb.)* thing or person that hinders 起妨碍作用的事物或人
yardstick	/ˈjɑːdˌstɪk/	n.	[C] a standard used for judging how good or successful sth. is（好坏或成败的）衡量标准；准绳；尺度
shift	/ʃɪft/	v.	1. to move, or move sth., from one position or place to another 转移；挪动 2. (of a situation, an opinion, a policy, etc.) to change from one state, position, etc. to another（情况、意见、政策等）变换；更替；变动 3. to change your opinion of or attitude towards sth., or change the way that you do sth. 改变观点（或态度、做事方式等）
soften	/ˈsɒfən/	v.	1. to become or to make sb./sth. more sympathetic and less severe or critical 使（态度）缓和；变温和；变宽厚

2. to reduce the force or the unpleasant effects of sth. 减轻；减缓；削弱

gritty	/'grɪti/	a.	1. showing the courage and determination to continue doing sth. difficult or unpleasant 有勇气的；坚定的；坚毅的 2. showing sth. unpleasant as it really is（对消极事物的描述）逼真的；真实的；活生生的
forecast	/'fɔːkɑːst/	n.	[C] a statement about what will happen in the future, based on information that is available now 预报；预测
		vt.	to say what you think will happen in the future based on the information that you have now 预测；预报
sticky	/'stɪki/	a.	1. made of or covered in a substance that sticks to things that touch it 黏（性）的 2. (infml.) difficult or unpleasant 难办的；棘手的；让人为难的
incidental	/ˌɪnsɪ'dentəl/	a.	1. small and relatively unimportant; minor 小的而较不重要的；次要的 2. accompanying, but not a major part of sth.; supplementary 伴随的；补充的 3. [pred.] ~ (to sth.) liable to occur because of sth. or in connection with sth. 易伴随发生；因相关而产生
delude	/dɪ'luːd/	vt.	to make sb. believe sth. that is not true 欺骗；哄骗
misapprehend	/ˌmɪsæprɪ'hend/	vt.	to interpret in the wrong way 误会；误解
carrot-and-stick	/'kærət ənd stɪk/	a.	rewarding people if they agree to do sth. and punishing them if they refuse to do it 软硬兼施的；威逼利诱的
insulting	/ɪn'sʌltɪŋ/	a.	very rude and offensive to someone 侮辱的；无礼的；污蔑的
prod	/prɒd/	v.	~ sb. (into/doing sth.) (infml.) (try to) make (a slow or unwilling person) do sth.; to urge（试图）促使或推动（某人）做某事；激励
demean	/dɪ'miːn/	vt.	1. to do sth. that makes people have less respect for you 降低身份；失去尊重 2. to make people have less respect for sb./sth. 贬低；贬损；使失去尊严
impede	/ɪm'piːd/	vt.	(fml.) to delay or stop the progress of sth. 阻碍；阻止
moribund	/'mɒrɪbʌnd/	a.	1. (of an industry, an institution, a custom, etc.) no longer effective and about to come to an end completely（企业、机构、习俗等）行将灭亡的；即将倒闭的；濒于崩溃的 2. in a very bad condition; dying 垂死的；濒临死亡的

undercurrent	/ˈʌndəˌkʌrənt/	n.	[C] 1. a current below the surface of a fluid 暗流；潜流 2. a feeling, especially a negative one, that is hidden but whose effects are felt 潜在的情绪（尤指负面的）
infraction	/ɪnˈfrækʃən/	n.	[C, U] (fml.) an act of breaking a rule or law 犯规；违法
flourish	/ˈflʌrɪʃ/	vi.	1. to develop quickly and be successful or common 繁荣；昌盛；兴旺 2. to grow well; to be healthy and happy 茁壮成长；健康幸福
nifty	/ˈnɪftɪ/	a.	1. skillful and accurate 有技巧的；精确的 2. practical; working well 实用的；灵便的
interchangeable	/ˌɪntəˈtʃeɪndʒəbəl/	a.	that can be exchanged, especially without affecting the way in which sth. works 可交换的；可互换的
stuck	/stʌk/	a.	1. unable to move or to be moved 动不了的；无法移动的；卡住的 2. in an unpleasant situation or place that you cannot escape from 陷入；困于 3. not knowing what to do in a particular situation 不知所措；(为某事)犯愁
cling	/klɪŋ/	vi.	(pt., pp. clung) 1. ~ (on) to sb./sth.; ~ on; ~ together to hold on tightly to sb./sth. 紧抓住或抱住某人/某物 2. ~ (on) to sth. to be unwilling to abandon sth.; to refuse to give sth. up 舍不得放弃某事物；拒绝放弃某事物
flex	/fleks/	vt.	to bend, move or stretch an arm or a leg, or contract a muscle, especially in order to prepare for a physical activity 屈伸；活动（四肢或肌肉，尤指为准备体力活动）
sustainable	/səˈsteɪnəbəl/	a.	1. involving the use of natural products and energy in a way that does not harm the environment（对自然资源和能源的利用）不破坏生态平衡的；合理利用的 2. that can continue or be continued for a long time 可持续的
resemble	/rɪˈzembəl/	v.	to look like or be similar to another person or thing 看起来像；显得像；像
subatomic	/ˌsʌbəˈtɒmɪk/	a.	[usu. before noun] (physics) smaller than, or found in, an atom（化学）亚原子的；比原子小的；原子内的
particle	/ˈpɑːtɪkəl/	n.	[C] 1. a very small piece of sth. 颗粒；微粒 2. (physics) a very small piece of matter, such as a photon, an electron or a proton, that is part of an atom 粒子
swell	/swel/	v.	1. to become bigger or rounder 膨胀；肿胀 2. to increase or make sth. increase in number or size（使）增加；增大；扩大

New expressions

take away	to make a feeling, pain, etc. disappear 解除；消除（感情、痛苦等）
get in the way	to prevent sb. from doing sth., or prevent sth. from happening 阻止某事发生
lock sth./sb. away	1. to put sth. in a safe place and lock the door, lid, etc. 将……锁藏起来 2. to put sb. in prison 把……关进监狱
front and center	in or into the most important position 在（或进入）最重要位置
from on high	from sb. in a position of authority 来自上级的；来自高层的
interact with sb./sth.	1. to communicate with sb. especially while you work, play or spend time with them 与某人交流；沟通 2. if one thing interacts with another, if two things interact, the two things have an effect on each other 相互影响；相互作用
in charge	in the position of having control or responsibility for a group of people or an activity 主管；掌管；负责
back off	to stop supporting sth., or decide not to do sth. you were planning to do 退出；放弃
cling to sth.	to continue to believe or do sth., even though it may not be true or useful any longer 坚持；墨守（某事物）
make sense	1. to have a clear meaning that you can easily understand 有道理；有意义；易于理解 2. to be a sensible thing to do 是明智的；合乎情理的

Notes

1. Himalayas（喜马拉雅山脉）: a mountain range in Asia separating the plains of the Indian subcontinent from the Tibetan Plateau. The Himalayan range has the Earth's highest peaks, including the highest one.
2. Broadway（百老汇）: a road in New York of America. It is known widely as the heart of the American theater industry.
3. SKU (Stock Keeping Unit, 库存量单位): a distinct type of item for sale, such as a product or service, and all attributes associated with the item type that distinguishes it from other item types.

4. HR (Human Resources, 人力资源): the people who make up the workforce of an organization, business sector, or economy.

5. subatomic particles (次原子粒子，又称亚原子粒子): particles much smaller than atoms.

Reading comprehension

Understanding the text

1. Answer the following questions.

(1) According to the text, how can we define corporate culture?

(2) Why does company culture matter to employees?

(3) What are the prerequisites for obtaining a great culture for a company?

(4) What would the corporate leaders do to grow a warm and human culture?

(5) Why might it be stupid for leaders to control corporate culture?

(6) What does "elephant" mean in the company? What kinds of negative effects do they exert on the corporate development?

(7) How do you understand the metaphor that "culture is an energy field"?

(8) What strategies can the companies utilize to tackle the dangerous myths?

Critical thinking

2. Work in pairs and discuss the following questions.

(1) Why does corporate culture stand out as one of the key components that are essential to the development of a great company?

(2) What is the relationship between corporate culture and company development? Do you believe or disbelieve culture plays a decisive role in its development?

(3) Researchers and consultants often point out that real change in how things are done inside a corporation cannot happen unless its culture is changed first. Do you think that corporate culture is a difficult thing to pin down and even harder to change?

(4) A great corporate culture assures that it is molded by the creativity of the employees from the bottom up, rather than by mandate from the top down. How do you interpret this very notion?

Word building

The prefix *mis-* combines with verbs or nouns to form verbs or nouns. Nouns formed in this way refer to "being bad or wrong, badly or wrongly".

Examples

Words learned	Add *mis-*	New words formed
interpret	→	misinterpret
construe	→	misconstrue
calculate	→	miscalculate
apprehend	→	misapprehend
representation	→	misrepresentation

The prefix *out-* combines with verbs to form verbs. Verbs formed in this way refer to "being greater, better, further, longer, etc".

Examples

Words learned	Add *out-*	New words formed
perform	→	outperform
smart	→	outsmart
grow	→	outgrow
last	→	outlast
play	→	outplay

3. Add *mis-* or *out-* to the following words to form new words.

Words learned	New words formed
mis-	
treat	
conduct	
judge	
handle	
behave	
out-	
number	
wit	

(continued)

Words learned	New words formed
live	
weigh	
shine	

4. Fill in the blanks with the newly-formed words in Activity 3. Change the form where necessary. Each word can be used only once.

(1) If found guilty of serious professional _____, he could be permanently erased from the medical register.

(2) Scientists know the body harbors trillions of such microorganisms—indeed, they _____ human cells 10 to 1.

(3) A spokesman denied that the police investigation had been _____.

(4) At present, we face unprecedented challenges and opportunities, but the opportunities _____ the challenges.

(5) They appear to have _____ the public mood on education.

(6) She went outside to talk to him, threatening all sorts of terrible punishments for anyone who _____ in her absence.

(7) There are some exceptions—parrots, seabirds, clams and tortoises which can all _____ us—but humans stand out as the longest-lived primates.

(8) Unfortunately, while there are many animal lovers in the world, there are also some people who _____ them.

(9) To win the presidency he first had to _____ his rivals within the Socialist Party.

(10) Shanghai hopes to _____ rivals Beijing and Hong Kong, but it also harbors a loftier ambition: to be the global capital of the 21st century.

Banked cloze

5. Fill in the blanks by selecting suitable words from the word bank. You may not use any of the words more than once.

A. disorganized	B. transforming	C. unpacks	D. ultimately	E. plastered
F. conversely	G. prevents	H. inconsistent	I. established	J. overestimated
K. asset	L. incentives	M. innovation	N. envisioned	O. transplanting

When Cholena Orr, director of Pac executive's human capital business, walks into the reception area of a workplace, she can tell you not only about that company's culture but also what kind of leader it has. Attentive and organized reception staff suggest a leader paying attention to investing in people, she says.

(1) _____, "if I walk into a(n) (2) _____ waiting room with a rude receptionist, I will go on to meet a company CEO who doesn't see people as their most important (3) _____, and who doesn't believe in training."

Orr adds, "Many leaders simply don't recognize just how much influence they have over their company's culture. Nor do they understand what culture is." That, she says, (4) _____ them from developing good approaches to creating and (5) _____ cultures.

Orr believes leaders shape culture and culture affects everything, from (6) _____ to recruiting and talent retention. When CEOs don't create culture, the culture will create itself, she says, and it's usually not what they had (7) _____.

Calling on business leaders to stop believing in common misconceptions, Orr (8) _____ her top five persistent myths about corporate culture. The most prevailing misconception among business leaders is that corporate culture is built much like a Disneyland theme park, where perks and "fun" are all that's needed for employees to work and live happily ever after.

Find out what truly motivates employees, she says, and match (9) _____ accordingly. If you ask seven different CEOs to define culture, you will receive seven different answers. Some will say culture is a "mood", others describe it as the shared values of a company's employees. Culture is not just the "vibe" you get when you walk into an office, nor is it the mission statement (10) _____ on the wall. Culture is how work gets done, says Orr. It shows up in the patterns, rituals and repeated behaviors of the people in the organization.

Structured analysis and writing

Structure analysis

Write an essay with paragraph coherence and unity

A coherent paragraph contains sentences that are logically arranged and that flow smoothly. And ties between old information and new information are highlighted to make the structure of ideas or arguments clear to the reader.

A well-written paragraph must have unity. That is, each paragraph is a block or unit of thought. It should present only one topic or one part of a topic. All the facts, examples, and reasons in a unified paragraph should explain this thought. Unity helps a writer speak clearly to a reader.

Now let's start with a brief structure analysis of Text A.

Introduction	Points out the topic: Corporate leaders began to realize the importance of organizational culture. But there are some misconceptions about corporate culture. The leaders are offered advice to build a great culture. (Paras.1–4) Brings out the thesis statement: There are five dangerous myths about the corporate culture which get in the way of your organization. (Para.5)
Body	Dangerous myth number one: Corporate culture doesn't matter. (Para. 7) Dangerous myth number two: It's all about pay and benefits. (Paras. 8–10) Dangerous myth number three: People can manage it from above. (Paras. 11–12) Dangerous myth number four: HR programs make culture great. (Para. 13) Dangerous myth number five: The point of culture-buildings is to please investors. (Paras. 14–15)
Conclusion	Concludes with a metaphor: Culture is an energy field. A great culture focuses on the waves swelling and crashing around you rather than the particles. (Para. 16)

In Text A, the structure of the text is clearly and logically presented. Five dangerous myths about the corporate culture which get in the way of the organization are respectively illustrated. In the body part, each paragraph interprets one misconception of corporate culture, achieving the effectiveness of coherence and unity of the whole text.

Structured writing

Read the sample essay and see how the essay is structured with paragraph coherence and unity.

Topic   Culture and leadership   **Introduction**   Culture and leadership are two sides of the same coin.

Unit 8 Why Corporate Culture Counts

Body

On the one hand, cultural norms define how a given nation or organization will define leadership.

On the other hand, it can be argued that the only thing of real importance that leaders do is to create and manage culture.

Conclusion

Leadership and culture are conceptually intertwined.

Sample essay

Culture and Leadership

When we examine culture and leadership closely, we see that they are two sides of the same coin; neither can really be understood by itself.

On the one hand, cultural norms define how a given nation or organization will define leadership—who will get promoted, and who will get the attention of followers.

On the other hand, it can be argued that the only thing of real importance that leaders do is to create and manage culture; that the unique talent of leaders is their ability to understand and work with culture; and that it is an ultimate act of leadership to destroy culture when it is viewed as dysfunctional.

Culture is the result of a complex group learning process that is only partially influenced by leader behavior. But if the group's survival is threatened because elements of its culture have become maladapted, it is ultimately the function of leadership at all levels of the organization to recognize and do something about this situation. It is in this sense that leadership and culture are conceptually intertwined.

6. Write an essay of no less than 200 words on one of the following topics. One topic has an outline that you can follow.

Topic

Key qualities a winner should own

Introduction

The three qualities a winner should own are intended to facilitate the journey to being a winner.

Body

A winner should highlight his uniqueness.

A winner should take a positive attitude toward life.

A winner should be full of confidence.

Conclusion

A winner should respond to life creatively and productively by being unique, positive and confident.

More topics:

- Key qualities of a great person who makes a difference in the world
- Common elements of creating a winning culture

 Translation

7. **Translate the following paragraph into Chinese.**

As we will see, many of these usages of the word "culture" display not only a superficial and incorrect view of culture, but also a dangerous tendency to evaluate particular cultures in an absolute way and to suggest that there actually are "right" cultures for organizations. As we will also see, whether or not a culture is "good" or "bad, functionally effective" or not, depends not on the culture alone, but on the relationship of the culture to the environment in which it exists. Perhaps the most intriguing aspect of culture as a concept is that it points to us phenomena that are below the surface, that are powerful in their impact but invisible and to a considerable degree unconscious. In that sense, culture is to a group what personality or character is to an individual. We can see the behavior that results, but often we cannot see the forces underneath that cause certain kinds of behavior. Yet, just as our personality and character guide and constrain our behavior, so does culture guide and constrain the behavior of members of a group through the shared norms that are held in that group.

8. Translate the following paragraph into English.

莫言出生在一个农民家庭,小学五年级都没有上完就辍学放牛了。那时他最大的特点是爱读书,在书荒的时代,他甚至反复诵读了一本仅有的《新华字典》。后来,他又读了大量的中国古典小说,加上喜欢听民间故事,特别是受齐鲁文化"泛神论"(pantheism)的影响,他对周围既熟悉又陌生的环境充满了奇特的想象,形成了他奇特的魔幻现实主义写作风格。最终莫言于2012年赢得了诺贝尔文学奖。莫言认为,"文学艺术永远不是唱赞歌的工具,而是应该暴露黑暗,揭示不公正"。在他看来,人性是多面的,好人身上也有缺陷,坏人身上亦有优点,优秀作品便应体现这些。

Section B

 Reading skills: *Passive voice*

When it comes to reading skills, sentences of passive voice and inversion are commonly used in the passage, which makes sentence patterns more diversified. Passive voice is used to indicate that the grammatical subject of the verb is the recipient of the action denoted by the verb. Passive sentences are usually used in news reports to highlight the actions of doers, such as "*woman killed by 4-year-old in Tennessee cookout*", emphasizing the action done by a 4-year-old child to draw readers' attention.

Let's read the following paragraphs in Text B and see how to identify the passive sentences in them.

Example 1

In a survey conducted earlier this year by Flexjobs, an employment site, culture was the most common reason people gave for quitting. A study published last year by Jason Sockin of the University of Pennsylvania found that workers rated things like respectfulness, work-life balance and morale as more important to job satisfaction than pay. (Para. 1)

Example 2

Offices are places where culture can be transmitted osmotically. Now that more workers are remote, firms increasingly write down their values. Justworks, an HR technology firm, subscribes to Camaraderie, Openness, Grit, Integrity and Simplicity. Lists like these can turn blandness into an art form, and are overly determined by what will create an acronym. They may not reflect what actually happens inside the company. Plenty of firms are characterized by Cluelessness, Rancor, Amateurism, Skiving and Stupidity, but you won't find that on the website. (Para. 3)

Example 3

Candidates seem to value this kind of information: a working paper published earlier this year by Jung Ho Choi of Stanford Graduate School of Business and his co-authors found that clickthrough rates for job postings rose for firms with higher diversity scores. (Para. 7)

The abovementioned examples show the diversity of passive wice forms. Some can serve as postpositive attributive, while some serve as active voices in a passive manner, and vice versa, such as "*The flower smells sweet*", "*The book is worth reading*", etc. In example 2, the phrase "*plenty of firms are characterized by...*" serves as an active sentence in a passive voice, which can be translated into Chinese, namely, "许多公司都具有……的特征。"

Fill in the blanks with appropriate words in the bracket by using passive voice. Change forms where necessary.

(1) President Xi Jinping's announcement of China's commitment at the recent United Nations General Assembly was doubly significant, given that the 2015 Paris climate agreement is _____ actively _____ by leaders of major governments, and _____ by inaction elsewhere, partly as a result of COVID-19. Although Xi did not elaborate in his speech on how the zero-carbon goal will _____, China has a track record of delivering on major initiatives in areas such as energy efficiency, renewables, pollution reduction, and poverty alleviation. But Xi's carbon-neutrality pledge is on a very different scale and must _____ in a different global context. (challenge; undermine; reach; fulfill)

(2) Initial details _____ by the Communist Party's Central Committee Thursday stressed the need for sustainable growth and also pledged to develop a robust domestic market. The communique _____ by state media following a four-day closed-door meeting didn't specify the pace of growth policy makers would target. (release; publish)

(3) Insider-dealing and manipulation rules also need to _____ to deal with new information flows. Price-sensitive data need to _____ widely available. And the plumbing must _____. (modernize; keep; renovate)

(4) Crutzen was indispensable to this scientific revolution. The concept of a planet that _____ on a geological scale had intermittently _____ for decades, even centuries, but never _____ seriously, and certainly not by the geologists. (human-dominate; moot; take)

(5) One of humanity's greatest achievements has been mastering routes across the world's oceans. Communities _____ by thousands of miles _____ into contact and religious ideas have spread across the waters, while artistic creativity _____ on by the experience of seeing the products of different civilizations. Customs have been decisively _____ by the movement of ships across the oceans. (separate; bring; spur; alter)

(6) In the 21st century, however, new factors have changed entirely the way goods are _____ across the seas, even though over 90% of world trade is carried on ships. Containerization means that goods can be _____ in Chicago and _____ in Warsaw without having to be unloaded at the port. The great port cities of the world have been _____ by automated docks full of gantries and cranes. (carry; load; unload; replace)

Text B

How to Read Corporate Culture?

1. Culture eats strategy for breakfast, runs the **aphorism**. It also **projectile vomits** employees who don't fit in. In a survey conducted earlier this year by Flexjobs, an employment site, culture was the most common reason people gave for quitting. And it matters more than high wages. A study published last year by Jason Sockin of the University of Pennsylvania found that workers rated things like **respectfulness**, work-life balance, and morale as more important to job satisfaction than pay.

2. The problem is that culture can be very hard to **fathom** from the outside. It resides in **quotidian** interactions between colleagues and in the hidden **threads** that bind decisions on everything from promotions to product development. You need to be inside an organization to really understand it. But more sunlight is getting in. Firms are doing more to signal what they stand for. Jobseekers have new ways to peer inside firms. So do investors, who share their interest in evaluating corporate culture.

3. Offices are places where culture can be transmitted **osmotically**. Now that more workers are remote, firms increasingly write down their values. Qualtrics, a software firm, may not believe in grammar but it does believe in "Transparent, All-in, Customer-obsessed, One-team and **Scrappy**". Justworks, an HR technology firm, subscribes to "Camaraderie, Openness, **Grit**, Integrity and Simplicity". Lists like these can turn **blandness** into an art form, and are **overly** determined by what will create an **acronym**. They may not reflect what actually happens inside the company. Plenty of firms are characterized by "Cluelessness,

Rancor, **Amateurism**, **Skiving**, and Stupidity", but you won't find that on the website.

4. But companies that **codify** their values are at least thinking about them. And their choices can offer meaningful clues. Kraken, a **cryptocurrency** exchange, sets out its beliefs in ten "Tentaclemandments". You need to see only that one word to know whether this is the workplace for you or whether you would rather be **hurled** into an active volcano.

5. Updates can also be instructive. In *ReCulturing*, a new book, Melissa Daimler lays out some of the changes that Dara Khosrowshahi made when he became CEO of Uber in 2017. The values of the previous **regime**, which included "Superpumped" and "Always be Hustlin", were **overhauled** for something a little less **hormonal**. The change from "**Meritocracy** and toe-stepping" to "We value ideas over hierarchy" told people something useful about the aspirations of the new leadership team.

6. Culture is increasingly readable in other ways, too. Since the pandemic, firms' policies on remote working have given outsiders greater clarity on how employers view issues like work-life balance. Under increasing pressure from employees to take stances, companies are likelier to offer opinions on political and social issues. Others go the other way: Coinbase, another crypto firm, has made it clear that it won't tolerate employee **activism** on subjects unrelated to its core mission. That's information, too.

7. Windows on cultural norms are being opened by regulators, who are pushing for greater disclosure about firms' workforces. Candidates seem to value this kind of information: a working paper published earlier this year by Jung Ho Choi of Stanford Graduate School of Business and his co-authors found that clickthrough rates for job postings rose for firms with higher diversity scores.

8. The behavior of CEOs used to be directly visible only to a limited number of people. Now bosses are everywhere, tweeting, posting and making **stilted** videos. In a recent survey by Brunswick Group, a PR firm, 82% of **respondents** said they would research the boss's social media accounts if they were considering joining a new firm. Even earnings calls offer insights. Academics at Columbia Business School and Harvard Business School have found that managers who invite colleagues to respond to analysts' questions on these calls are more likely to work in firms that have more **cohesive** leadership teams.

9. Employee-review sites like Glassdoor are another source of insight. These sites can be **distorted** by **embittered** ex-workers. But, says Kevin Oakes of the Institute for Corporate Productivity, a research **outfit**, they are also likely to contain "**slivers** of truth". And all these slivers add up. There is no **substitute** for being at a firm day in, day out, if you want to understand what it is really like. But the outlines of corporate culture are more **discernible** than ever. That ought to lead to fewer cases of **indigestion**.

(719 words)

New words

aphorism	/ˈæfəˌrɪzəm/	n.	(fml.) a short phrase that says sth. true or wise 格言；警句
projectile	/prəˈdʒektaɪl/	n.	1. an object, such as a bullet, that is fired from a gun or other weapon（武器发射的）投射物；枪弹；炮弹 2. any object that is thrown as a weapon（作为武器的）发射物；导弹
vomit	/ˈvɒmɪt/	v.	to bring food from the stomach back out through the mouth 呕吐
respectfulness	/rɪˈspektʃlnɪs/	n	courteous regard for people's feelings 尊敬；敬意
fathom	/ˈfæðəm/	v.	to understand or find an explanation for sth. 理解；彻底了解；弄清真相
quotidian	/kwəʊˈtɪdɪən/	a.	(fml.) ordinary; typical of what happens every day 寻常的；普通的；司空见惯的
thread	/θred/	n.	an idea or a feature that is part of sth. greater; an idea that connects the different parts of sth. 线索；脉络；思绪；贯穿的主线
osmotically	/ɔzˈmɔtɪk(ə)lɪ/	ad.	by means of osmosis 渗透地
scrappy	/ˈskræpɪ/	a.	1. consisting of individual sections, events, etc. that are not organized into a whole 散乱的；不连贯的；支离破碎的 2. not tidy and often of poor quality 不整洁的；糟糕的
grit	/grɪt/	n.	[U] 1. very small pieces of stone or sand 沙粒；沙砾；细沙 2. the courage and determination that makes it possible for sb. to continue doing sth. difficult or unpleasant 勇气；毅力
blandness	/ˈblændnəs/	n.	1. the trait of exhibiting no personal embarrassment or concern 平淡；温和 2. the quality of being bland and gracious or ingratiating in manner 温柔 3. lacking any distinctive or interesting taste property 平淡乏味
overly	/ˈəʊvəlɪ/	ad.	(before an adjective) too; very 很；十分；过于
acronym	/ˈækrənɪm/	n.	a word formed from the first letters of the words that make up the name of sth. 首字母缩略词
rancor	/ˈræŋkə/	n.	feelings of hatred and a desire to hurt other people, especially because you think that sb. has done sth. unfair to you 怨恨；怨毒
amateurism	/ˈæmətərɪzəm/	n.	the belief that people should take part in sports and other activities as a hobby, for pleasure, rather than as a job, for

Unit 8 Why Corporate Culture Counts

			money 业余主义（认为享受体育和其他活动的乐趣比从中谋利更为重要）
skive	/skaɪv/	v.	(infml.) to avoid work or school by staying away or leaving without permission 逃避工作；旷工；逃学；旷课
codify	/ˈkəʊdɪˌfaɪ/	v.	to arrange laws, rules, etc. into a system 把……编成法典
cryptocurrency	/ˈkrɪptəʊkʌrənsi/	n.	a kind of digital currency that is created and exchanged using cryptography 加密电子货币（使用加密法确保付款安全支付及收取）
hurl	/hɜːl/	v.	1. [VN+ ad./prep.] to throw sth./sb. violently in a particular direction 猛扔；猛投；猛摔 2. [VN] ~ *abuse, accusations, insults, etc. (at sb.)* to shout insults, etc. at sb. 大声说出（辱骂或斥责等）
regime	/reɪˈʒiːm/	n.	a method or system of organizing or managing sth. 组织方法；管理体制
overhaul	/ˌəʊvəˈhɔːl/	v.	1. to examine every part of a machine, system, etc. and make any necessary changes or repairs 彻底检修 2. to come from behind a person you are competing against in a race and go past them 赶上；超过（赛跑对手）
hormonal	/hɔːˈməʊnəl/	a.	of or relating to or caused by hormones 激素的
meritocracy	/ˌmerɪˈtɒkrəsi/	n.	[pl. ~ies] 1. [C, U] a country or social system where people get power or money on the basis of their ability 精英领导体制；英才管理制度 2. *the* ~ [sing.] 精英管理班子
activism	/ˈæktɪˌvɪzəm/	n.	the process of campaigning in public or working for an organization in order to bring about political or social change 行动主义
stilted	/ˈstɪltɪd/	a.	(disapproving) (of a way of speaking or writing not natural or relaxed; too formal（言谈或写作）生硬的；不自然的
respondent	/rɪˈspɒndənt/	n.	a person who answers questions, especially in a survey 回答问题的人；（尤指）调查对象
cohesive	/kəʊˈhiːsɪv/	a.	1. forming a united whole 组成一个整体的 2. causing people or things to become united 使结合的；使凝结的；使内聚的
distort	/dɪˈstɔːt/	v.	1. to change the shape, appearance or sound of sth. so that it is strange or not clear 使变形；扭曲；使失真 2. to twist or change facts, ideas, etc. so that they are no longer correct or true 歪曲；曲解

embittered	/ɪmˈbɪtəd/	a.	making sb. feel angry or disappointed about sth. over a long period of time 使怨恨的；牢骚满腹的
outfit	/ˈaʊtˌfɪt/	n.	a group of people working together as an organization, business, team, etc. 团队；小组；分队
sliver	/ˈslɪvə/	n.	a small or thin piece of sth. that is cut or broken off from a larger piece（切下或碎裂的）小块；薄片
substitute	/ˈsʌbstɪˌtjuːt/	n.	a person or thing that you use or have instead of the one you normally use or have 替代者；代替物；代用品
discernible	/dɪˈsɜːnəbəl/	a.	capable of being seen or noticed 看得见的；辨认得出的
indigestion	/ˌɪndɪˈdʒestʃən/	n.	pain caused by difficulty in digesting food 消化不良（症）

New expressions

fit in	*(with sb./sth.)* to live, work, etc. in an easy and natural way with sb./sth. 与……合得来；适应
be rated as sth.	to think that someone or something has a particular quality, value, or standard 被认为……；被评价为……
reside in sb./sth.	to be in sb./sth.; to be caused by sth. 在于；由……造成（或引起）
be characterized by sth.	to give sth. its typical or most noticeable qualities or features 使……具有特点（或最吸引人注目的特征）
now that	because of sth. or as a result of sth. 既然；由于
set sth. out	to present ideas, facts, etc. in an organized way, in speech or writing（有条理地）陈述；阐明
lay out sth.	to present a plan, an argument, etc. clearly and carefully 清晰谨慎地提出；策划（计划、论点等）
take stances on sth.	the opinions that sb. has about sth. and expresses publicly（公开表明的）观点；态度；采取立场
add up	to increase by small amounts until there is a large total 积少成多

Notes

1. Flexjobs（美国知名招聘网站）: an online service that aggregates flexible, work-from-home, telecommuting, and online jobs. The jobs that appear on FlexJobs.com come from one of two sources: (a) the FlexJobs' staff scours the Internet to find real jobs with telecommuting options, and (b) screened employers post jobs on the site.

2. *ReCulturing* (《文化重构》): the playbook for building a business in which employees are clear on the why, what, and how they are working. *ReCulturing* is not a one-time change effort because culture is not something we ultimately have, but rather something we do. One of today's most renowned thought leaders and practitioners on the issue, Melissa Daimler provides a modern definition of culture that is more of a verb than a noun. Culture needs to be reviewed consistently, just like strategy and purpose. Focusing on these three areas leads to higher performance and engagement.

3. Clickthrough Rate (CTR, 点击率): a way of measuring the success of an online advertising campaign for a particular website as well as the effectiveness of an email campaign by the number of users that clicked on a specific link.

4. Coinbase (美国加密货币交易所): the special name given to the first transaction in every block. These can also be called "Generation Transactions".

5. Brunswick: committed to being the most diverse, equitable and inclusive advisory firm in the world. It aims to help the leaders of the world's great value-creating organizations operate successfully across the increasingly complex and fast-changing arenas of finance, politics and society at large.

6. Glassdoor: an American site where employees and former employees anonymously review companies and their management.

7. Dara Khosrowshah (达拉·科斯罗萨西): became the new CEO of Uber in 2017. He is an Iranian American businessman whose business acumen is held in high regard by everyone.

Reading comprehension

Understanding the text

1. Choose the best answer to each of the following questions.

(1) According to the text, what do workers rate as more important to job satisfaction than pay **EXCEPT** _____.

A. mutual respect   B. work-leisure balance

C. strategy   D. morale

(2) What jobseekers cannot find on the website about a firm is _____.

A. cluelessness   B. team spirit

C. transparency   D. customer obsession

(3) The reasons that culture can be very hard to understand from the outside lie in the following statements **EXCEPT** _____.

   A. culture resides in ordinary interactions between colleagues

   B. firms always attempt to cover what actually happens inside the company

   C. culture resides in hidden threads that bind decisions on everything

   D. jobseekers cannot find what actually happens inside the company from the outside

(4) How do regulators contribute to providing insights into a firm's cultural norms?

   A. By analyzing earnings calls of CEOs.

   B. By encouraging employee activism on social issues.

   C. By requiring firms to disclose information about their workforce.

   D. By conducting surveys on job satisfaction.

(5) Jobseekers need to see only that one word to know whether this is the workplace for them or whether they would rather be hurled into an active volcano. What can be inferred from the sentence?

   A. Jobseekers' decision to work in a firm depends on nothing but its culture.

   B. Jobseekers' decision to stay or leave depends on the firm's location.

   C. Jobseekers' decision to stay or leave rests on their instinct.

   D. The values of a firm determine whether jobseekers decide to stay or leave.

(6) What can be concluded from a recent survey by Brunswick Group?

   A. Jobseekers are interested in the boss's tweeting, posting, etc.

   B. Boss's social media accounts are taken into consideration when they seek employment.

   C. Jobseekers are more curious about the boss's earnings calls.

   D. Jobseekers are more likely to work in firms with more cohesive leadership teams.

(7) If employees want to understand what the firm is really like, they will _____.

   A. browse employee-review sites

   B. learn about the firm from ex-workers

   C. work in the company every day

   D. learn about the firm from the behavior of CEOs

(8) What do employee-review sites like Glassdoor provide insight into?

   A. The financial health of a company.

   B. The market value of a company's products.

C. The work-life balance at a company.

D. The academic background of a company's employees.

Critical thinking

2. Work in pairs and discuss the following questions.

(1) In your eyes, how do you understand corporate culture?

(2) Why was culture the most common reason people gave for quitting?

(3) What type of firm is your team more likely to be dedicated to? Illustrate your views with specific reasons.

 Language focus

Words in use

3. Fill in the blanks with the words given below. Change the form where necessary. Each word can be used only once.

| fathom | distort | overly | substitute | discernible |
| embittered | respondent | indigestion | overhaul | thread |

(1) Employers may become _____ cautious about taking on new staff.

(2) When marriages break down children are swept into the vortex of their parents' _____ emotions.

(3) The course teaches you the theory, but there's no _____ for practical experience.

(4) Night fell, but the outline of the factory buildings was still _____. The factory buildings were silhouetted against the growing darkness.

(5) It is hard to _____ the pain felt at the death of a child.

(6) The study says there must be a complete _____ of air traffic control systems.

(7) Newspapers are often guilty of _____ the truth.

(8) A common _____ running through the evolution of virtually all electronic technologies is miniaturization.

(9) Only 2.7% of the survey _____ said they had plans to buy a home in the next six months.

(10) _____ is a catchall term for any kind of stomach distress.

Expressions in use

4. Fill in the blanks with the expressions given below. Change the form where necessary. Each expression can be used only once.

| fit in with | reside in | set out... | rate... as |
| lay out | take a stance on... | add up | be characterized as |

(1) Production of the goods must _____ the needs of the society.

(2) Rhode is currently _____ the top junior player in the country.

(3) The environmental footprint of different bricks reflects multiple factors including the type of kiln, fuel, and transportation. But with so many produced, their impact _____.

(4) The group _____ being well-educated and liberal.

(5) Happiness does not _____ strength or money.

(6) He _____ the reasons for his decisions in his report.

(7) The financial considerations are _____ in a booklet called "How to Borrow Money".

(8) The President has _____ a tough _____ terrorism.

Sentence structure

5. Restructure the sentences by using the inverted structure "not only... but also...; neither/nor...; only when/if...; though/as...; so...". Make changes where necessary.

Model:	The countries <u>not only</u> had found a path to the future that did not run over the relics of the past, <u>but they had also</u> learned that it was possible for countries to work together to build a better tomorrow.
→	<u>Not only had the countries</u> found a path to the future that did not run over the relics of the past, <u>but they had also</u> learned that it was possible for countries to work together to build a better tomorrow.

(1) Straitford, Inc., a private intelligence-analysis firm based in Austin, Texas, is among the firms making the biggest splash in this new world.

Unit 8 Why Corporate Culture Counts

(2) Although it sounds very odd, cosmic inflation is a scientifically plausible consequence of some respected ideas in elementary-particle physics, and many astrophysicists have been convinced for the better part of a decade that it is true. (though)

_____
_____

(3) The children become so involved with their computers that leaders at summer computer camps often have to force them to break for sports and games. (so... that...)

_____
_____

(4) Americans no longer expect public figures, whether in speech or in writing, to command the English with skill and gift. And they do not aspire to such command themselves. (neither/nor)

_____
_____

(5) Both nonstop waves of immigrants and bigger crops of babies played a role as yesterday's "baby boom" generation reached its childbearing years. (so)

_____
_____

(6) Students learn critical thinking and communication skills. They also develop an intimate understanding of and appreciation for how scientists come up with evidence and develop conclusions. (not only... but also...)

_____
_____

 Collocation

> Qualtrics, a software firm, may not believe in grammar but it does believe in *Transparent*, *All-in*, *Customer-obsessed*, *One-team* and *Scrappy*. (Text B) Justworks, an HR technology firm, subscribes to *Camaraderie*, *Openness*, *Grit*, *Integrity* and *Simplicity*. Lists like these can turn blandness into an art form, and are overly determined by what will create an acronym. (Text B) Plenty of firms are characterized by *Cluelessness*, *Rancor*, *Amateurism*, *Skiving* and *Stupidity*, but you won't find that on the website. (Text B)

> Loneliness has become a "*plague*", an "*epidemic*" or "*pandemic*" that afflicts young and old alike. (*English Digest*, July. 2020)

6. **Fill in the blanks with no less than three coordinated words to complete the sentence.**

   (1) Our connection to the world and to others includes a wide range of senses, including _____, _____ and _____.

   (2) Now, artificial intelligence technologies are streamlining the process, reducing the _____, _____ and _____ needed to doctor digital images.

   (3) Paresky is especially worried about the impact on college-age students who were just getting their first taste of independence, only to be sent back home into a family setting that could be filled with _____, _____ and _____.

   (4) The premier called on government officials to make progress in an array of areas including _____, _____, _____ foreign investment, meeting the public's basic living needs and ensuring the stability of industrial supply chains.

   (5) Booksellers are among the most _____, _____ and _____ of people, and bookshops have been swift to adapt to the obstacles of social distancing and self-isolation to provide incredible services for their customers.

   (6) This political interest in happiness has been underpinned by the new academic discipline of positive psychology that emerged in the late 1900s, which puts forward a concept of happiness as something that can be expertly _____, scientifically _____ and _____.

   (7) As the world returns to shopping, traveling and consuming, we return also to _____, _____ and _____.

   (8) Rising _____, unchecked _____, groundwater _____, and rapid urban population growth have left millions vulnerable to natural disasters—scientists warn the city itself may not survive the century.

 Translation

7. **Translate the following passage into English.**

   就文化学体系而言，企业文化无疑是一个社会文化体系中的亚文化。任何一个企业的文化，都要受到所在国家、民族文化传统的影响。管理者与被管理者的思想和行

为都必定受到他们自身所处文化的影响。对于中国企业文化而言，几千年积淀形成的中国文化传统依然影响深远，渗透到企业文化的方方面面。近年来随着阿里巴巴、方太集团、春秋航空等一批优秀中国本土企业走出国门参与全球市场竞争，其出色的表现，令国际管理学界逐渐意识到，东方社会在几千年文明发展中形成的丰富管理思想所包含的独特管理智慧，对中国本土企业的成功有深远影响。

Unit project

Write a report on corporate culture based on a comparison of cultural similarities and differences between Chinese companies and foreign counterparts.

> This unit is focused on the critical role of corporate culture. The two texts have expounded the dangerous myths that stand in the way of a great company's development, and introduced some interesting and helpful tips for employees to read corporate culture. Both texts hold the view that a company's key to success lies in its heart and soul, that is, creating a unique and winning culture.
>
> In this unit project, you are asked to write a report on a comparative study of corporate culture between Chinese companies and foreign ones. Divide the class into 3–4 groups and assign each one with the task of conducting research on the culture of some specific company. To complete the project, you can follow the steps below.

(1) Work in groups and design a survey or interview on the critical importance of corporate culture. The following questions can be included in your interview. Add more questions if you can.

- How do you define your company's culture? And what distinguishing features does the company possess?
- What is the core value that explains your company's success over the years?
- What are the advantages of your company to build a winning culture?
- Is there any dangerous myth in your company that hinders its healthy development?

...

(2) Each of your group members is required to interview some leaders or staff of the company via telephone, e-mail or face-to-face talks. Take down their answers to your questions and highlight the key points of their corporate culture.

(3) Analyze and interpret the uniqueness, core values and existing problems of each company's culture. Each group needs to prepare a 5-minute report presentation with PPT in class.

(4) Compare your survey result with other group members'. Make a comparison between 3–4 companies. Summarize the common characteristics and differences of the companies' culture and draw a conclusion from your comparative study, highlighting some core values of corporate culture that constitute each company's competitive advantage.

Glossary

A

abandon	Unit 2B
abandonment	Unit 2B
absence	Unit 4B
abstraction	Unit 7B
accelerate	Unit 1B
accolade	Unit 4B
accountable	Unit 3A
accreditation	Unit 1A
acquaint	Unit 7A
acquaintance	Unit 2B
acronym	Unit 8B
actionable	Unit 5A
activism	Unit 8B
acumen	Unit 1B
acutely	Unit 5A
adaptable	Unit 1A
address	Unit 6A
adroit	Unit 2A
advantageous	Unit 6A
adversarial	Unit 4B
adversity	Unit 3A
agonize	Unit 4A
agreeable	Unit 3A
alarmingly	Unit 6A
altitude	Unit 7A
amateur	Unit 2A
amateurism	Unit 8B
ambiguity	Unit 4B
amelioration	Unit 6A
amplify	Unit 7B
analogy	Unit 2B
analyst	Unit 4B
aphorism	Unit 8B

applicable	Unit 1A
appraisal	Unit 5A
apprentice	Unit 1A
architect	Unit 3B
arise	Unit 3B
articulate	Unit 6A
assimilate	Unit 2A
assist	Unit 1A
assumption	Unit 4B
attain	Unit 4A
audible	Unit 7A
authority	Unit 4B
autocrat	Unit 4B
autonomy	Unit 7A
avail	Unit 7A
avenue	Unit 1B

B

ballistics	Unit 6B
banal	Unit 6B
bang	Unit 7A
beguile	Unit 7A
believer	Unit 4B
bias	Unit 4B
bicker	Unit 4A
bigotry	Unit 6A
blacksmith	Unit 7A
blandness	Unit 8B
blast	Unit 7A
bolster	Unit 6A
boost	Unit 1B
bullet	Unit 4A
bureaucratic	Unit 4B
bypass	Unit 3A

C

calculation	Unit 3B
camaraderie	Unit 4A
cancerous	Unit 2A
carrot-and-stick	Unit 8A
cascade	Unit 3B

254

Glossary

catastrophic	Unit 4A
cater	Unit 5B
centricity	Unit 5B
champion	Unit 4B
channel	Unit 5A
chunk	Unit 3B
clarify	Unit 3B
clarity	Unit 4A
cling	Unit 8A
clue	Unit 2B
codify	Unit 8B
cohesive	Unit 8B
collaborate	Unit 1B
collaborative	Unit 5A
comparatively	Unit 2B
complexity	Unit 4B
complicate	Unit 5B
comply	Unit 3B
comprise	Unit 6A
compromise	Unit 5A
compulsory	Unit 1B
concerted	Unit 6A
concisely	Unit 2A
confine	Unit 7A
confirm	Unit 3B
consecutive	Unit 4A
considerable	Unit 2B
constituency	Unit 5B

D

daunt	Unit 1B
daunting	Unit 1B
debacle	Unit 4A
decay	Unit 2B
deficiency	Unit 5A
delegate	Unit 3A
delegator	Unit 4B
deliberately	Unit 5A
delicate	Unit 2B
delude	Unit 8A
demanding	Unit 4A

demean	Unit 8A
demise	Unit 6B
denial	Unit 4B
dependency	Unit 2B
dependent	Unit 7A
derail	Unit 4B
derelict	Unit 2B
derive	Unit 4B
deteriorate	Unit 2B
dictate	Unit 1B
digitize	Unit 5B
discern	Unit 3A
digitized	Unit 7A
discipline	Unit 6A
disclosure	Unit 2A
discrimination	Unit 6B
distort	Unit 8B
distribute	Unit 4B
diverse	Unit 2A
diversify	Unit 6A
documentation	Unit 2A
draft	Unit 3B
drag	Unit 2B
dramatic	Unit 7B
draw	Unit 5A
dummy	Unit 2B
dummy data	Unit 2B
dumpster	Unit 2B
dysfunction	Unit 4B

E

earnestly	Unit 2A
ego	Unit 4B
elaborate	Unit 3A
elusive	Unit 5B
embittered	Unit 8B
embrace	Unit 3A
empathize	Unit 3A
empower	Unit 5B
empowerment	Unit 6A
enchilada	Unit 8A

Glossary

energizing	Unit 3A
engaging	Unit 3A
engender	Unit 2B
engross	Unit 2A
entail	Unit 6A
enterprise	Unit 6A
entrepreneur	Unit 6B
entropy	Unit 2B
entrust	Unit 2A
envision	Unit 3A
epicenter	Unit 4A
equate	Unit 7B
estimate	Unit 3B
ethnography	Unit 5B
evangelist	Unit 1A
excursion	Unit 5B
exert	Unit 7A
expedite	Unit 4B
expertise	Unit 7B
explicitly	Unit 3B
externalize	Unit 3B
externally	Unit 3B

F

fabulous	Unit 3A
facilitate	Unit 1A
faction	Unit 4B
fad	Unit 2B
faint	Unit 4A
fathom	Unit 8B
feat	Unit 6A
feedback	Unit 4A
fiasco	Unit 4A
firework	Unit 7A
fiscal	Unit 6A
fizzle	Unit 7A
flaw	Unit 7B
flex	Unit 8A
flog	Unit 8A
flourish	Unit 8A
fluid	Unit 4B

forceful	Unit 7A
forecast	Unit 8A
fortify	Unit 3A
foster	Unit 5A
front-end	Unit 4A
front-line	Unit 4A
functionality	Unit 2B
fuzzy	Unit 4A

G

geometrical	Unit 6B
geophysics	Unit 2A
gibberish	Unit 6B
gigabyte	Unit 2A
gloss	Unit 2A
gospel	Unit 6A
graffiti	Unit 2B
granularity	Unit 3B
gratification	Unit 1A
gratifying	Unit 2A
grit	Unit 8B
gritty	Unit 8A
groundwork	Unit 4A

H

hail	Unit 6B
halve	Unit 3B
heed	Unit 1A
herald	Unit 5B
hexadecimal	Unit 6B
highlight	Unit 4A
high-profile	Unit 6A
hindrance	Unit 8A
hobbyist	Unit 1A
hone	Unit 5B
hook	Unit 1A
hormonal	Unit 8B
hose	Unit 2B
hostile	Unit 5A
hotshot	Unit 2A
hulk	Unit 2B

Glossary

hurl	Unit 8B
hypothesis	Unit 3A

I

ideation	Unit 5B
immaculate	Unit 2B
immune	Unit 2B
impart	Unit 4A
impede	Unit 8A
implement	Unit 1A
implication	Unit 4A
implicit	Unit 8A
incentive	Unit 5A
incentivize	Unit 7B
incidental	Unit 8A
inclination	Unit 6A
indentured	Unit 7A
indigestion	Unit 8B
inevitability	Unit 3A
inflict	Unit 4A
infraction	Unit 8A
infuse	Unit 5B
ingenious	Unit 6B
inhabitant	Unit 2B
initiative	Unit 5B
inquisitive	Unit 1A
ins-and-outs	Unit 1A
insight	Unit 1B
instill	Unit 1A
instinct	Unit 4B
institutional	Unit 8A
instructive	Unit 5A
instrumental	Unit 1A
insufficient	Unit 2B
insulting	Unit 8A
intact	Unit 2B
interchangeable	Unit 8A
interface	Unit 4B
intermediary	Unit 6B
intermingle	Unit 2B
intuition	Unit 4B

invasive	Unit 2B
invigorate	Unit 3A
invigorated	Unit 3A
irrelevant	Unit 6A
irrespective	Unit 1A

L

laboriously	Unit 6B
lackluster	Unit 5A
lapse	Unit 5A
latitude	Unit 8A
launch	Unit 1B
lawmaking	Unit 5A
lean	Unit 4B
lengthy	Unit 1B
lens	Unit 5B
leverage	Unit 7B
lieutenant	Unit 6B
lightweight	Unit 2A
like-minded	Unit 1B
limitless	Unit 7B
litany	Unit 1A
litter	Unit 2B
lottery	Unit 4A
lousy	Unit 4A

M

machinery	Unit 5A
magnitude	Unit 7B
manageable	Unit 3B
maneuver	Unit 5A
manipulate	Unit 8A
manually	Unit 5A
manufacture	Unit 1B
marginally	Unit 3A
marketable	Unit 7A
materialize	Unit 6B
maternal	Unit 5A
maturity	Unit 4A
maximize	Unit 6A
maximum	Unit 2B

measurable   Unit 7B
medieval   Unit 7A
mediocre   Unit 4B
mentality   Unit 6A
mentoring   Unit 7B
meritocracy   Unit 8B
meticulous   Unit 3A
mingle   Unit 3A
minimize   Unit 4B
misapprehend   Unit 8A
miscalculation   Unit 4B
misinterpret   Unit 3A
misperception   Unit 6A
mold   Unit 1A
momentum   Unit 3A
morale   Unit 4B
moribund   Unit 8A
multidisciplinary Unit 5B
multiply   Unit 7B

N
necessitate   Unit 7A
neglect   Unit 2B
nifty   Unit 8A
non-disclosure   Unit 2A
notification   Unit 1B
notional   Unit 3A

O
objet d'art   Unit 2B
oblige   Unit 5A
obscene   Unit 2B
obscenely   Unit 2B
obstacle   Unit 6A
occult   Unit 6B
odds   Unit 3B
omit   Unit 3A
onboarding   Unit 7B
opt   Unit 7B
optimization   Unit 4B
orientation   Unit 4A

osmotically	Unit 8B
outcome	Unit 4A
outfit	Unit 8B
outlet	Unit 1B
outweigh	Unit 4B
overblow	Unit 3A
overhaul	Unit 8B
overlook	Unit 5A
overly	Unit 8B
oversee	Unit 4B

P

pandemic	Unit 1B
panel	Unit 6A
paradox	Unit 4B
paramount	Unit 4B
particle	Unit 8A
patrol	Unit 1A
payroll	Unit 6B
pedigree	Unit 1B
permutation	Unit 3B
perpetual	Unit 2A
persuasive	Unit 4B
pester	Unit 5A
phenomenal	Unit 7A
pipeline	Unit 6A
pitfall	Unit 2A
plateau	Unit 7B
plethora	Unit 1B
ply	Unit 4A
pomp	Unit 3A
ponder	Unit 7A
portfolio	Unit 5B
potential	Unit 1B
potentially	Unit 7A
precinct	Unit 1A
predominately	Unit 6A
priesthood	Unit 6B
principal	Unit 5B
prioritize	Unit 2B
probability	Unit 3B

Glossary

processor	Unit 6B
procrastinate	Unit 2B
prod	Unit 8A
professionalism	Unit 2A
progress	Unit 1A
projectile	Unit 8B
promote	Unit 1A
propagate	Unit 1A
proponent	Unit 5B
proportional	Unit 7B
prosper	Unit 1A
punch	Unit 2A

Q

qualify	Unit 4B
quantify	Unit 5A
questionable	Unit 3B
quotidian	Unit 8B

R

rally	Unit 3A
rancor	Unit 8B
real-time	Unit 4A
recipient	Unit 2A
reckon	Unit 6A
recruiter	Unit 7A
recruitment	Unit 6A
recur	Unit 5A
refactor	Unit 2B
regime	Unit 8B
rein	Unit 5B
remedy	Unit 3B
reminiscence	Unit 4A
rental	Unit 5B
replace	Unit 2B
resemble	Unit 8A
resonate	Unit 1A
respondent	Unit 8B
responsive	Unit 5B
restrict	Unit 1B
revenue	Unit 5B

reverse	Unit 6A
revise	Unit 7A
revolutionary	Unit 1B
rip	Unit 2B
ripple	Unit 4A
robust	Unit 5B
roster	Unit 5B
rot	Unit 2B
rung	Unit 7B

S

saga	Unit 1B
sage	Unit 1A
satisfying	Unit 1B
savvy	Unit 1A
scrappy	Unit 8B
scrutinize	Unit 3B
seasoned	Unit 1A
self-sustained	Unit 2A
setback	Unit 2B
sexism	Unit 6A
shave	Unit 7B
shepherd	Unit 4A
shift	Unit 8A
showcase	Unit 6A
sideline	Unit 1A
simplicity	Unit 4B
sink	Unit 4A
skeptic	Unit 4B
skepticism	Unit 4B
skive	Unit 8B
slip	Unit 3B
sliver	Unit 8B
smash	Unit 2B
smooth	Unit 1A
soar	Unit 7A
soften	Unit 8A
solicit	Unit 5A
solidify	Unit 3A
sorely	Unit 1A
specialist	Unit 7A

Glossary

specific	Unit 7A
sporadic	Unit 1A
squander	Unit 4A
standpoint	Unit 1A
standstill	Unit 2B
sticky	Unit 8A
stilted	Unit 8B
strategy	Unit 4B
streamline	Unit 5A
strengthen	Unit 4A
stuck	Unit 8A
stumble	Unit 2B
stumbling block	Unit 2B
stunning	Unit 2A
subatomic	Unit 8A
subconsciously	Unit 3B
subdivision	Unit 3B
subscribe	Unit 6A
substitute	Unit 8B
subtlety	Unit 4B
summit	Unit 8A
superb	Unit 4A
supplement	Unit 4A
supposition	Unit 3B
surface	Unit 3B
surrogate	Unit 5A
sustainable	Unit 8A
swell	Unit 8A
swing	Unit 5A
symptom	Unit 4A

T

tangible	Unit 1A
tapestry	Unit 2B
target	Unit 3B
tedious	Unit 6B
thermodynamics	Unit 2B
thread	Unit 8B
tinker	Unit 1A
titan	Unit 1B
torturous	Unit 3B

英语读写教程 2（第二版）
Intermediate IT English Reading and Writing 2 (2nd Edition)

trait	Unit 1B
transparent	Unit 6B
trauma	Unit 4B
triage	Unit 4B
trigger	Unit 2B
trivial	Unit 2A
troubleshoot	Unit 1A
trustworthy	Unit 1B
tutorial	Unit 1B

U

unbounded	Unit 6A
undercurrent	Unit 8A
undoubtedly	Unit 1A
unfold	Unit 3A
unforeseen	Unit 3B
unintentionally	Unit 5A
unreliable	Unit 3B
update	Unit 2A
updated	Unit 2A
uplifting	Unit 3A
upskill	Unit 2B

V

verdict	Unit 6A
vindicate	Unit 6B
vine	Unit 4A
visibility	Unit 4A
vision	Unit 6B
visionary	Unit 6B
vocal	Unit 6B
vomit	Unit 8B

W

whereas	Unit 5A
wide-ranging	Unit 5A
wrestle	Unit 4A

Y

yardstick	Unit 8A
yield	Unit 7A